Hyper**Healing**

Hyper**Healing**

The Empowered Parent's Complete
Guide to Raising a Healthy Child
with ADHD Symptoms

AVIGAIL GIMPEL M.S.

gatekeeper press™
Columbus, Ohio

HyperHealing: The Empowered Parent's Complete Guide to Raising a Healthy Child with ADHD Symptoms

Published by Gatekeeper Press
2167 Stringtown Rd, Suite 109
Columbus, OH 43123-2989
www.GatekeeperPress.com

ISBN (paperback): 9781662903342
eISBN: 9781662903359

Dedication

To Daniel, my husband and best friend. The journey is so much more exciting with you at my side.

To my children, Aliza, Gavriel, Ayelet, Yonatan, Yosef, and Levonah. You have inspired me to love better, to improve every day, and to live a life of meaning.

Contents

**Part Three:
Check Your Environment**

Acknowledgments

ALTHOUGH ONLY ONE name appears on the cover of this book, *HyperHealing* was a production involving input from so many talented and dedicated people. I would like to take this opportunity to express my gratitude to all those who have contributed to the writing of this book.

I begin with my parents-in-law, Drs. Lynn and Amnon Gimpel. You have not only opened doors to professional opportunities but also challenged and guided me through conversations and debates, helping me construct my intervention plan. To my brothers and sisters-in-law Micah, Gila, Jeremy, and Tehila for your encouragement, feedback, and genuine friendship. We have been raising our kids together as a team, which really is the best way to go at it.

I would like to thank my parents, Nomi Perlman and David Perlman, for providing me the chance to spread my wings and choose my direction with clarity and conviction. To my brothers and sisters Bezalel, Rif, Chev, Paul, Eli, Elisheva, Sony, Yaelli, Kivi, Tamar, Sara, Jesse, and Shim for your support, interest, and enthusiasm for this project. Your pride in me is heartwarming! An additional thanks goes to my sisters, Chev and Sara, for reading through the manuscript and giving invaluable constructive feedback. To my niece Batya for helping create content and editing the back cover. All of you are so precious to me.

Many educators, doctors, and therapists are quoted in this book. These remarkable people have developed programs that have greatly enriched anyone who has encountered them. I would like to thank each of them: Dr. Ross Greene, Dr. Allen Kazdin, Dr. Victoria L. Dunckley, Dr. Carol S. Dweck, Mr. Richard Lavoie, Dr. Carolyn Dean, Dr. Marcia Angell, Dr. Michael Gershon, Mr. Charles Duhigg, Ms. Wendy and Mr. Larry Maltz, Dr. Matthew Walker, Mr. Richard Louv, Dr. David Perlmutter, and Dr. John J. Ratey. I highly recommend reading their work, cover to cover.

To my dear friends Caryn Zamir, Ilana Sperer, Isha Esses, Sara Zadok, Anita Berman, and Yarden and Gilly Frankl for reading through the manuscript and giving priceless honest feedback. The reader will benefit greatly from your contributions.

To colleagues who read, reviewed, and critiqued the manuscript: Vivienne Glasser, Toby Klein Greenwald, Ijeoma John-Adubasim, Danya Saitowitz, Tzvi Broker, and David Hochberg. Your professional contributions have upgraded my content.

To Dr. Sara Givon and Mrs. Leah Gura at Herzog College for entrusting me to teach your students. This book began as lectures to my beloved students, to whom I have the utmost gratitude. Your questions, contributions, and challenges to my lectures forced me to be disciplined and to dig ever deeper to provide worthy content to you. You may hear your voices in this book.

A special thanks goes to my clients. You have shared your stories over the last many years with honesty and faith. It has been my greatest honor to accompany you as you raised your healthy children with ADHD symptoms, bravely making choices and guiding your children towards success.

To my two editors, Sarah Mandel and Margarita Martinez, who both totally got me and dove into this project wholeheartedly. It's a pleasure working with editors who seem to be thoroughly enjoying the content. To Eden Tuckman, my project manager at Gatekeeper Press, who helped turn a manuscript into a fantastic, published book. Many thanks to Andy Meaden for the beautiful cover design.

My husband Daniel has been running around with a copy of my manuscript under his arm for over a year now, correcting, editing, discussing, and processing. None of this would be possible without you, my dear. Thank you with all my heart for your love, dedication, and all the stories about you that you graciously allow me to share with the world. Keep making me laugh.

This book is really a love story to my children Aliza, Gavriel, Ayelet, Yonatan, Yosef, and Levonah. You guys have challenged and inspired me to get my act together and love and care for you better every day. I look forward to enjoying the next many years together.

The writing process was rough! Every stage presented its own challenges. But the book had to be written, so I persevered. My feeling throughout has been gratitude to God for allowing me to be the conduit through which this information can get to anyone searching for it. With a humble heart, I present *HyperHealing* to you, dear reader. We are now partnering in raising the next generation of healthy children. May God continue to bless and inspire us all.

Introduction

MY CHILDREN SHOWED up in rapid succession, six of them in eleven years. I was delusional enough to think I knew what I was doing for a short blissful spell. But then I noticed that my oldest was the *only* kid in the park to run headlong into moving swings regularly to get to a specific destination. She was also too busy playing to sit and do schoolwork. Did any of my friends have a child that preferred to sit under his desk rather than near it? Were my husband and I incompetent? Why did the other parents seem to have it figured out?

Everyone had advice for us, from the relatives and well-meaning parents of rule-following children to doctors and teachers. Their advice pointed in one direction: children with these behaviors are wired wrong—get them help! Wouldn't it have been a lifesaver if my children had shown up with a user manual?

My journey to understanding why my children were struggling, and the discoveries I made that contradicted the "advice" I got, are enumerated in my book *HyperHealing: Show Me the Science*. It was a fascinating, heartbreaking, and truly illuminating process, which has led me to an immensely powerful conclusion: my children are healthy! And my children are also struggling. Why?

The why question is what led me to start researching and developing programs for my own children, my students, and my clients. Why are seemingly healthy children doing so poorly socially, academically, and emotionally? Why are very bright children failing? The books I read either pathologized children or suggested one specific cause of

ADHD symptoms and offered helpful yet incomplete advice. I was left with a choice: rely on pharmaceutical interventions, pay for expensive coaching or educational assistance, or develop a program of my own. So, as a teacher, college lecturer, and by now a weathered mom, I set out to write the manual.

My students, clients, and children have reaped the benefits of these years of dedicated work, but my parent education program was not accessible to you, a parent faced with the same choices I had. The training programs I offer are too expensive for most families, and medicating healthy children comes at a cost as well.

This book is dedicated to you, dear parent. You know your struggling child needs help, and you would like to consider all your options. I am offering my program to you. You will be able to follow and implement it step by step. We will examine the many causes of ADHD symptoms. I will present intervention programs just for your child.

Parenting is the most important job of our lives. We must not allow guessing and bad advice to inform our decision making. This is the parenting manual that should have been delivered with our unique and beautiful child at birth, the one I surely could have used in those confusing early years.

Here's an important fact: your child is not damaged; he is struggling. His brain is intact. He's healthy. ADHD symptoms often arise due to a clash between personality and environment, and you *are* your child's environment. You have not caused her symptoms, but you can do much to help align her personality and environment. In this book, we will discuss the many triggers of ADHD symptoms, both environmental and genetic.

We bang down the door of the psychiatrist's office for a diagnosis and medication because our kid is making life too hard! Not because *she* is too hard, but because we are reading the instruction manual for a blender, and we have an iRobot! Let us link arms and move forward with confidence, knowing that our child will succeed. I am here to journey with you, understand your struggles as they are my own, and celebrate each and every step you take to help your child.

How to use this book

This book is the culmination of many years of research and refinement, in which I built effective parent education courses and a college curriculum and have worked extensively with a range of clients.

- **Part One: Powerful Parenting – Let's Begin with Us:** Getting ourselves disciplined has a cascade effect on our child. This section is a how-to guide to better communication, rule setting, and discipline.

- **Part Two: Healthy Habit Formation – Now It's Our Child's Turn:** In the second part, we invite your child to take the leading role in his HyperHealing program. It may seem strange that we are inviting the star of the show so late in the book, but our extensive work—stage setting—is so powerful and critical, we must get it right before our child can get involved and succeed. We will go through a process of habit formation (behavior modification) and emotional intervention to boost our child's problem-solving skills and help her become more socially graceful. This section will also include a chapter on building a bridge between home and school, getting your child's teacher to be a vital partner.

- **Part Three: Check the Environment:** The third section will discuss other important factors that contribute to ADHD symptoms. We will create a physical exercise program, plan an optimal diet for the growing and developing brain, and understand the role screens and sleep are playing in your child's development. We will examine the effects of physical, sexual, or emotional abuse on the development and behavior of a child.

Each chapter ends with a "cheat sheet," a quick review of the chapter, for your reference. There is a lot of information in this book, and there are many interventions. As you interact with your family, you may want to go back to the book and get a quick reminder of the programs you planned to implement.

This is a workshop in book form, so each chapter has a follow-up action plan. Don't skip the exercise like you might have done in high school! We can't help our children if we don't practice.

If you are looking for online support as you progress through the HyperHealing program, go to www.hyperhealing.org to join our online community and be part of a live parent training and support workshop with a HyperHealing facilitator or me. We provide all the support you will need to help your family progress.

I get calls from parents, years after they participate in a workshop, with questions about a specific topic or to tell me a success story based on what they learned in the course. Developing new skills and changing well-worn habits is hard. We all need reminders. When I run a group, it is as much to review the material and strengthen myself as it is for my participants. With renewed strength, I can refocus on being my children's improved parent, and so can you. I encourage you to use the book in the same way, always refreshing and reinforcing.

I am here by your side to congratulate you for jumping right in and being open to developing new skills for the sake of your family. I've been there, I'm still here, and "I'm still standing," as my favorite song says. And I'm also still smiling!

There is a lot of information here. It's all important and should be learned. But don't get discouraged! Every small rung you climb is a great achievement. The ripple effects of every change, every positive word, every moment of self-control and loving discipline will be felt for years. We are embarking on a vital and worthwhile process; embrace the journey and feel great about every success. I will lay out the entire program. You decide what parts you can implement now, and what you will save for later.

"How long will the program take to implement? How many hours of the day will I have to set aside to do the exercises?" I am often asked. Great question. Here's my answer. How many hours a day do you spend interacting with your child (or trying to avoid interacting with said child)? Count the hours. How much of that time is satisfying, and how much of it is stressful? **I will not add a minute to your schedule**, I promise. You're busy enough as is. The goal is to upgrade and infuse that time with high-quality, effective interactions. Your choices will make all the difference to your child and her progress. You can take control of that time and make it meaningful and satisfying for all of you. Choose to empower yourself and your child, and you will be very proud of your achievements. Enjoy the process!

PART ONE

Powerful Parenting,
Let's Begin with Us

CHAPTER ONE

Introducing
"Instant Gratification" Child

AFTER YEARS OF searching, failures, and terrible advice, I have learned a few things about my ADHD kids.

1. The problem does not reside within my child, but rather in the clash of her personality with her environment. Am I clashing with her?

2. I did not cause her challenges, but I can help her work them out.

3. If I do not fully understand him, how he processes, what he loves, and what shuts him down, I cannot be the appropriate messenger to get my child on the right track.

In this chapter we will first discuss the reason we became parents in the first place. We will then understand why much of the modern western approach to child-rearing runs counter to our real mission, and sets us on a collision course when trying to raise a child who needs a different rulebook.

It is one hard job to raise this child. Why did we volunteer for the job?

A couple of weeks ago I got an invitation to a baby naming. The invitation said, "Please join us as we name our sweet, joy-providing angel." I was thrilled for the young couple, but just a little worried about the parents' expectations. Let's say Joy-Provider ruins their morning. She may decide to be difficult, make a mess often, or embarrass her parents in public.

Kids have little life experience, poor manners, even worse hygiene, lots of charm, and explosive potential. They are not born to give us joy, although we are filled with joy at their mere existence.

So, how did we get ourselves entangled in this parenting project? Are we mad?

Philosophers explain what we parents feel intuitively, that raising children is the most significant thing we ever do in this world.

"All animals reproduce," says the late Rabbi Lord Jonathan Sacks, former chief rabbi of Great Britain, and leading theologian of our generation. "Humans alone need a reason to reproduce, a reason that connects us to some larger scheme of meaning. Those who deny that there is any such meaning rob us of any compelling reason to undergo the many sacrifices that having and raising children inevitably entails" (Sacks 2010).

Consider the child-raising process for a moment. The baby is born totally dependent, enchanting us with his pure and beautiful helplessness. As we grow with our child, we start to gain some skills such as loving consistently, self-control, reasoning, listening, perseverance, negotiating under pressure (kind of like a hostage negotiation), and the ability to give selflessly and build a meaningful relationship with this precious child. We commit for the long haul and grow and develop and become better people through the challenges of raising healthy, productive children. Our hard work and endurance lead to satisfaction and joy.

But we do not embark on the journey of parenting with a blank slate. We approach this tremendous task with tools and assumptions that are a combination of the environment in which we raise the child and our life experiences before parenting. If we can develop a deep understanding of our own motivations, and how they are molded and often derailed by western modernity's agenda for our parenting, we will have much greater insight into how we need to change to parent our child with ADHD symptoms.

We are often advised that along with hoping for our children's success and well-being, we are also supposed to help our kids be happy and build their self-esteem. But this may be a trap. How did we come to adopt this "keep your child comfortable and protect him from pain" notion? Explains Rabbi Sacks:

> It happened when big business discovered that children represent an immense potential market, not just for toys but also clothes, music, films, video games, soft drinks, junk food, the whole paraphernalia of street cool. So began the transformation of children into consumers . . . (Sacks 2004).

If a child is meant only to be accommodated and protected, then discipline, discomfort, earning second place, and any kind of effort or pain becomes taboo. Setting limits reduces her joy, so go easy on that too. As adults, when we reflect on our most joyful and life-changing moments, were they not ALL rewards for fighting through challenge and discomfort, working hard, broadly expanding our comfort zone, and working towards deeper meaning?

Rabbi Sacks continues,

> Childhood needs its visions and aspirations. Joseph— the first person described in the Bible as a teenager— was the great dreamer of dreams. The young Moses, moved by the plight of his people, began the fight against injustice and slavery that was to become his life and legacy . . . When we are young, we want to change the world. *If that instinct is frustrated,* there is a danger that children will turn to drink, drugs, sex, danger, violence, anger and the many other pathologies of our age (Sacks 2004; italics added).

> If we want our children to become active citizens, we have to induct them early into the habits of *responsibility.* They need the space to write their own chapter in the story we share, and they need to know that we trust them to do so—making mistakes along

the way but learning from them . . . All we can do is to
give them the chance to give—to others, to society and
to the world that will one day be theirs (Sacks 2004).

When we allow our children to grow up with responsibility and a
dream, we allow them to fail and learn, succeed and grow, and find
their own meaning. Our job is not to shield them from discomfort;
it is to be by their side as they find their voice and become unique,
contributing members of society. Happiness and strong self-esteem
come from within; we can't infuse them by proxy. We must model
responsibility and perseverance, guide our children lovingly with clear
rules, discipline, and positive feedback, and create opportunities for
our children to grow.

**What happens when that beautiful child we dreamed of is too
hard for us to raise? Do the above rules still apply? The doubt
creeps in . . . maybe he is somehow defective? How do disillusioned,
depleted parents find the strength and faith to proceed?**

This "raising kids to reach great potential and meaning" notion is
very romantic. We all get the whole "achievement and growth process"
concept when watching the neighbors raise their perfect kids. What
happens when Mr. Touch-Everything-Bother-Siblings-Impossible-
to-Discipline-Off-in-Dreamland shows up? You know, the kid who is
about to be diagnosed as ADHD?

The idealism dissipates. We feel exhausted and have no clue how
to proceed. We punish, make all sorts of empty threats, and bribe him
to get moving with promises of exciting activities to follow all chores.
And then we feel terrible for having expectations of our diagnosed
child. We feel we should be more gentle, help her more, make life
easier. We feel sorry for our poor, struggling child. We hear from
those around us: treat him sensitively, accommodate, don't expect too
much, and certainly don't punish, as he is not capable of fulfilling your
expectations. Gentle whispers say, "Keep *this* kid happy." Is this kid
different?

When my husband and I met with the teacher of one of our sons,
we were impressed with the grades the teacher showed us. Our boy
seemed to be paying attention, and his efforts were paying off. You

could imagine our surprise when the teacher told us he was worried about our son. "You see," he explained, "Your son has a really hard time focusing. It's so hard for him! My heart goes out to him when I see how hard he must work to keep up with us."

What? Was the teacher complaining that our son was working too hard?

I was sure I had misunderstood the teacher. I asked, "When he works hard and really focuses, does he succeed?"

"Sure, 90 percent of the time," was the teacher's reply.

"I fail to see the problem, dear teacher. Why are you distraught that he is working hard and succeeding? Isn't that what kids are expected to do in school?"

And then I understood . . . since my child had been diagnosed with ADHD, instead of expecting my son to exercise a weaker muscle and learn to concentrate like the rest of his friends, the teacher was trying to accommodate him and felt it inappropriate to expect my son to sweat too much. For my part, I was thrilled that my healthy son figured out that if he really tries, and he succeeds at focusing, he is rewarded with excellent grades.

It sure is lucky that our son didn't catch on to his teacher's attitude and cash in on the exaggerated sympathy. There are so many problems with this encounter. Why had the teacher lost faith in a kid who demonstrated that he could work hard? Why was it considered problematic for a student to exert too much effort?

Most of all, why do we buy the story that this child is less capable and needs accommodation?

1. We have been told by his teachers and doctors that due to his neurological disorder, he is limited. His brain is wired differently. They add that it would be unfair and painful to put excess demands on him. We feel sorry for our child, so we turn him into a sorry child.

2. It is SO hard to raise him, and we begin to believe their story in order to make sense of the situation. Our culture gives us a binary choice. Either the child is limited, or we are failing.

While neither is true, we choose the former, which somehow has more external support.

3. As good parents, we don't want to force our son to do something he can't do, causing him to suffer. Remember the message: don't allow him discomfort. Never let him fail! He hears this message loud and clear, and our collective low expectations become a self-fulfilling prophecy.

None of this is true; he's not limited! One source of his ADHD symptoms is his instant gratification personality. (We will examine other potential causes of ADHD symptoms later in the book.) Your child is an inventor, entrepreneur, artist, scientist, a builder, a high-tech guy or girl . . .

But also . . .

- a procrastinator (when the activity is not engaging, the expectation is too big, or he is not sure where to start)

- transition phobic (when he is engaged in something awesome, and we are demanding that he shift to something less enticing. Example: getting into the shower may require calling in the national guard. Once under the steamy water, he's having so much fun, singing his heart out, that no one can get him out. I know this does not only happen in my house.)

- attention-demanding and energy-draining (there is nothing more gratifying than getting attention from Mom and Dad, even negative attention)

- a disorganized mess (cleaning and organizing require engaging in the same boring activity daily, thereby developing new habits)

- a routine resistor (routines, like waking at the same time every morning, doing chores or homework, or getting to bed on time, directly clash with novelty)

- highly impulsive (excitement is more important than caution, so caution is thrown to the wind).

An organized, compliant child will flourish in school and can assist a struggling friend to get by. But how well will the compliant child fare as an adult in a competitive job that demands a lot of out-of-the-box, creative thinking? An instant gratification personality type may struggle in school, but in that same competitive job, she may persevere and teach her friend to be spontaneous and take risks. Both types must be raised to nurture their natural talents, develop their weaker ones, and know when they should reach out for help and build a team.

We fail dismally when we try to raise Instant Gratification child as if he were "Agreeable Kid." He's not! And that's good. Let's get to know him better through these two examples.

I'm reminded of the enormous final project my daughter was assigned as a high school art major. Since she had a dual major, she decided that the project was causing too much pressure, and after three years of art class, she was going to drop the major.

"No way!" I said lovingly, and rolled up my sleeves to help. We spent many long hours planning. There was some crying (read: full-blown tantrums, door slamming, and stair stomping included), anger, and unfun hard work on her part. Finally, the project was complete, and it was beautiful. What an achievement. The glow on my daughter's face as she presented her project proudly at the exhibition is fixed in my memory. I asked her that evening how she felt. She replied (blessedly, she agreed to talk to me), "I have never been so happy!"

Did I make her happy? Nope! I was the catalyst of much misery. If my goal was a happy/comfortable experience, or even shielding her from failure, I would never have pushed my daughter to persevere. It would have thrilled her to drop art. But what would she have missed? The entire process of tapping into her creativity, pushing herself to work hard, experiencing the deep joy of her own personal success, and the responsibility of completing the course.

I followed Rabbi Sacks' sage advice that:

> Children grow to fill the space we create for them, and
> if it's big, they grow tall. But if we turn them into mini
> consumers, we rob them of the chance of greatness, and

I've not yet met a child not capable of greatness if given
the opportunity and encouragement (Sacks 2008).

*I cherish the sweet email I got from a twenty-year-old client, about half
a year after we concluded our work together. He didn't write much—he
hated writing, but he attached a picture. It was his high school diploma.
Two years after officially graduating high school, he had finally handed
in his last assignments and earned his degree. When we met two years
earlier, he spent the first half hour of our meeting explaining that due to
his ADHD, he could not finish his assignments, and he was just fine with
that. I asked him if he had a dream of what he would like to be one day.
He shared that he would like to open a mountain rappelling company
one day.*

*After we talked a little about what ADHD really was—a list of
symptoms—and how everyone had challenges to overcome, I asked if
he would like to consider tackling earning his diploma as the first step
in fulfilling his dream. He was doubtful but open to the suggestion. We
made a plan that involved a strict behavioral structure, short- and long-
term goals, and positive feedback.*

*That diploma was indeed the first step in fulfilling his dream. Last
I checked in, he now works for a rappelling company and continues to
build his credentials to start his own business.*

Both of these children were struggling with the desire for instant
gratification. Had they been accommodated, they would have felt
fantastic for a short while, but would have ached for the joy and
satisfaction that achievement ultimately brings.

> The majority of children who have difficulties with
> the world around them are not primarily hyperactive
> but are reacting to an environment that does not
> provide them with the necessary ingredients for
> their development. An understanding of these
> developmental needs can only be gained when we
> assess the total life-space of a child, which includes
> school, family, and the child himself... These
> children most often need people who they can trust,
> rather than drugs (Minde 1975, 130–1).

Instant Gratification child demands strong instant feedback all the time. Any strong response is rewarding. If we get excited about his newest invention, great. If he bothers his younger sister and she makes a crazy, ear-numbing shriek, even more fantastic. How about if we jump in and yell at him, escort him to his room, and hold the door closed? We nailed it! Best. Reward. Ever. The reason we struggle so much to discipline this child is because we are disciplining with too much energy, being too generous with the commodity he so craves.

In his personality temperament and character traits inventory, Cloninger (Cloninger 1987; see also Cloninger et al. 1993) described four temperamental traits:

- Harm Avoidance (HA)

- Reward Dependence (RD)

- Persistence (P)

- Novelty Seeking (NS).

Novelty seeking (instant gratification) is a personality trait with a tendency to act, explore, and respond to novelty and make impulsive decisions. This type of child has extravagant approaches to reward cues, and rapidly loses his temper. He cannot tolerate monotony; he may be inconsistent in relationships due to a lack of self-reflection. When frustrated, he quickly disengages.

A novelty-seeking person also has many advantages to her personality. She is excitable, curious, enthusiastic, and engages quickly with new and unfamiliar stimuli, thereby expanding the likelihood that she will learn from her environment.

I prefer "instant gratification," but you can use "novelty seeking" if you feel it describes your child best. What's crucial to understand is that our Instant Gratification, novelty-seeking child is nondysfunctional. In fact, his personality actually contributes to adaptive functioning. In this beautiful world of many varied personalities, Instant Gratification child adds his own strengths, thereby completing the picture.

Since our yelling or loud criticism is inadvertently rewarding our Instant Gratification kid and reinforcing his ability to get the negative feedback in a heartbeat, it's time to STOP!

Easier said than done.

We parents are not flourishing; we are caught in a habit cycle that we are struggling to break. Jonny picks on his brother. Parent yells. Jonny gets strong negative feedback and unconsciously registers that feedback as something he may want to try to trigger again. So Jonny goes right back at it, this time picking on his sister. We up the punishment. He cries. We cry.

Help! Seems Jonny is now in charge, and he is way too young for that responsibility! He makes TERRIBLE decisions; we can do much better than him. Instead, we cower in the corner, hoping his explosion will simmer down quickly, with as little collateral damage as possible. To handle ever-escalating tantrums, we desperately make up new rules as we collapse, utterly defeated, at the end of each day.

It's time to take charge, to become that parent you dreamed of being. This will require some self-care. When the oxygen drops on an airplane, you put the mask on yourself first. Only when you can breathe, do you quickly strap the mask on your little one. You deserve to be your best you; your family craves the emotional and mental skills you are about to develop.

Action Plan

1. Get yourselves a glass of wine, find a peaceful (or at least not totally chaotic) spot, and relax.

2. Remind yourself that this child is a gift from God. He is not disordered; he is healthy, and he needs your help. You are his environment.

3. Review in your mind or write down what is special about your child. Imagine her in your mind's eye and see where she shines.

4. Know that you have not caused her struggles; you have been trying to figure out how to help her since the moment she was born. You are not the cause of her challenge, but you are the leader in the home, and with your patience, curiosity, and guidance, she will do great.

5. Make a list of the instances where you and your child are too frequently butting heads. Go through the day. Remember the moments when you wanted to run away or put him up for adoption.

The next chapter is just for you.

THE CHEAT SHEET

Chapter One:
Understanding "Instant Gratification" Kid

- ☛ We begin this book with a parenting program because your child's challenges do not live in your child alone; the symptoms are a manifestation of a conflict between your child and his environment.

- ☛ YOU are your child's environment.

- ☛ Things I have learned through trial and error while raising my children with ADHD symptoms:

    1. I did not cause this problem, but I am powerful and can help my child overcome his challenges.

    2. I am here to help my child make sense of her world, not to coddle, fix, or accommodate.

    3. My child is healthy and struggling.

- ☛ Why did we become parents to begin with? Parenting is the most significant thing we will ever do. Giving to others, sacrificing, and expanding our comfort zone makes us better people. The challenge of raising kids makes us great if we are paying attention. All people grow from their challenges.

- ☛ We must give our children responsibilities and allow them to dream. Their challenges will help them grow.

- ☛ Why are we told to accommodate this child or give her fewer responsibilities?

    1. We are told by doctors and teachers that she is "disordered" despite the lack of evidence.

    2. It's HARD to raise him, so we begin to believe they must be right; this behavior can't be normal.

    3. We don't want our child to suffer.

CHAPTER TWO

If Mama Ain't Happy,
Ain't Nobody Happy!

(This illustration is based on real-life family experiences.)

"MOM, I'M HOME! What's for dinner?" shouts Joey as he bursts through the door, hurling his backpack.

Mom starts to sweat; there is no good answer to this question, no way to predict Joey's response. One day "salmon and mashed potatoes" gets rewarded with a huge "that's my favorite!" Two days later the same response could lead to a full-blown hour-long tantrum and major property destruction.

Mom is terrified, bracing for the onslaught. Joey senses the terror and lets it rip. Mom yells back. Let the games begin!

If we are going to discipline this child, we must make four very important decisions today.

- **Decide** to see our child as a healthy child who is capable of learning to behave like a civilized person.

- **Decide** to own our parenting role and see it as crucial and powerful, a role that may not be abandoned or outsourced.

- **Decide** to accept that raising children is a long and valuable process, there are no shortcuts, and our perseverance will help our child succeed and give us the most valuable life skills we can ever develop.

- **Decide** to realize that this child is a blessing to us, the very child God gifted us with. We and our children are a perfect match, and with all the glitches and bumps along the way, this is our journey together. There is no return or exchange policy because the child we got is the one we need. If we are raising our child but dreaming that he be more like the neighbor's kid, this process cannot work. Only when we embrace the gift we have can we proceed.

If Mom saw Joey as healthy and capable, would she let this behavior drag on indefinitely? Would she be understanding that Joey had a hard day and needs to let off steam? Would she run to pick up the backpack and put it in its place? Would she yell back? No way! Healthy, normal kids are not permitted to behave this way.

Why has Mom backed away? What is she thinking? What are WE thinking when we nurture destructive behavior?

Mom and Dad are not thinking. They have been triggered and have gone into automatic response mode. At this point, it is nearly impossible to pull back from the unhelpful response that follows.

Why is that? Let's understand the habit loop better so we can become deliberate, effective parents.

In this chapter we will:

- Focus on our response to our child's triggering behavior

- Understand that we are not simply responding to the behavior; we are also grappling with our avalanche of emotions, feelings, and experiences from the past

- Examine what happens to us when we are triggered, and why our responses are not aligned with the presenting situation

- See that due to the emotional overload, we stop using our thinking brain and drive our high-speed response car down a dangerous, emotionally charged, winding road with no brakes.

When we become cognizant of our internal process, we can get the help we need to work out our stress and separate the behavior of the child in front of us from all the ghosts of the past. We only develop new communication habits when we respectfully and lovingly care for ourselves.

What is our Cue-Routine-Reward cycle? The first step towards respectfully repairing our own pain.

As a child, Michael Phelps was highly emotional and undisciplined. His coach, Bob Bowman, realized that although Michael had great physical potential, if he was going to compete and win swimming competitions, he would have to do some serious work on his mental preparation and stop acting impulsively. Michael's parents had recently divorced, and he was struggling under the weight of the separation. He had already been diagnosed as ADHD. Coach Bowman knew he had to replace the negative triggers coming from Michael's emotional load and causing outbursts and lack of focus, and replace them with new positive triggers. In this way he could help Michael develop a positive habit loop.

Every day after practice in the pool, Bowman sent Michael home with a "videotape" to watch. There was no actual video; it was a mental visualization exercise that was practiced twice daily. Phelps would imagine every move in the competition in slow motion repeatedly. He focused on his past successes and choices and dealt with any future challenges. He practiced so many times in his mind that when he stepped into the pool and his coach called out "videotape" (his new positive trigger), he moved automatically.

When Phelps dived into the water at the 2008 Summer Olympics, his goggles instantly filled with water. He was calm. He had already practiced swimming in the dark countless times in his "videotapes." When he broke through the water with his final powerful stroke, the cheers he heard were deafening. Upon removing his goggles, he discovered "WR"—world record—next to his name on the scoreboard. He had won another gold and demolished every previous swimming record, and he had done it blind!

Parenting successfully is as powerful an act as winning a gold medal at the Olympics. Parenting a kid with ADHD symptoms bumps the task up to swimming with water in our goggles. Water in the goggles throws us off course. We don't know how to do that! It's frightening and isolating, causing us to immediately escape to our least successful emotional responses: panic, anger, fear, resentment. Can we break through these, like world swimming champion Phelps did? Only if we become aware of the possible triggers and play our own videotape.

We need to recognize and break our habit cycles and begin acting deliberately. Just like Phelps, we approach our most important job in a fashion that is a little undisciplined, and highly emotional. Why are we so emotional despite our assumption that we are rational adults, ready for the job?

In case you suspected you were the only one regularly making emotional nondecisions, I'll put myself out there first.

There are a lot of kids wandering around my house on a regular basis. They have all these needs like showering, eating, playing, constructing, and eating some more, which leaves a constant trail of stuff all over the place. One would think I would just train my kids to clean up after themselves; case closed. But I have an old, deep-seated need to get things organized. And I'm also allergic to the chaos of mess. My stress caused by the mess is much greater than my need to teach the kids to tidy up after themselves.

Are they incapable of learning to clean, or have they made it just hard enough for me to get them mobilized so that I trade calm, rational thought for emotionally triggered, knee-jerk behavior and clean it all myself? My irrational response nurtures their messy habits and does not help them mature; it enhances my feeling that I can rely only on myself and increases my resentment; the feelings and habits become entrenched as we repeat the cycle over and over.

Old voices are at play here. One says, "Let the kids play and enjoy; you'll have time to train them in responsibility later." The other says, "The chaos is too deep and too large. I would rather return my mental state to 'calm' than educate my child." The combination leads to spoiled kids, and an explosive, resentful mother. I **know** better, I really do, but my emotions take over; my old voices drown out rational thought; and yes, I am a bit emotional and undisciplined. We will pick this story up again later and unearth more triggers along with hopefully better responses.

What is the mechanism of action that causes us to circumvent our rational brain and respond so quickly and poorly to emotional triggers? How can we change it?

The first step to dismantling emotional barriers is to identify them and then create rational, respectful discipline.

We have had ample time in our pre-parenting lives to create habits, good and bad. We have been triggered many times! Some of the triggers have been positive and have built confidence. As an example, when creating "works of art" and being rewarded with many compliments about our diligent, creative work, we learned to work even harder to get the same results again. The more positive feedback we received, the more we were motivated to work hard, and this attribute turned into a habit.

Other triggers, such as making mistakes and being shamed, could lead to avoiding bold behavior and fear of failure. Being treated aggressively could reduce our sense of self and confidence. Being compared to others could lead to a feeling of unworthiness or a need to constantly prove oneself. When our childhood experiences continually trigger these responses of fear, avoidance, and other negative emotions, we develop unhealthy habits. When we become adults and our kids inadvertently step on the land mine of our old and sore emotion, we go directly into a habit loop. The old cringe or desire to attack or escape returns. Each of us has many triggers, which lead to multiple and unexpected internal emotional voices.

Charles Duhigg, in his fantastic and highly recommended book, *The Power of Habit,* explains what the habit loop is, how we develop it, and how to reset our undesirable habits.

This is what a parent habit loop looks like:

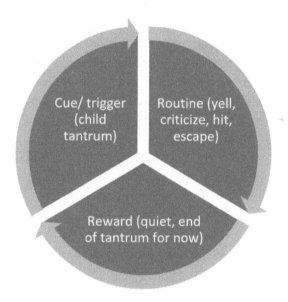

Our child tantrums; we have a need to return to quiet or control. The tantrum triggers in us an emotional and physical discomfort that demands resolution. That is the **cue**. There are rational responses to tantrums, as we will learn about in the next few chapters. Yelling, hitting, and criticizing are not only the least effective choices, but they are also damaging. We would not choose them if we were thinking. But we are not; we have been triggered by the tantrum, and the behavior must be eliminated NOW! (Are we panicked that the child is not normal? Are we terrified that it will never end? Do we lack a strategy and feel powerless? Was tantrumming an inexcusable sin in our homes growing up?) Whatever the deep cause, we make a terrible choice and go into a **routine** that **rewards** us in the short term by producing a startled, quiet child. But will he tantrum again? You bet!

As we get more "positive" results (temporary calm or quiet) from irrational responses, we develop a habit and suspend thought. The more we repeat a behavior, the stronger the habit we create. Once something becomes a habit, our rational mind does not have to get involved for us to carry out the task. The next time the cue happens, we go directly into our routine, and only afterward do we hate ourselves for breaking every one of our parenting red lines. We can't understand why we couldn't just stop yelling, punishing, and behaving so poorly.

The cycle repeats itself. Our rational selves are no longer in charge because the behavior has been practiced and reinforced so many times. **We develop habit loops, and our kids mimic us. Can we break out of the symbiotic emotional entanglement and build a new, healthy attachment with our children?**

Our kids are also developing habit loops. Instant Gratification child likes a lot of attention, wants things now, hates to hear "no," and would prefer you leave him alone when he's having fun.

Here is Instant Gratification child's habit loop:

We are intertwined.

Our child triggers us because of her need for a strong response (positive or negative—as long as it's strong); we are triggered by her outburst. We develop a need to de-escalate or punish. Thus we respond vigorously, thereby rewarding her! And the cycle goes on and on and on.

Until . . .

We remember that we are the adults!

We must stop feeding into this toxic exchange. How is that done? By moving our unconscious habit loop back to the conscious and resetting it. Easier said than done, but it is possible. Do you know why? Because respecting our emotional overload and our stress and rebalancing ourselves is the best gift we will EVER give ourselves and our child. When we regain self-discipline and self-respect, we establish ourselves as the leaders in our home. When we separate our emotional process from that of our child's, our child can safely go back to being a child, knowing that he can no longer trigger a response in us, and becoming able to rely on us to set the tone.

How can we break unhealthy habit loops and replace them with new, constructive ones?

Are you ever driving, and you find yourself in your driveway without being cognizant of how you got there? Do you remember how much effort it took to learn how to drive when you were sixteen? How is it that now driving is so simple, to the point that you are almost not aware that you are driving? Our minds create habit loops to free us up to work out more complex problems. In the case of Michael Phelps, the cue was "videotape," as shouted by his coach as he entered the water. His reward was winning the competitions. He started with small wins and built up from there. If "videotape" was followed by success often enough, a craving was established to repeat the behavior, and it became as natural as driving. We must find our own "videotape" trigger to replace the old triggers and form a new, positive habit.

Follow these steps carefully to become aware of your habit loops and start to change them:

1. **Emotional Cue: Identify your emotions and write them down.** Do you have any alone time, just for you and your thoughts? If not, create some. It helps to put your phone down, because the phone demands more attention from us than our kids do. During this quiet time, **meditate** on the interactions you have been having with your child. Watch your most recent interactions on a "videotape." Do the interactions go in circles? What triggers you? What emotion do you feel

every time you get triggered? Is it despair? Humiliation? Disappointment in yourself or your child? Concern for his future? Anger? Do you feel unappreciated? Maybe you have no idea how to respond?

Understand that your emotional feeling launches you directly into a behavioral response, so identifying the emotion is key. Keep your personal story in mind as you travel inward. We carry all our old responses and triggers in a huge suitcase of emotions on our shoulders. We sometimes link our children's behaviors to our pre-parent past, thereby exaggerating our response and expressing rage that we cannot even understand. (For example, our child reminds us of a relative who was controlling or intimidating. Even a hint of those old feelings [a cue] can trigger a response just to escape the feeling that interaction imposed on us.)

Ask yourself why a behavior triggers you to feel a specific emotion and where that response comes from. Speak to a friend, spouse, or therapist and trace your strong emotion back to its original trigger. Talk about your pain, confusion, rage, powerlessness, or any other legitimate feeling you have had in response to past experiences. Not all experiences are from the distant past; even trouble with a boss can trigger emotional responses at home. Give yourself the time to examine how new situations are connecting you to the past. That may help you be less disappointed in yourself. Write down how you feel. Name the most dominant emotions.

2. **Physical Cue: Identify your physical response.** Every strong emotional feeling is accompanied by a physical response; we feel our stress in our body. Where do you feel yours? Nausea? Headache? Tight shoulders or chest? Get in touch with your body; feel the tightness. When we feel that physical discomfort, it is a sign to us to pull back. The better you get in touch with your physical feeling, the faster you will be able to disengage.

3. <u>Routine:</u> **This is the automatic behavior following the trigger. We must visualize choosing a more productive response. What is your routine now?** While you watch yourself on the "videotape," what is counterproductive about your response and what do you like? Are you listening well, or are you blocked by panic? Are you complimentary to your child, or are the loud voices of the criticism you have absorbed redirecting you? Do you take the time to play a game or read a book to her, or do you have the urge to be constantly "productive" and process playtime as wasted time? Do you share some laughs with him, or is it all business? Celebrate your strengths and successes. Become aware of the automatic routines you slip into and their origin.

4. <u>Triggers to Routine:</u> **Feel your environment. What is contributing to your stress buildup?** Is it the baby crying? Are your kids treating each other unkindly? Is the house messy? Did the blatant disrespect bring you down? Have you spent any time by yourself today, doing something you like or speaking to a friend who fills you with energy? Are you running on an empty emotional tank?

   Review the scenario from today when you yelled at or threatened your child. What overwhelmed you? Were you hungry, tired, or suffering from a headache? Could you not accept once again that you are stuck raising this kid and not the compliant one? Study the pitfalls that may repeat themselves (think water in goggles). Be kind to yourself. If your emotional weight is too heavy, you will have no oxygen left for anyone else. Know that stress plus mess can lead anyone to shut down.

5. <u>Reward:</u> **The same triggers, a different response.** So far, we have identified the trigger and visualized it. We have examined our routine, seen what exacerbates it, and identified what responses we have that we like. Now we must anticipate the stress and change the response. <u>Visualize a response that</u>

will give you much more satisfaction than the previous, more aggressive responses. How can you calm yourself down? You will now visualize yourself using your calm response repeatedly. For this to be successful, we must link our calm leadership behavior to an enjoyable outcome.

The following are a few calm-maintaining suggestions. Of course, we each must find the reward that works best for us.

- Counting to ten or breathing generally doesn't work well because we tend to forget to do those things when stressed. One mother gave me a different idea. She said she never yells, but she goes to the bathroom an awful lot. If you can anticipate the trigger, sometimes a quick exit to catch your breath is very valuable. Even a minute out of the storm could rescue you from a toxic response. This option is only available if you are not leaving a younger child to become the target of your frustrated child's behavior. Hanging an EXIT sign in the kitchen with an arrow to the escape room might help. If the kids ask about the new sign, explain that you sometimes need time to think or take a break and don't always remember that you need it, so the new sign is your reminder. Kids love to hear that their parents work hard to be better, not just them.

- Prepare a joke, something that *really* tickles you. One father chose to say "serenity now" (apparently from *Seinfeld.* Look it up; I hear it's funny). He would say it out loud each time his daughter triggered him with a disrespectful comment. (Just to calm you down, dear parent, we will not be tolerating or nurturing disrespectful behavior; we will address that soon. The first step is becoming a leader.) Think of a funny situation, something that made you belly laugh, and visualize it or repeat it to calm the building stress.

▫ Make a mantra. Some examples: "One moment of self-control will pay huge dividends"; "I am stronger than my need to yell"; "My calm is the biggest gift I can give my child"; "I love my calm response."

▫ Create something external as a reminder to remain calm. Put a stop sign on the fridge. Find a meaningful quote and write it down. Do you feel calm on the beach? Hang a picture of the beach in the kitchen (most of the tantrums go down in the kitchen in my experience).

▫ Here's my favorite (sorry, fathers, this is only useful for the mothers): I like to visualize the challenge of childbirth and how bravely I battled each contraction. I knew that if I tightened every muscle, the contraction would be more difficult. But if I gained control, I could focus on my calm muscle, and the contraction would end more easily. There is an end to every contraction and to every temper tantrum. The only part that's in my control is my response.

▫ Get some help! If you feel that you will not manage to contain your frustration, ask someone in your home to say a previously agreed-upon word or phrase that will remind you to disengage. Phelps needed his coach to get started. Your "coach" can be a spouse, relative, or friend. Be careful here; if you will feel criticized by the reminder, it will not work. Only use this technique if you will see the intervention as helpful rather than critical.

6. **Share:** The final step is **sharing** this process with a spouse, partner, friend, or relative. Talk through your successes and celebrate them, even the small ones. Every tiny choice that brings you closer to a calm leadership response is a great achievement. Get your frustrations out, not on your child but to a fellow parent who is probably dealing with similar issues. Visualize together in the evening, after a long day's

interactions, the challenges and the achievements. Remind yourself daily that you are blessed and that you are raising a first-rate child. The more you practice in your mind, the more you reframe your reality.

This next story is a continuation of the one I began at the start of the chapter. The theme is still mess. I'm making some progress.

I come from a big, beautiful family with five brothers and two sisters. We were a sociable bunch, so on a weekend afternoon, each of us could easily have between two and five friends over. Do the math; that's a lot of mess. As the evening of these very enjoyable days approached, I would notice a creeping, uneasy feeling in my stomach, knowing that as one of the older children, it would be my task to clean the chips from the food fight out of the carpet, collect the tinker toys that had been hurled between the two forts in the living room . . . You get the picture? Suddenly I was yelling at all the little kids to stop throwing, to clean up, to get out. Not pretty.

Fast-forward a bunch of years. Now I'm blessed to be the mother of six beautiful children, also a sociable lot. They are welcome to invite friends to jump on the trampoline and enjoy kid fun on Saturday afternoons. I'm not a big yeller. But suddenly, I find myself shouting at the happy, messy kids to clean up, or I start frantically zipping around, making a nuisance of myself, packing games away while the kids are playing. The house starts getting back in order, but I have triggered my husband, and he starts demanding that everyone get up and clean.

It works; the kids are mobilized! Some progress is made—I am not doing all the cleaning myself while acknowledging that the mess is too much for me. But I am still behaving poorly—yelling, giving mixed messages. I give no clear instructions to my children and little guests, and I am still completely out of touch with the deeper internal emotional panic and feeling that I am in some way being taken advantage of.

Here is my loop:

Cue:
Emotional: feeling out of control and distressed by mess in my house, triggered by panic from the past.
Physical: headache

Routine:
Yelling at my children and guests, cleaning in an unreasonable way, not giving clear instructions about my need

Reward:
Husband and I mobilizing kids to "help Mom," thereby enforcing my unreasonable behavior, but rewarding me by getting the home back into the order I needed.

I was triggered, and the behavior that followed, the yelling and frantic cleaning, was rewarded by a clean house. What was the price? Total loss of control, disrespect for my children who had been permitted to invite friends over, and loss of a valuable process of teaching my children to be more responsible.

Now what? How can this be repaired?

Most often we either continue the pattern because we are so deep in the habit loop and are unaware that it is even happening, or we have no idea that we have the power to stop it. We may also lash out by not permitting guests to come to play or decide that our behavior is so unjustified that we choose to cut out the yelling and instead suffer in silence. The suffering in silence option usually causes us significant pain; the price is too high. We deserve better! Below is an alternative **cue-routine-reward** habit that I committed to adopting.

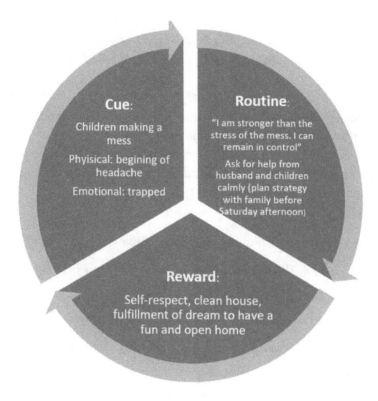

One more example.

This involves a father of four children, one of whom "has a little ADHD," as the father reports. "She [his daughter] moves slowly when given instructions and has trouble following through." It exhausts the father, who is responsible for getting the children out the door in the morning.

"Who does this child remind you of?" I ask.

"Oh, she's just like me!"

That's a clue. If something really triggers you, it is bringing up strong emotions from the past. It is either a repeat situation or characteristic.

What is triggering the father? He tells me he needs order, and when things don't move along smoothly, he feels chaotic and desperate to return to order. Desperation turns instantly to anger, which drives a need for resolution by yelling. "Does it work, the yelling?" I ask.

"Sure, the kids get the message and start moving."

What's the price? Poor Dad, he's crushed; he was NEVER going to yell at his kids. The problem is, he's been triggered by ghosts of the past and his needs in the present, and the yelling has "worked" enough times to create a habit loop.

"What are the ghosts of the past? Were you also a little spacey? How did your family respond to you? How closely does your behavior today mimic that of the adults of your childhood?"

"I was yelled at a lot, and everyone wanted to understand why I couldn't figure out how to get things done right. There were strong feelings of shame and guilt. I now sound very similar to my parents."

Old loop:

- **Cue:** Daughter moving slowly, not following instructions

    □ Physical trigger – unknown, needs further investigation.

    □ Emotional trigger – shame and feeling unable to behave "normally"; need for order.

- **Routine:** Speak sharply or yell; criticize child for her incompetence.

- **Resolution:** Father rewarded by the child getting scared and moving quickly.

    □ The price: damage to father/daughter relationship; daughter feeling shame and wanting to be normal; father distraught by his lack of control.

New loop (meditate on and practice your new loop in advance so you are not guessing in the heat of the moment):

- **Cue:** Daughter moving slowly; not following instructions

    □ Physical trigger – N/A

    □ Emotional trigger – shame, fear of chaos

- **Routine:** Close eyes and breathe; leave the room to stay calm

    □ Invite child to understand the father's stress

▫ The father can offer a more sensitive way of communicating and getting the result of the child moving along more efficiently. It can be a gentle touch or an agreed-upon sentence.

- **Resolution**: Calm morning environment, a self-respecting father, a respected daughter.

Now it's your turn.

What sends you into behavior patterns that make you feel disappointed in yourself? You deserve self-respect! You deserve to be the calm parent you dreamed you would be. Give yourself the gift of figuring out and changing your habit loop. Once you are rewarded frequently enough for your conscious choices, this behavior will become your new habit loop.

Identify your "engine." What is the cause of your decision-making process yet lurks in your internal shadows and you are not aware of it? What do you hold as the highest value, so you sacrifice other values to ensure this need is realized?

Identifying our engine is a technique I have developed over years in conversation with many clients. The concept of the "engine" emerged as I was talking with a young client. He had suffered some serious abuse and had redefined himself as a loser, someone who could do nothing right. I told him to imagine himself as a beautiful Ferrari—red, shiny, ready to tear up the road. Unfortunately, his sparkling Ferrari engine had been stolen (by the abuse, neglect, false expectations, poor examples), and a Subaru engine was inserted in its place.

Would the car hum? Would its driver experience the joy of the ride? Nothing would work; he would be spluttering at the side of the road. Should he blame himself for the car's breakdown? Never! The engine is there and hurting him. His job is to identify it, understand the damage it is doing, and replace this engine with the one that's just right for his magnificent self.

I will explain this process through a few examples:

1. *Shauna chose to be a stay-at-home mom, giving haircuts on the side. She has one small child. All she craves in life is an organized, neat home,*

to take her little boy to the park in the afternoon, and have a tasty, gourmet dinner waiting for her husband when he comes home from work. But everything about how she runs her life contradicts these stated goals. The house is a mess. They never make it to the park. She comes late to every doctor's appointment, avoids booking haircut clients, and she and her husband often eat oatmeal for dinner. Why is she not even close to achieving her goals?

Shauna's engine is much louder and stronger than her stated desire and dream. After asking a few questions, we begin to get a picture of what is blocking her from her goal.

- Who do you view as the ideal person?

- What about that person do you so admire and see as a value above all others?

- What makes you secretly jealous of others?

- What is a compliment you would love to get but would never ask for?

Here are a few of Shauna's responses:

- Her mother never stops; she does everything, and does it well. She hosts elegant dinner parties while working full time and keeping a sparkling home. She is involved in charity work and volunteers at the local church.

- Work never ends for her dad. No matter how much work he has put into a project, there is always more to be done.

- Her parents are the "ideal" people. She admires their ability to keep going, using every moment of their lives in a productive way. She obviously feels jealous of people who are highly effective, getting things done all the time.

- What she actually craves deep in her heart is to be that efficient person, catching the dust as it falls before it hits a gleaming surface in her home.

More questions for Shauna:

- Has this value you see in others been a blessing to them?
- What happens to you when you attempt to mimic the values you admire?

Shauna's responses:

- "My mother did not sit and play with us; she was always doing something. We had everything we needed and more, but not that calm time where there was no race, that we could just sit and enjoy time together. Time was a commodity, never to be wasted. Reading, watching a movie, going to the beach for a lazy afternoon were not permitted. My mother never relaxes; my father doesn't either."

- "When I have somewhere to go, for some reason, I suddenly have the urge to organize the refrigerator, to my husband's dismay. I can't even explain to him why I am shoving in so much and running late. In the afternoon, I either race around cleaning up or collapse in disgust and do nothing. I don't play with my son. I don't go to the park. I don't make money; I read a novel. And I can't stand myself!"

What is Shauna's engine, her underlying need that frustrates her ability to set up her dream home and family? Her engine is her need to be productive. Productivity in itself is wonderful, but when it takes over as the sole need, all else falls away. She looks at her parents and says, "How did they pull it off?" They didn't, but she can't see that. They didn't play with their kids; they didn't enjoy any relaxation; and they didn't teach their kids responsibility because they were doing everything productively themselves. They were loving and kind and generous—very good parents—which makes this confusing. Their chosen values contradict her deepest desire, but she is trapped in the need to mimic them.

Identifying an engine does not mean that we then reject our past or the people we try to copy because of our admiration for them. We simply reflect on and thereby reduce the need to imitate them. We make it just one of our values and strike a healthy balance.

When someone is raised in a home in which productivity is the supreme value, but where the parents allow that child to observe passively and do not teach their child *how* to be productive, the child is doomed to fail. She has only two options: be very busy in an unsystematic and chaotic way or collapse. If she is already being busy, she must shove in everything so she is as productive as possible. If she has a lazy afternoon, all is lost, and she may as well burn time. She will not replace the lack of productivity with a nice trip to the park, which would just confirm her laziness. So, the child doesn't play; the mother is frustrated and distracted, and neither knows why.

Once we identify the engine, we can see how it is harming us. We can get to the root of the desire and compare it to our chosen adult values. We then review scenarios and decisions from life today and see how this engine is directly harming every decision. We can understand our feelings of internal stress, disappointment, or anger are a result of this engine. We can then begin the process of changing the habit loop.

2. Dan is a husband, father, and on unemployment benefits because he can't hold down a job. He suffers from bouts of depression, severe anxiety, and listlessness. He is very disorganized, which is how he landed in my office to begin with. He loves his family, wants to get a good job, and knows he is very intelligent and capable. During conversation, I shared with him that my friend was having brain surgery that day, and I was very concerned. I expected him to wish my friend well, to show an appropriate level of concern and move on. Something else truly surprising happened. Dan said, "You know, once the doctors thought I had a brain tumor. I suffered a lot, and I'm still suffering from headaches every day."

Question for Dan:

- Who do you feel jealous of, and why?

Dan's response was impressive in its honesty.

- He said he felt jealous that everyone felt sorry for this other person and not him. He felt sad that the other person had "out-suffered" him.

Many people secretly hold victimhood and suffering as their highest value. Most of them have had their real voice stripped from them through some form of abuse. Dan was no different. I asked about his relationship with suffering and illness as a child. He responded that his father was verbally and physically abusive. Dan was desperate for the adults around him to see his pain, but they did not. The only time he got loving attention was when he was sick or if his parent felt he was weak and needed pity. Weakness became a value. Being a victim was his engine.

How does the need to be a victim hamper success in every area of life? If a person feels valued only when he suffers, he must always be suffering. That means he may not allow himself to succeed, as that would make him normative and even powerful. In a relationship, he must be "wronged" often, leaving the spouse confused as to why she is always inadvertently hurting him. Children are treated to a heaping dose of "you are making life so hard for me," "do you know how hard I work, and you never appreciate me and my efforts!" Although he has a genuine desire to be healthy and strong and successful, his inner core says, "Your only power is in your weakness. Make sure you are always in a sorry state."

Only when we found the engine could he clearly see how the need to suffer and be a victim was taking over every area of his life. Now Dan must pay attention to the stress that mounts the minute someone suggests he is doing well or someone is suffering more than he is, or not enough people are paying attention to his pain, and then create a new healthy success- and relationship-oriented habit loop.

3. Jeff is an architect, but only in his fantasy world. He's actually a computer programmer who was supposed to be an architect. He was supposed to go to Harvard. He was surely smart and capable enough to attend an Ivy League school, but his fear of failure forced him into the very prestigious New York University. He is now a dad, a programmer, and "just" a suburban husband. And he does the suburban dad routine poorly. He blames his running late, messiness, and inability to discipline his children consistently on his ADHD. What's the engine? It took a while to reveal.

Question for Jeff:

- What are you most ashamed of?

Jeff's response:

- "My diploma from NYU."

What? Yup, he was supposed to be a famous architect, and he is a middle-class suburban dad with a nine-to-five job. No travel, no excitement, no dream. His engine was the need to be special, the best, the edgy, smart guy, but fear held him back. Resentment filled the void.

When his children or wife needed something that looked like regular, boring life, he froze or ran. The chaos that ensued was quickly medicated but will not dissipate until he makes peace with this engine and learns to embrace the life he has or finds the courage to make a change. Jeff's spouse and children should never absorb the frustration, although they can be a part of his healing.

Finding our old broken-down engine and replacing it with the shiny bright one that fits our Ferrari requires a journey back in time. We must also answer a few very direct questions as honestly as possible. Never feel shame in answering these questions. You are brave and care for yourself and your family so much that you are willing to look yourself in the eye and finally examine what has been holding you back for so long. You have not caused your own problems, nor did you invite them, but you can choose to examine and change them.

Here are the questions you can ask to direct you towards your engine:

1. What pattern continually repeats in your life, which you feel powerless to change?

2. What have you been blaming on others that may be coming from an old habit in you?

3. Do you need to be blamed by others so that you can hang onto a harmful behavior?

4. Who do you most admire, and for what attribute?

5. How does that attribute play out in the other person? Has it enhanced or hindered their life? Are you copying the behavior, and is it doing the same for yours?

6. Who are you secretly jealous of? Why?

7. What compliment do you crave most (you work so hard; you are always put together; you do everything yourself . . .), but would either never ask anyone for, or would feel ashamed if you did get it?

It's HARD to self-critique, let alone try to identify where our difficult responses come from and understand how to root them out. Since we are often dealing with childhood trauma or old patterns, we do not store the memories in our conscious mind but rather shove them down and absorb them in our bodies. We function admirably for years, with only some slight snags along the way.

When our kids show up, they bring those old painful feelings right back to the surface in a complete jumble. Raising our children is the surest way to force us to get back in touch with ourselves (this is another reason our children are such a blessing to us). We face the choice of either grabbing this opportunity to dig up and heal the pain of the past or continue to repeat our patterns. We are already a few steps ahead. When we understand that the problem behavior does not "live" inside our child or in ourselves, but in a toxic loop between us, we can begin to take responsibility.

Another very helpful way to identify and heal painful patterns is through somatic therapy. According to studies, our bodies hold onto past traumas, which then reflect in our posture, reactions, and body language. We may also experience physical pain, indigestion, and other physical or emotional symptoms, triggered by old skeletons. EMDR (Eye Movement Desensitization and Reprocessing) and EFT (Emotionally Focused Therapy) are two therapies that I have seen produce very positive results. Talk therapy may be effective as well, but I recommend the other two for resolution of destructive repetitive patterns that are creating stress in your parenting and blocking your ability to parent with your complete self. We all need some help. Go get the help you need.

We must also learn to take care of ourselves:

Here is a final yet vital piece of advice for us parents on managing our stress for the sake of our own health and that of our children. David J. Palmiter Jr., PhD, author of *Working Parents, Thriving Families* (Sunrise River Press, 2011), states,

> Parents receive some of the best parenting advice every time they take off on an airplane. If the cabin loses pressure and you must put on an oxygen mask, put one on yourself first before you help your child. I see households all across America where the oxygen masks have long since dropped and all of the oxygen is going to the children . . . Investing in the relationship with their partner is one of the most giving things a parent can do.

Amy Novotney, author of "Take Care of Yourself First," adds,

> . . . the research makes it clear that children are negatively affected by their parents' stress. That's why modeling good stress management can make a very positive difference in children's behavior, as well as how they themselves cope with stress, psychologists say . . . Palmiter recommends that parents make time for exercise, hobbies, maintaining their friendships and connecting with their partners. That may mean committing to spending regular time at the gym or making date night a priority . . . Single parents should establish and nurture meaningful connections in other contexts. A satisfying relationship with a colleague, neighbor, family member, or friend can help to replenish one's energy for parenting challenges (2012, 44).

Any worthwhile achievement takes time. We must enter the inner recesses of our subconscious to discover why our child's lack of success or struggles paralyze us and make us feel so inferior and out of control. Often it has less to do with her and more to do with our own mentality.

Action Plan

1. Chart your habit loops. Chart your child's loop. See how they interact with each other. Are you each responding to the other's needs? Is this creating an unhealthy cycle? (A habit loop chart can be downloaded free of charge from my website, www.hyperhealing.org.)

2. Make a plan to recreate your loop. This can be challenging. Talk it over with someone you trust; run through examples of your behavior. Practice your new loop. Imagine your trigger, how you feel, and how you will choose to respond differently from now on. Put in your "videotape."

3. Spend time in the evening, reviewing how you responded throughout the day. Congratulate yourself on any successes, and strategize how you will improve on the responses that were less positive.

4. What is your "engine," and how is it hindering your relationship with your spouse or child? Answer the engine questions. Be honest and kind to yourself. Get help from a professional if the process is too difficult.

5. How are you going to destress? Will it be a once-a-week coffee with a friend, date night, or getting to the gym with a gym partner? These are not just nice suggestions; these are keys to your sanity and the health of your family. Make a choice, and get started on it tomorrow morning.

THE CHEAT SHEET

Chapter Two: The Parent Self-Care Program

☛ Why do we often have a toxic relationship and chaotic discipline with our children?

☛ To understand our less-than-optimal responses, we must first know our child is healthy; know we are in this for the long haul; know we can't outsource parenting to a teacher, therapist, doctor, or pill; and see our child as a great gift.

☛ Would we allow our child to tantrum or destroy property if we saw him as capable and healthy? No! Why are we allowing this behavior?

☛ We are responding poorly more because of our own emotional triggers and less because of our child's actual behavior, however terrible it may be.

☛ What triggers parents to respond emotionally instead of rationally? Shame at self or child, fear that the child will fail or the parent will not have the resources to raise the child, having been yelled at or overcoddled as a child, having lived in chaos, having been abused or neglected, and much more.

☛ How can we identify and heal the trigger so we stop going into an emotional response loop?

☛ Follow the healing behavior loop steps.

  1. Write down your negative feelings towards your child, and the negative responses you display. Try to understand their source. Why are they causing you to feel unempowered? Talk over your responses and triggers with a friend or therapist.

2. Physical cue: How does your body feel when you begin to get stressed? What hurts?

3. Routine: Review your response now and imagine a better response for the future. Practice it in your head.

4. Triggers to routine: What factors in your present environment are exacerbating your negative response? (Baby crying, mess in the house, tired, hungry)

5. Reward: Reject the reward you have been getting until now (quiet, shaky, calm) and replace it with an in-control, bonding, loving reward.

6. Share your process with your spouse or friend to get honest and productive feedback.

☞ Identify your engine. What is getting in the way of you fulfilling your dreams? What is stopping you from being your best self? Ask these questions to identify the engine that was wrongfully installed in the beautiful Ferrari that is you.

1. Who is your ideal person, and why? What attribute about that person do you admire above all else?

2. What makes you secretly jealous of others?

3. What compliment do you dream of getting but are too ashamed to ask for it?

4. Has the value you admire been a blessing to the other person?

5. What happens to you when you mimic that value?

6. What pattern do you continually repeat that destroys you, but you feel powerless to change?

☞ Put the oxygen mask on yourself first, and then assist your child. A parent who is ignoring his pain cannot raise a child with respect, calm, and joy. Instant Gratification children need strong leadership and clear rules and consequences. They need a well-cared-for parent to care for them. Spending time and effort on yourself will help your family thrive. Meet with friends, go to the gym, get a massage, watch a movie, go on vacation, and then come back to your beautiful child with the energy and desire to journey on together.

CHAPTER THREE

Exchange Curses
for Blessings

FIFTY PARENTS OR so shuffled in, a nice crowd for a chilly winter evening. These motivated fathers and mothers came to listen to a lecture on the causes of ADHD and treatment options. One woman, sitting in the front row, caught my attention. She was totally focused, her eyes trained on my face, scribbling every word frantically. And then she started to cry! I thought I was giving a stirring presentation, but had I really moved her to tears? Unfortunately, that was not the case.

The weeping mom came over to talk after the lecture. She told me that she had two sons, both diagnosed with ADHD. After hearing me explain matter-of-factly that children with ADHD have altered brains (yes, back then I was still blaming the brain, and I am ashamed to say I was telling parents that their children were less capable than their "normative" peers), she wanted to know why she should even consider having more children after having produced two defective ones. I tried to comfort her, telling her that her children could accomplish great things if only she applied the right techniques. She refused to be comforted. In a mere hour-long "scientific" lecture, I had told her that her children "couldn't." They couldn't focus; they couldn't act maturely; they couldn't make friends as well as others.

Laying aside the factual inaccuracies of my claims, who had given me the authority to declare anyone incapable of anything? How could I know how far a person can go? Could I declare the potential of these children? I had "cursed" her family.

The crying mom incident stirred me from my follow-the-crowd slumber, and I began to research how faulty the "brain blame" narrative was. Fast-forward a few years, and I was invited to be a member on a panel focused on ADHD treatment in the classroom. Another member of the panel was a well-respected child psychologist. When each of us was asked about the abilities of a child with ADHD, I discussed ADHD symptoms, how science has yet to determine the cause of the disorder, and that we should consider all students healthy and capable of succeeding.

My psychologist colleague disagreed emphatically. She read a prepared statement, confidently claiming that children diagnosed with ADHD had a brain disorder and lacked the same potential as other children. She then instructed a room overflowing with teachers to accommodate these children and not overload them with expectations because it would cause them unnecessary stress and set them up for failure.

I watched her message sink in. She was preaching to the converted; this is what most of the teachers already believed. It was validating for them to get professional confirmation. I lost the crowd. And the children? The sweet, unsuspecting, diagnosed children? They lost way more than the crowd that day. Their potential was sealed before they were given a chance to dream.

Has anyone you respected, someone you perceived as more powerful or knowledgeable than you, ever told you that you "can't"? Has that person determined who you are—whether smart, big-mouthed, talented, wild—without giving you the chance to discover who you could become on your own? What were the consequences?

I remember one of my curses well. It was in tenth-grade geometry. I was not doing well. The principal summoned me to her office and gave me two choices. I could either drop math because it was too hard for me, or I could suffer. "I choose to suffer!" would have been the correct answer, but both she and I failed. I believed her declaration that I was incapable of passing geometry, and she let me give up without a fight. I shrank that day. I was the girl who could not pass math. And the curse lingers still. Even though half the class cheated off my math tests in college, I was the girl who couldn't learn math. Why did I pass college math? It was a summer course. It was an easy course. It was in a community college . . . nothing could break the spell.

In this chapter we will examine the effects of the messages we hear and we give. We will see that we can be cursed by both positive and negative assessments stated by those more powerful than us. The process of understanding and removing curses and never passing them on is "a game-changer" in the words of a therapist friend of mine. I agree. Once we have identified our engine, changed our habit loop, and banished curses from our lives, we are prepared to take on the most important and impactful role of our lives.

Understanding the curse through the brilliant work of Carol S. Dweck

If there is any psychologist who can explain the reaction of the crying mom or my strange relationship with math, it's Carol S. Dweck, PhD. In her groundbreaking book *Mindset* (Ballantine Books, 2006), Dweck introduces us to two different mindsets: the "fixed" mindset and the "growth" mindset.

Someone with a growth mindset will see failure as an impetus to work harder, and hard work as a challenge that will lead to growth. If a growth mindset child gets a low grade on a test, she may look it over to understand her error and figure out what method to use to do better next time.

What about the fixed mindset child? She will be crushed by a bad grade. She will label herself as stupid, incapable, a total failure, and resolve to work less or drop out altogether.

How did these kids develop growth or fixed mindsets, and how do these mindsets affect them? What does any of this have to do with raising a child with ADHD symptoms?

Growth mindset children are hearing a message from a parent, teacher, older sibling, or other people of influence in their lives that intelligence can grow, talent can develop, and with hard work and effort, anyone can become better at anything—even at focusing and concentrating. They see the challenge as an opportunity, and approach it with curiosity and excitement.

In contrast, children developed fixed mindsets from being "diagnosed" or labeled with something.

What happens to a child who has been "diagnosed" with ADHD? The diagnosis itself comes loaded with a "fixed" message. The implication of the label is that a problem resides within a child and cannot be altered or changed. He "has" a problem, rather than he is struggling with a challenge.

Fixed (read: diagnosed) mindset kids hear that intelligence is something very basic and cannot be changed. They have been labeled as "smart," "talented," "inattentive," "unfocused," etc., and they need to constantly prove that the title they have been given is correct.

The growth mindset kids are always using their energy to stretch beyond their present ability because they don't have a set finish line. No one told them they can't or they must; all possibilities are open to them, and mistakes and questions are a welcome part of the process.

Even a positive label can set a person on the path toward a fixed mindset. A fixed mindset leaves a person trapped. If he has been told he is "smart," can he reveal that he's not smart? If he is "the talented one," can he slip up and produce mediocre art? While one child is exerting all his effort to explore, ask, and learn, the other is exerting all her efforts to protect the image others have of her. A child who has been labeled is always protecting the label, not perfecting it. He has a big secret to hide: he fears he is not nearly as smart as everyone says he is. If he makes a genuine friend, that friend will discover his terrible secret, that he actually has to study, that he doesn't understand everything, that he makes mistakes. No one can be allowed close enough to become privy to this information.

Another way people develop a fixed mindset is by experiencing any kind of abuse. When a person is physically, sexually, socially, or verbally abused or experiences severe neglect, no labels are required to tell this child exactly who he is. He hears it loud and clear through the actions of the abuser. He has redefined himself and now spends his time fearing being that person, while all along knowing that he can't escape the curse. He will then spend many years protecting himself so that no one will reveal how terrible he is. (His engine has been replaced, causing trauma and shame and a redefinition of self.)

Other messages that trigger a fixed mindset begin with "You never . . ." and "You always . . ."

A woman, well into adulthood, told me that when she was younger (thirty years younger!), it was her job to clear up and put the food away every Sunday night after dinner. She did what she thought was a great job each week. One Monday morning, her mother said casually, "You always leave one thing out. Why can't you ever finish the job?" To this day, this woman, now a mother herself, struggles to finish any chore. She feels an internal battle raging; she wants to leave just that one last thing undone.

According to the Oxford Living Dictionary, a curse is defined as: "A solemn utterance intended to invoke a supernatural power to inflict harm or punishment to someone." Of course, mental health professionals don't intend harm when they solemnly proclaim from their position of medical authority that a person has a lifelong psychiatric disorder/disease, as is defined in the psychiatric disease model of human emotional suffering and is codified in the Diagnostic and Statistical Manual of Mental Disorders (DSM).

"But over and over I've seen the aftermath of that powerful ritual of receiving and internalizing a lifelong, pathologizing diagnosis. Such disease model labels don't consider how personal losses, unmet needs, isolation, traumas, and social toxicity impact our lives in painful ways," says Michael Cornwall, PhD, in his Sept. 24, 2017, *Mad in America* article "Does a Psychiatric Diagnosis Have the Impact of a Medical Curse?"

When a person is labeled as disordered, depressed, or limited in some subjective way, his abilities have been confined; his potential has been established. What is not considered is his process, his history, his environment. He is told that he is not responsible for his limitations, and those limitations are fixed. This is the mirror image of the "smart" and "talented" child. Both children have been cursed. Both judge every experience and interaction through the lens of an unchangeable individual. They both are protecting their egos, avoiding challenges, blaming external factors for their perceived failures, and are unwilling to ask for help or reveal imperfections.

"Becoming is better than being," says Dweck (2006, 25). Unfortunately, the fixed mindset does not allow the luxury of becoming. Children must already be. We clearly see the damage caused by a fixed mindset when a person is labeled with positive attributes. What happens when negative characteristics become your permanent markers? "If failure means you lack competence or potential—that you are a failure—where do you go from there?" (Dweck 2006, 35).

Beware the curse of low expectations. We want to protect our children from failure at all costs, even though failure in a safe setting will make them more resilient. When we expect less of our children, when we don't ask them to help in the kitchen (she is clumsy; she makes a mess; she will feel bad about herself) or help around the house (he is so disorganized; the house looked better before he began; I will do it for him so he doesn't feel disappointed with his inability to get the job done), the message we are sending is that they can't! They can't bake; they can't organize; they can't get a good grade.

Children know we are attempting to shield them from pain, and the result is often devastation. Our children become adults who can't organize their house, can't complete a project, and can't finish a degree. This shielding is done with the best of intentions, but when, through our actions, we give over the message that they can't . . . they won't. And the results? Many of the ADHD symptoms on the DSM list.

It is not only our kids. What about us? Have we been told we can't? Have the powers that be declared who we are and what our capabilities are? Sure! Has this helped or hindered our ability to flourish? What is your story, dear parent? What fixed mindset symptoms are you displaying as a parent?

What are the symptoms of parenting with a fixed mindset?
Most of us have heard fixed messages from a helpful parent, teacher, or society. The mindset is that you must be a "good" parent, always

there for your kids, never failing. You approach parenting with the expectation that you must succeed, that your children will be just right, and that seeking advice would expose you as not having everything figured out. What would your real parenting experience look like, seeing as a "perfect" parent does not and never will exist? Your child tantrumming in public would be a humiliating disaster because the scene would display your lack of natural skill.

Let's up the challenge. You have a fixed parenting expectation of yourself and, oops, your child is an Instant Gratification kid with ADHD symptoms. You are supposed to be smart, capable, talented (if your curse was of a positive nature), or you were told you would fail at parenting (negatively worded curse). What are you to do? You are intent on proving everyone right or wrong and doing the best job ever.

There is nothing more painful for a fixed-mindset parent than a child publicly announcing through his actions that he is different, difficult, or in any way less than the other kids. I know how devastating it can be because I have been there myself. The energy output is directed away from focusing on this child and his needs and put towards appearing to be in control, all the while feeling the lie burn inside.

How the fixed and growth mindsets look in the parent of a child with ADHD symptoms

Fixed-mindset parent	Growth-mindset parent
Do you expect yourself to know exactly how to raise your child even though you have never done this before, for a child of this age with this temperament?	Do you seek help?
Are you ashamed when your interventions don't work out?	Do you see the failed intervention as an opportunity to learn from your mistakes?

Fixed-mindset parent	Growth-mindset parent
Do you feel intimidated when your child challenges you?	Do you love to discover that he knows something you don't yet know?
Do you overreact when your child misbehaves in public because others now see what a failure you are?	Do you take it easy on the response because everyone has children who sometimes misbehave?
Do you overreact to your children's flaws because you expect them to be as perfect as you were expected to be, or are you worried they will be as flawed as you fear you are?	Do you see your children's misbehavior as part of growing up, with room for improvement?
Do you panic when you don't know what's wrong with your child, assuming something is very wrong with him?	Do you find someone who has more experience than you to consult with?
Do you need to make everything you do seem effortless (think Wonder Woman with all her inborn perfections in all areas) so that people are impressed, and maybe a little jealous, of your "how does she do it all" abilities?	Are you open to sharing your challenges and battle wounds with friends or professionals?

If you find that you are of the fixed rather than growth mindset, it's time to reevaluate this perspective, because parenting is incompatible with "fixed" anything! Our children are dynamic, growing, changing human beings. We must be ready to grow with them and not spread the curse.

Combating the fixed mindset in parents and moving to a growth mindset

As always, improvement begins with us. The first step in shifting to a growth mindset is having gratitude for what we have. Embracing and cherishing the present helps us combat the need for it to be different or better. Gratitude signals a dynamic process, a level of joy in the part of a process rather than the expectation of a finished product. We must take a step back and see the gifts we are so fortunate to have right now. Our child is exactly the way he needs to be right now and will continue to grow with time. This moment is precious and should be acknowledged.

Take a few moments every day to be grateful for being a parent, for the sparkle in your child's eye, for the roof over your head, your job, your friends. Ask yourself, "What is great right now?" without adding "but"! Don't look for perfect; look for good. The way to halt "fixed" dead in its tracks is by being truly grateful for NOW, not planning for what will be, but for the tremendous abundance of now. Say it out loud for your child to hear. Say it often. Tell her how lucky you are to have her as your child. Tell her she was chosen just for you, and you love her as she is. Be grateful for who you are, the uniqueness of your personality, how you love, how you care, who you are right this very minute.

Next, we must abandon any notion of what is supposed to be (who decides that anyway?!) and evaluate where we are, what our goals are, and **engage in the journey of life**. Raising ourselves and our kids is a journey, with different aspirations and goals at different stages in our travels. If we realize that **our goal is improvement and not perfection**, we can begin to engage in a healthy way. We cannot get our child to develop great habits in every sphere right now, but we can take note of one area that needs improvement—for example, organization—and begin to help him with that.

Our measure of success will no longer be reaching the goal; it will now be remaining engaged in the process and taking steps to improve. We must celebrate the daily steps and choose the next one.

- Was I more patient today than yesterday? Fantastic!

- Did I discipline more clearly today? Great.

If the answer is no, why not? Is your lack of success because you are a failure? Not at all. Figure it out.

- Why did I yell today? Am I stressed because of work? Am I tired?

Talk it out. Think it through. You are not expected to know how to do this right; you are learning on the job. You are only expected to be willing to try your best and learn from your mistakes. The process is exhilarating.

My friends are always surprised that I know a thing or two about fixing cars. They wonder if I took a course. No, I did not. When I learned to drive, we had a string of cars that broke down constantly. Had I been "fixed," I might have been humiliated about driving cars that were unreliable. Instead, each time the car broke down I paid close attention at the repair shop, asked a million questions, and learned a very useful new skill. No one expected me to know how to fix a car. All that stuff under the hood of a car is as mysterious as figuring out how to raise a child, just a little simpler.

After a "breakdown" in your home, are you feeling sore that you have a car that doesn't just work, or did you learn how to change a tire today? Who would have known that I would be better positioned than my peers, who had reliable cars, to handle inevitable breakdowns?

Make a choice.

Either see the breakdown as an opportunity to get to know your child better and hone your skills or simply feel bad that only your kid "breaks down" constantly. Once we begin to implement the two-step plan to shift from being a fixed to a growth mindset parent, we notice the impact that the fixed mentality has had on our children. We can begin to see that the curses our children receive each day form some of the ADHD symptoms they exhibit.

What symptoms are we seeing in our fixed mindset "ADHD" kids?

- They are unwilling to stick to something that is hard; they quit and run away easily.

- They blame others for their perceived failures.

- They are protecting their egos; they can't be wrong.

- They have trouble building real friendships because they are busy exerting all their effort in not letting others see their flaws. They are protecting the terrible secret that they are imperfect.

- They don't engage in hard activities; they don't have the bandwidth to fail.

- Eventually, they stop studying because not trying and failing is less painful than working hard and failing.

Can we help our children switch from a fixed to a growth mindset? A person can be put in a growth mindset by being told that an ability can be learned. "The growth mindset is the belief that abilities can be cultivated. But that doesn't tell you how much change is possible or how long change will take" (Dweck 2006, 50).

Dweck and her team conducted a study on hundreds of early adolescent children. The children were given a set of ten questions from a nonverbal IQ test. The students did fairly well. Right after concluding the ten questions, they got feedback. Half of the students were told, "You did really well. Wow, you must be really smart" (putting them in a fixed mindset). The other group was told, "You got eight right; this is a good score. You must have worked very hard." This second group of kids was not made to feel they had a special gift and therefore were naturally succeeding; they were told they were doing the hard work it takes to do well.

The second part of this study is fascinating.

Both groups of students did equally well on the first test. Right after the feedback received from the researchers, the two groups of kids parted ways. Half the children were pushed into the fixed mindset, and they immediately started rejecting challenges. They refused to do anything that would expose their flaws. These children stopped enjoying the process even though they had originally succeeded. Even when they were offered easier questions, they rejected them.

When students were praised for effort, 90 percent wanted a

challenging new task they could learn from. The growth mindset children continued to improve.

Here's the final and most startling point: when children were asked to report their scores in order to help other students, 40 percent of the fixed mindset kids lied about their scores by inflating them.

If this happens with positive labels, how about negative ones? Can we turn this fixed mindset in our children around? Absolutely, and we must, because a festering fixed mindset continues to wreak havoc on both parent and child until it is addressed.

What steps can we take, when communicating with our children, to shift their mindset?

1. Let them know that now is great, that you are grateful for them, and they are fantastic the way they are.

2. Give them the message that they (and you!) can improve in every area; nothing is fixed.

3. Speak about yourself in growth and process-oriented ways.

   □ Tell your child about a setback you had and what you learned from it.

   □ Never call yourself names. Say, "That was a poor choice; I can do better. What did I learn?"

4. Don't label your children—not positive labels and not negative ones.

   □ Discuss their choices and their progress. Let them know you notice how they use their skills to work hard.

   □ When giving a compliment, don't compliment the child's native talent (smart, funny, beautiful, artist). Rather, compliment the process she is engaged in. For example, "You chose and blended the colors beautifully for this painting. You are really paying attention to details." Or, "Your handwriting gets better every day."

5. Discuss big goals, and then break them down into smaller steps so your child understands that you want progress, not perfection.

◻ Celebrate each step.

Finally, use the "brick" method. This is a method I created together with a few young clients. They felt very bad about not being perfect or the best.

We talked about building a home. One person would try to draw up plans to build a home but would be so discouraged that it was not yet built and that it was not the most beautiful on the block. Because of these difficult feelings, he would avoid building, the fear of failure being too threatening. The other builder would see the open lot and think about the potential. He would begin to put one brick on top of the next until his home started taking shape.

I tell my clients that they cannot possibly build their beautiful home, make best friends, or get a perfect grade in one day. It's impossible for everyone, not just them. All they must do is add a brick today. At the end of the day, they ask themselves if they added just one brick toward their goal. Sometimes we plan the brick together, and sometimes the child chooses to be very brave and plans the brick himself. What we always do is celebrate the accomplishment of adding the brick and enjoy that moment, instead of looking at what we have not yet done.

As I was putting the finishing touches on this chapter, my oldest son came home from completing the Israeli version of BUD/S, which is the grueling entry exam for the Navy SEALs. My son has dreamed of serving in an elite unit and has trained consistently for three years. But, despite his best efforts and great physical achievements throughout the week, he was not accepted into the coveted unit. I was devastated for him, and quite frankly terrified of how he might react to this perceived failure.

My son had a thing or two to teach his mom about growth mindset. His response truly took my breath away. After taking some time to quietly absorb the new reality at the beach for a few days, my remarkable boy announced, "I am going to be the very best combat soldier in whatever unit I am placed." I asked him if he felt sorry for himself, to which he responded, "Why should I feel sorry for myself? I know how to work hard, build myself up, and I'm just starting from a different place than I expected." He had defeated his internal "victim" voice. He knew that a winner is someone who has internalized the secret that we grow and learn from every situation, and that our choice to engage challenges makes us ever stronger.

Action Plan

1. Identify your mindset.

   ▫ Are you fixed or growth mindset dominant? We can sometimes be both, but in different situations.

2. Have you been cursed?

   ▫ Dig up the fixed messages of your past and internalize the weight these messages have been putting on you.

   ▫ Understand that no one is perfect; no one can be perfect; and all we can do is embrace each challenge as an opportunity to grow and become stronger and more successful.

3. Are you beating yourself up?

   ▫ Do you call yourself names like "I'm such an idiot! What a loser!"? That's the curse talking. **The beatings end here!**

   ▫ You deserve to be proud of your efforts and of your love and dedication to your family, not beaten for not knowing things you could not have known yet.

   ▫ Be proud of your investment and of your bravery for becoming a parent.

4. You are exerting lots of energy now to protect yourself from discovery.

   □ Use that same energy, but this time when something is difficult, choose to see it as an opportunity to grow.

   □ Choose to engage in the process and learn something new.

   □ Choose to reach out to a friend or mentor and ask for advice.

   □ And finally, choose to be proud of yourself for being engaged, a person open to growth, someone who engages life with curiosity and is often surprised by the outcome.

5. When you are in any social situation, do you compare yourself to others and then feel bad about yourself?

   □ Pay attention to the comparison and understand that you are two separate people. That person has her strengths, and you have yours. If you perceive her as more capable in one area, maybe you can learn from her. The comparison devastates us; the admiration and hope to learn build us.

   □ Be grateful for who you are.

6. Spread the message to your family.

   □ Speak in growth mindset language.

   □ Tell your children about the mistakes you made and how you worked through them.

   □ Celebrate your efforts; celebrate their efforts.

   □ Embrace the process.

   □ Tell yourself and your family what you learned from your hard work, even when the result was not what you were hoping for.

▫ Forgive yourself *out loud* for messing up, and plan to do it differently next time.

7. Set goals and focus on the small steps and successes.

▫ Communicate that the goal is improvement, not perfection.

8. State out loud what you are grateful for each morning.

▫ For best results, conclude your day with a grateful statement as well.

Are you ready now to get right into direct intervention with your Instant Gratification kid? You are calmer. You have faced your true self and made friends with it. She is ready and waiting for you. Let's dive in.

THE CHEAT SHEET

Chapter Three: The "Growth" Mindset Program

☛ Has anyone told you that you "can't"? You have been cursed.

☛ Kids develop a "growth" or "fixed" mindset based on our communication.

☛ What is a growth mindset?

- The knowledge that intelligence can grow; talent can develop; and we must apply ourselves to achieve.

- Challenges are opportunities and are good for us.

☛ What is a "fixed" mindset?

- Intelligence can't change.

- You are defined by your diagnosis; you are stuck with your labels of "smart," "hyper," etc. You fear failure and avoid asking for help.

☛ How does a "fixed" mindset develop?

- Labeling (ADHD); fixed compliments

- "You never" or "you always" statements

- Having low expectations of our child/not allowing her to fail

- A child experiencing abuse.

☛ How do "fixed" mindset adults parent their children?

- They expect to know how to raise their children even though they have not been guided.

- They feel ashamed when a parenting intervention does not succeed.

- They feel intimidated by their child if the child challenges them.

- They overreact when their child misbehaves in public.

- They overreact to flaws in their children.

- They have the need to be "super" parents.

☛ How do "growth" mindset adults parent their children?

- They seek help when they do not know how to proceed or an intervention fails.

- They see this failure as an opportunity to learn.

- They know that all kids make mistakes and never expect perfection.

- They continually consult with more experienced parents.

- They are open and willing to share their battle wounds with friends, hoping for guidance.

☛ How can parents help transform their own mindsets and the mindsets of the whole family?

- Be grateful always for what you have. Set aside time to see the blessings of today and let your child know how fortunate you are to have him as your child.

- Embrace the present.

- Remember always that our goal is improvement, not perfection. Celebrate every step.

☛ What "symptoms" do fixed mindset kids exhibit? How similar are they to ADHD symptoms?

- They don't stick to projects, especially if the project is hard and there is risk of failure.

- They blame others for their failures.

- They spend a lot of time protecting their egos.

- They struggle with building friendships because they don't want to reveal their flaws.

- They avoid demanding activities, making them look lazy or spoiled.

☞ We must rescue ourselves and our children from fixed mindsets and become growth mindset people. How can we do this?

- Let the children know that we love them just as they are now, and that everyone has challenges to overcome as well as stronger attributes.

- Let them know they can always improve in any way they choose, and they are capable of working hard to improve. Set a big goal and break it down into smaller steps.

- Speak about yourself in growth language. Let your children know how you struggled with something and chose to learn from it. Get help. Improve.

- Never label yourself or your child with anything. Both positive and negative labels are curses. Discuss their choices and effort, not their attributes.

CHAPTER FOUR

The Art of the Compliment

*A*MY COMES IN *from a fun hour of swimming. She's tired, but she puts her swimming bag where it belongs anyway! Nice! There's only one problem: she leaves all her wet swimming paraphernalia in the bag, which is now closed into the hallway closet. Amy is super pleased with herself!*

And you? Are you imagining the mold developing on the soggy towel? Do you fear that this child will never figure out how to be fully responsible? Do you need to swoop in and save the situation? Be honest!

The guests are on their way, and you are trying to get everything done before they all arrive. Stephen is sitting on the couch, completely absorbed in his video game, oblivious of you speeding back and forth, right in front of his nose at ninety miles per hour.

"Stephen, get up and help!" *you shout.*

He gets up! That was some quick listening.

"Set the table quickly, sweetheart. The guests will be here soon!"

He gets working. Result: No napkins, and the fork is on the right side of the plate.

He must know by now that we always set the table with napkins, right? He is the main consumer of the napkins at every meal.

How are you doing now? "It's his ADHD. He never gets it right!"

Perhaps? "Why can I NEVER depend on him? First he sits around, and then when he finally gets up, he can't finish the job?"

Is that it?

In this chapter we will explore the **power of compliments** to help our children grow. First, we will understand why negative events have such an impact on us, and then we will discuss what types of positive experiences counteract the negative ones. Finally, we will look at how we parents can reduce the negative output and transform ourselves into positive parenting powerhouses.

You may be wondering when we get to the part where the kids stop acting out and making us nuts. Parents say to me, "Okay, I'll give compliments, I promise! But how do I get her to BEHAVE?" I hear you loud and clear. But we still have to take a deep dive into positive communication because there is one iron-clad rule about parenting an Instant Gratification kid that I would like to remind you of. It goes like this: **this child wants our strong attention, and he will take it positively or negatively.** Therefore, we must provide a positive environment for him so that we allow him to *choose* to behave well.

If we get triggered quickly by our child's misbehavior, he will misbehave again very soon, guaranteed. If we remain calm when he has an outrageous tantrum (but don't ignore it) and get super animated when he gets ready for school quickly, he can now choose to get our attention through his positive behavior.

Right after we practice complimenting our kids, I promise we will move seamlessly into other discipline methods. I hope you are convinced that positive communication is not just a fluffy step, but vital to healthy discipline and our child's success.

Why do we respond to and remember negative situations much more than positive ones?

Alina Tugend, in her insightful *New York Times* article "Praise Is Fleeting, but Brickbats We Recall," explains why we naturally notice, process, and remember negative experiences more than positives ones. "This is a general tendency for everyone." Tugend cites Clifford Nass, a professor of communication at Stanford University and author of *The Man Who Lied to His Laptop: What Machines Teach Us About Human Relationships,* "Some people do have a more positive outlook, but almost everyone remembers negative things more strongly and in more detail" (Penguin, 2012).

Why is that? We handle different types of information in different areas of our brain, explains Professor Nass. We process negative thoughts and emotions more thoroughly than positive ones, and therefore they stick around in our minds longer and continue to upset us. When we have bad experiences, past or present, they create more discomfort. Thus we remember them and re-experience them for a long time. This is human nature. Think of a recent painful or demeaning experience and compare it to a compliment you just got. Which one drums up a stronger emotion?

It isn't our fault that we process the negative more strongly. Not at all. We are hardwired that way, but we are capable of reversing it. Those who are "more attuned to bad things would have been more likely to survive threats and, consequently, would have increased the probability of passing along their genes," the article states. "Survival requires urgent attention to possible bad outcomes but less urgent with regard to good ones." Additionally, "We tend to see people who say negative things as smarter than those who are positive. Thus, we are more likely to give greater weight to critical reviews" (Tugend 2012).

A mother recently told me about an interaction between two of her children. The older sister said to her undoubtedly confident younger brother as he was singing with full emotion, "You know, you carry a tune well, but you don't have a great voice." The mother reported that the next day while she was taking the young boy to a doctor's appointment, he commented, "Our whole family has good voices. It stinks that I'm the only one who has a bad voice."

Negative feedback is a quick and vicious process. It leaves no prisoners.

What kind of experiences counteract the power of the negative ones?

In a fascinating study reported by Tugend, Teresa M. Amabile, professor of business administration and director of research at the Harvard Business School, asked two hundred and thirty-eight professionals, working on twenty-six different creative projects from different companies and industries, to fill out confidential daily diaries over several months. The participants were asked to answer questions based on a numeric scale and briefly describe one thing that stood out that day.

"We found that of all the events that could make for a great day at work, the most important was *making progress on meaningful work— even a small step forward*," said Professor Amabile, a coauthor of *The Progress Principle: Using Small Wins to Ignite Joy, Engagement, and Creativity at Work*. Furthermore,

> After analyzing some 12,000 diary entries, Professor Amabile found that the *negative effect of a setback at work on happiness was more than twice as strong as the positive effect of an event that signaled progress*. And the power of a setback to increase frustration is over three times as strong as the power of progress to decrease frustration (*Harvard Business Review Press*, 2011; italics added).

If parents knew this, how would it reshape their communication with their children? First, they would be more aware of **the power** of their choice of words. Also, they would direct their message towards praising meaningful achievements rather than throwing around meaningless compliments. Most importantly, they would not avoid criticism, but use it constructively and very sparingly.

Professor Roy Baumeister, in his book *Bad is Stronger Than Good* (Florida University Press, 1996), suggests a ratio of **five goods comments for every one bad**. For most of us, the ratio is inversed. It is vital to flip the trend and begin flooding our children with "many good events" (Tugend 2012).

When I ask parents at our intake meeting about their communication with their children, most parents emphatically insist that they're enthusiastic complimenters. "What are five things about this child that you feel he's fantastic at?" I enquire. Dead silence. Some stuttering. Because our feedback is so vital to the health or our children, we've got to get it right.

There is one additional factor that makes learning the art of the compliment so pressing.

Rabbi Sacks explains in his 2014 essay "How to Praise":

> I discovered the transformative power of focused
> praise from one of the more remarkable people I ever
> met, the late Lena Rustin. Lena, who was a speech
> therapist, worked with stammering children. She
> believed that in order to help the young, struggling
> child she had to understand and treat the entire family
> and only then could she help heal the child. Why is
> that? The family creates an equilibrium and adjusts
> to the struggles of a particular family member. If
> there is to be improvement, everyone has to shift and
> understand their role in making a change.

Let's apply this to our child with ADHD symptoms. We have all
grown accustomed to his negative behavior. If he is to change his
behavior, the entire family will have to readjust.

"By and large, we tend to resist change," continues Sacks (2014).
But change we must. How can we create an environment that makes
change manageable and unthreatening?

Lena showed that the road to family change is through praise. She
instructed the family members to catch one another doing well and
lavish that member with a specific and grateful compliment. With this
method, she was creating a new respect within the home, boosting
everyone's self-respect and self-confidence, and therefore allowing a
safe space for change. Not only did the struggling child change, but
the entire atmosphere became positive, allowing for all to shift their
unhelpful habits.

Becoming a positive parenting powerhouse

Alan E. Kazdin, author of *The Kazdin Method for Parenting the Defiant
Child*, an absolute must-read for all parents, takes us through the
process of revamping our internal negativity-response mechanism. Go
out and get the book. I will highlight my interpretation of the most
relevant parts for our purposes. The examples and commentary are
based on work I have done with my clients.

Kazdin says praise is "one of the strongest ways to influence your child's actions" (Kazdin 2009, 21). The way we communicate either reinforces negative behavior (like giving in to a tantrum or nagging request from a child) or builds positive momentum.

A mother once told me that she is very strict with her children until they start to nag. She was signaling to her kids that they could break her resolve through nagging, and this encouraged them to refine nagging to an art form. Why? Because they were being rewarded for nagging, and the results were always satisfying.

Can we turn this around?

Yes, and we must. Earlier, we discussed responding calmly to triggering behavior. We calmed ourselves down. Yay us! We also inadvertently created an attention void. Our kids used to get ample negative feedback, but we have reduced the negative response. Now there is no response, which does not suit our Instant Gratification kid, or any child. Children need a strong response from us. No problem; we will replace anger and frustration with powerful compliments.

Let's follow the rules set out by Kazdin to become powerful communicators. Our goal is to give our Instant Gratification child strong and gratifying compliments and use those sweet words to replace the loud, angry feedback he has been demanding from us until now. He wants our attention, positive or negative. Once we establish a steady flow of compliments, he will be quite confident of receiving positive feedback from us. Therefore, he will start craving instant gratification for his *good* choices and will act accordingly.

Rule #1: Be enthusiastic!

Guess why this is so important. Imagine yourself in an angry moment. Really see yourself crazy upset. How enthusiastic are you? When we get angry at our kid, there is no stopping us. We raise our voices, perspire, get right in his face, and he knows we meant it! When he does something praiseworthy, we say something bland like, "Good job. Keep it up!" If our kid is an instant gratification seeker, he will make a quick (unconscious) calculation and choose to elicit our scolding response.

He gets more feedback that way. It's not fun for him to get yelled at; it is strictly a fulfillment of his internal need.

We must completely reverse this process. Let's raise our voices with joy when she does something right and be bland when responding to negative behavior. We must smile, get close, speak louder, and say it like we mean it. Also, name the deed, "_____ was so respectful, responsible, kind, thoughtful . . ."

Let's catch our children being good.

I was presenting this method in a parent workshop several years ago. A woman raised her hand and said, "I can't do that."

"What can't you do?" I asked.

She replied, "I can't be enthusiastic. You don't understand, I'm Hungarian."

I understand you, sister. I'm German. I get that it may feel unnatural to start overflowing with enthusiasm. Firstly, some of us may not have examples from childhood of this kind of communication. In addition, it may feel "fake," like we are putting on a show. We can be very genuine with our negative feedback, but when it comes to compliments, suddenly we get self-conscious; it just doesn't feel natural. We are used to noticing the negative. But we must do better, and we can. Despite the challenge, it's important to reset our communication. Start slowly. With a smile, raise your voice just a tad. Your child will do the rest.

Rule #2: Be specific.

We are great at making long lists. "You came in and threw your backpack down. You didn't take out your sandwich, which will now get moldy. You demanded a treat and immediately started bothering your sister!!!!" Sound like anyone you know? Somehow, we expect our critical, never-ending barrage to magically create better behavior. It NEVER does. Our victim is not listening. Do *we* listen closely and take notes while we are being yelled at? If we truly want to educate our children to improve their behavior, **we must use *their behavior* as an example**.

How can we ensure he will be able to repeat the behavior he just got complimented for? By complimenting very specifically. As you break a child's behavior down into smaller segments, you are giving him instructions. "You walked in, warmed my heart with your smile, (*okay, now he knows that smiling when he comes in is a great way to* start) and asked for a treat so respectfully (*got it . . . respectfully asking is the right way to go*)." We gave instructions, and now he can get the emotional candy next time. The more specific we are with our compliment, the more instructions we are giving for the future.

Rule #3: Say it right away.

The closer a compliment follows a deed, the more a child links the two in his head. We are, of course, invited and encouraged to repeat it later. Tell Grandma! Tell Daddy when he gets home! But it is of utmost importance to say it right away.

Rule #4: Do not caboose (don't add a "but"; keep it pure)!

If we want our child to hear our compliment and receive it and choose to behave well, we must never *ever* add "fixer-upper" critical comments! Never! They don't fix; they destroy. We must grant our child the respect he deserves for his positive behavior without highlighting what he could have done better. When we add a negative comment to the end of our enthusiastic compliment, he only hears the end.

Perhaps our child did something well but did not do it perfectly. **Our goal is not perfect; it is progress**. Say she came home from the pool and remembered to put her pool bag in the closet, as in the example above. That's great! But . . . she forgot to take its contents out.

We can either compliment what she did well and then we can close our mouths, or we could compliment what she did, and make sure to let her know that she also messed up. Now she feels like a loser and is less likely to put the bag away again.

I am often invited to give lectures in the evenings. That means I come home late—and tired! My dear husband gets the kids showered and to bed and gets the kitchen in order after dinner. One evening I came in particularly tired. I was thrilled to find the kitchen tidy and went directly to bed. My heart sank in the morning, though, when I noticed that my husband had indeed cleaned up the kitchen but had left the food out on the counter. I was upset! I worked hard on that dinner, but now it had to be thrown away.

I had a choice. My husband had done great. The kids were happy, well-fed, well-rested, and the house was in order. I could focus on what was done well and then shut my mouth, or I could make sure he knew how upset I was about the food. I wish I could report that I zipped my mouth.

There is a lesson to be learned. Why did I feel the need to point out my husband's "failure"? I wanted to fix him (good luck with that, ladies) and make him more perfect, and I wanted to be sure it didn't happen again. How did I do? Poorly! By pointing out his failure after letting him know how great he did, I canceled the positive feeling. Who wants to keep trying when the person receiving a gift only notices the bad? Not only did my husband get a terrible feeling about his care for our children, but he also had less of a desire to work hard the next time I left the house in the evening.

Here is the key. Whatever your child did wrong, the same scenario will repeat itself soon enough. She will go to the pool; you will go out to work. She will come home from school; bath time will happen again tomorrow. Can you hang on to your "fixing" urge just until next time? Instead of extinguishing this compliment, you can remember the more challenging behaviors and give instructions next time. This way everyone wins. Your child/spouse will feel great about his success and has practiced a good behavior for which you are now rewarding him with a compliment, and now you are more aware of what needs strengthening next time.

Here's another example, because this is too important not to master.

You prepare a beautiful meal for family and friends; the food is tasty and abundant. Everyone enjoys dinner. As you clean up, your friend says, "Avigail, that was such a great meal! Healthy, delicious, thanks so much! What was up with the dessert? Was that a new recipe? It was a little dry and bland."

How do you feel? Frankly, I feel like saying, "You cook dinner next time and host *my* entire family! Are you such a great baker?"

Is that fair? She said so many nice compliments. Yeah, I'm sure she did . . . I just don't remember them. I'm too focused on my dessert. This is a learning process. If we want our children to learn from their own behavior, we must help them highlight the good, and strengthen the not-yet-good behavior through reminders, but **not** at the time of the compliment.

Rule #5: Reach out and touch.

Touch is the glue to our compliment. Give a high five, a shoulder pat, a hug. It's all good. If the child is sensitive to touch, stand close or ask permission before touching. While we never want to touch aggressively when mad, we always want to infuse more warmth into our positive communication.

A couple of warnings:

1. **Don't lie:** Never add a lie to a compliment! Sometimes we think that if we tell a child he is being so organized, he will become more organized. This trick does not work; our kid is smart. He will just trust us less and feel sad that he is not worthy of a real compliment. Be very honest. We cannot mold our children to the shape we wish them to be; we can encourage them in the good choices they chose to make.

2. **Take it slow:** Many kids are not used to compliments, especially enthusiastic ones. They have no experience of receiving them. They may be uncomfortable or embarrassed if you come on too strong. If she can't yet tolerate a compliment, instead of complimenting, just notice the behavior. "I noticed that you brought all your books home from school." That's it. Once she can handle being noticed for doing well, move on to full compliment mode, step by step.

3. **Don't make him feel childish:** Compliment according to your child's ability level, not below. We don't want to compliment a ten-year-old for getting dressed unless this is still a real challenge to him. Compliments are meant to help children reflect on their own good behavior; he will feel

childish and foolish when we notice a behavior that he has been competent at for years.

4. **Include your other children in the compliment if you can:** Kids get jealous when they see a sibling being complimented. They hear you say, "Jorge, look how nicely you cleared your plate. That was so responsible. Now I will have much less cleaning up to do," and their immediate response is, "What about me! What, I didn't clear my plate? I clear my plate every day!" Our instinct as parents is to get annoyed at the child for not allowing his brother to get a compliment. We think, "Why does everything have to be about you all the time?"

   The uncomplimented child is expressing a raw emotion. It's best not to judge him but to help him through it. Try something like this. "Hey, Marco, did you notice what a good job Jorge did clearing his plate? Wasn't that great? What can *we* say to him because we are so proud?" You have asked Marco to be your partner, so now he is included and has permission to enjoy his brother's behavior instead of seeing it as a direct threat to his own honor.

5. **Compliment progress:** Only compliment progress and process, not ability. Remember the curse? We can help our children towards a growth mindset when they hear us specifically notice their hard work and effort, and how they are one step stronger than yesterday. Or, we can place a curse upon them by giving fixed mindset compliments such as how smart, funny, talented, or cute they are. Instead of, "You are so smart!" say, "You are working so hard!" Or "Your beautiful singing created such a happy environment" rather than "You have such a fantastic voice!"

6. **Don't over-compliment:** It cheapens the compliment, and your child will instantly know that she doesn't deserve it. Let her earn her compliment and then be proud. Don't fabricate exaggerated behavior and then gush about it.

7. **Don't hand out candy wrappers without the candy inside**:
   A vague "good job!" is a tease. Can your child understand
   what he has done well? Can he replicate it and receive another
   "candy" from you?

*Mom really wanted her daughter to attend synagogue with her. Her
daughter, fifteen years old and more inclined to sleep in on Saturday
morning, begrudgingly agreed to come along. She rolled out of bed, got
herself dressed, not in her Saturday best, but good enough, and grumbled
all the way to synagogue. When they got there, instead of picking up a
prayer book and joining the singing, the teenager found a comfortable
seat and put her head down on the pew to continue her morning snooze.
Mom was humiliated!*

*As they left the synagogue, Mom had a choice to make. She could
either lecture her daughter about proper synagogue behavior; she could
remain quiet; or she could remember what her goal was to begin with,
and give her daughter a compliment. What? A compliment? Why would
this behavior deserve a compliment?*

*This process-oriented mom knew why. Her daughter could have
stayed in bed, but she didn't. Out of respect for her mother, she made this
gesture. That's fantastic. Not only that, but she attended prayers. Okay,
she didn't pray, but she chose to bring herself to the right place at the
right time. Good for her, a very good choice.*

*If the goal is to get the daughter to join the family more often, Mom
has exactly one choice. This is what she said: "My dear, thanks so much
for respecting my request to come to prayers this morning. It made my
day to have all my children together. It must have been hard to get up
and come with us instead of sleeping in. Good for you. Excellent choice."
And with that, she planted a big kiss on her daughter's cheek.*

You may be thinking, "That kid acted like a brat! Her mother asked
her to come, and she couldn't even have enough respect to keep her
eyes open! How will this naive mother ever teach her daughter proper
synagogue conduct!" If you were in the mindset of fixing all the wrongs,
you would be correct. But we must be progress minded if we want our
children to progress. If this daughter gets positive feedback, she will
want it again. But, if you choose to fix it all and put her in her place, she

will not be showing up again; end of process! Take a deep breath, and keep asking, "What's my goal?"

Here's the rub. We are hardwired to notice the bad way before we lay our eyes on the good. When we enter a room, especially one filled with our children, we tend to scan it to stop dangerous or inappropriate behavior. It's nice to suggest we make this big change, but is it doable? I know it is because I have seen fantastic parents embrace this positivity challenge and succeed.

I would like to add one more suggestion that I recommend parents follow when they rewire their communication network. We must make one conscious decision as we are about to engage in any interaction. We must decide to notice one good thing about the other person right away.

A struggling teacher was in the habit of spending his day scanning the classroom to decide who deserved punishment, determined to change his approach. He resolved that following any instruction, he would now focus his attention for ten seconds on who got moving and obeyed, who had already placed their book on their desk, etc. After that he was free to catch the slackers. What happened was miraculous. After each instruction and ten seconds of compliments, there were fewer and fewer slackers. Let's commit to ten seconds at the beginning of each observation or interaction, where we permit ourselves to see and comment only on the good.

Powerful compliments for the whole family

Here is one more great idea to help boost the positive, complimentary environment in your home. I have been doing this for years, and my family loves it. Get yourself a simple binder and place it on your kitchen counter, open with a pen in it. This will be your compliment book. You can call it anything you want. You will write compliments throughout the week for each member of the family. Write as many or as few as fit into your busy schedule—one a week per person, one a day; any amount is great. Not just any compliments will do for this book, though. Focus on compliments that indicate that a child (or adult) had to put some effort into the good deed they did.

For example, a child comes in from school with a piece of cake from a birthday party at school. He sees that his brother is already home and offers him half of his cake. Wow! That goes in the book. Or a child has a very hard time in math class, but she pushes herself to get the homework done anyway. These are the deeds that build our children. **Making a decision to do something good, and then overcoming adversity and stepping out of our comfort zone to accomplish it is the recipe for greatness.**

I encourage parents to include themselves in the book so children can learn by example that anything worthwhile needs effort and choice. It's imperative for them to know their parents' process so they can imitate it. Dad went to the supermarket with a very incomplete shopping list, but when he tried to call Mom to get the rest of the list, she had turned her phone on silent by mistake. Dad decided not to get frustrated and instead to think about what his family usually needs from the supermarket. He also stayed calm when he realized he would probably have to run out again for the items he forgot. Go, Dad!

Choose a meal when the family will be together each week and read the compliments out loud. We like to cheer for each person being complimented with a fun little tune. Make sure to write an equal number of compliments about each child; they keep track.

You know how kids love to tell on each other? If they have something juicy to tell, they get an even more satisfying response from the parent. I invite my children to tell on each other, but only nice things. When a child tells me something special her sibling did, I write it in the book, and write down who told me. Both kids get credit when the compliment is read out, the doer and the teller. This has dramatically reduced sibling rivalry and the constant parental judge and jury job. It has also turned complimenting one another into a natural process. Try it at home.

The first compliment goes to you, dear parent, for taking the time to learn a new strategy to raise your child better. The goal of changing your communication with your child is challenging but very worth your effort. Keep at it!

Action Plan

1. Think of a few things your child does well consistently.

   □ Write them down.

   □ Think of something you do well often. Write that down too.

2. Plan to give a compliment at least once a day, but preferably three times a day. Some parents have a hard time finding something to compliment.

3. Don't manufacture compliments.

   □ Catch your child doing something well and jump on the opportunity. If you are seeking, you will find it.

4. Focus on keeping negative feedback quiet and emotion-free.

   □ Infuse positive feedback with lots of emotion.

5. If you are struggling with the need to fix and can't find any positivity in your child's behavior, ask yourself, "What is my goal?" That will help you focus.

6. Practice complimenting yourself and other adults in your life. Compliments are contagious.

7. Go out and get that binder.

   □ Leave it in a very visible place so you don't forget about it, and start your compliment book.

   □ No one is too old, too young, or too much of a teenager not to enjoy a compliment.

THE CHEAT SHEET

Chapter Four: The Positive Communication (Compliment) Intervention Program

- Why do we respond negatively to our children? Why do we notice misbehavior more often than good behavior?
    - Negative circumstances and events leave a stronger and longer-lasting impression on us. We are wired to scan for danger and point out mistakes because, back in the day, mistakes could be fatal. Let's forgive ourselves and rewire.
- How can we counteract the effects of negative events and harsh words?
    - When people engage in meaningful activities where they feel they are making progress, negativity has less of an effect.
    - Also, we have to balance the positivity and negativity with a ratio of five positive expressions to one negative one.
- Our Instant Gratification child craves our attention and will take it positively or negatively. If we flood his world with strong, positive communication, he will begin to crave it and adjust his behavior to deserve it.
- Become a positive parenting powerhouse by following these five golden rules:
    1. When you give a compliment, be enthusiastic! Shout it like you mean it. Smile!
    2. Be specific! Tell your child exactly what he did right, every detail. You are giving a candy; your details are instructions for further good behavior.
    3. Say the compliment right away so that you link the behavior to the reward/compliment.

4. Don't caboose! Don't add a negative fixing remark to the compliment. You are not looking for perfection; you are looking for progress. You will have plenty of reminder moments.

5. Touch your child while giving the compliment. A kiss, high five, pat on the shoulder are great.

☛ Here is what we may never do when we are complimenting:

□ Never lie! Your child will lose confidence in himself and you.

□ Take it slow! Your child may not be used to compliments, so pace yourself.

□ Don't make her feel childish; compliment her on actions that are at her ability level and not below.

□ Include other children in helping you give the compliment.

□ Only compliment progress.

□ Do not exaggerate.

□ Be specific, never vague. "Good job!" is not a good compliment. Good job on what?

☛ Get a binder and begin writing in it good deeds you notice your family doing. Read it out once a week at dinner.

□ Focus on progress-oriented behaviors or behaviors where the child or adult demonstrated self-control and overcame a significant challenge.

☛ Eliminate toxic "telling" on each other between siblings by allowing them to come "tell" on a family member who did something good and then write it in the book with the name of the "teller" included. The results will be magical.

CHAPTER FIVE

Punishment is Not
A Dirty Word[1]

*T*HE THREE-YEAR-OLD TWIN *boys scurried up the jungle gym at the park. There was a mischievous sparkle in their eyes. When they got to the tippy top, they pulled down their pants and proceeded to make a water (pee?) fountain off the top. Dad, who had thought it would be fun to bring the two to the park that day, was mortified. All the moms on the bench were vacillating between stifling a laugh, judging the harried dad, and feeling blessed that these were not their sons.*

Dad bellowed up to the boys, "Get down here right now! You are punished!"

The kids climbed down and walked over to their father with trepidation. One bravely asked, "Daddy, what's our punishment?"

Exasperated, the father replied, "I don't know, but when I figure it out, it's going to be really bad!"

In this chapter we will explore all the ins and outs, dos and don'ts of punishment. First, we will understand why we are so uncomfortable with the entire concept of punishment, which leads directly to why we are so bad at it. Next, we will see that punishing our children is not only

---

1   This chapter is based on my interpretation and embellishment of the book *The Kazdin Method for Parenting the Defiant Child* by Alan E. Kazdin, PhD (Mariner Books, 2009) plus other sources. Have you bought the book yet?

inescapable, but we engage in it vengefully every day, so we may as well do it right. Is everything punishable? No, and we will figure out how to punish fairly and justly. Upping the ante, we will discover that proper punishment is a message to our child that we believe in her and respect her and know she can do better. We will then present the "how-to" of punishment, and each of you parents will plan to tailor the punishment guidelines to your family's individual needs.

We are bad at this punishment thing. Why is that?

- We have been influenced by a societal message that our children are fragile, and we must protect their feelings.

- We have been told that it is best to discipline only through positivity and example.

- We want to be our child's friend, so we are afraid that if we punish, we will be rejected by her.

- We hear that we have no right to impose our will on our child.

- We simply have no idea how to do it right; correct punishment requires guidance.

Even the word "punishment" makes us feel uneasy. When I broach this topic with parents, they politely correct my use of words and suggest that maybe we should not use the word punishment, but rather "natural consequence." Let me share an illustrative story as my response to the correctors.

My children and I went to visit a friend one afternoon. My friend was holding her baby on her hip, helping another child set up a game, and straightening the living room all at once. Her older daughter thought this would be a great moment to have some fun. She took a blanket that was sitting on the floor and threw it over her mother's head. The blinded and confused mother stepped on this very same daughter while trying to disentangle herself and her infant from the blanket. The stepped-on kid started to wail, "You hurt me! Why did you step on me?"

That is a natural consequence, my friends. The child blinded her mother and consequently got stepped on. Mom had no voice or role in the sequence of events. What did the child learn? It's unclear. What she did not learn is that her mother disapproves of the potentially dangerous and disrespectful decision her daughter made. This was fate, not intervention.

Why is choosing to give an active punishment so important?

Our children must know not only that we believe they can do well, but also that we are right there with them, helping them along. If we choose not to respond clearly when a child misbehaves, we are sending two harmful messages: one, that we don't think this child can do any better than he has just done (which was well below our expectation of him), and two, that we are not present to give him guidance and redirect him. No child deserves to be abandoned like that.

In addition, if a child continues to misbehave with no clear message that we disapprove of the behavior, eventually the behavior and the child will begin to grate on us. You know what happens next? We will punish anyway, but more violently and in a less controlled fashion than we would have done if we respected our child and ourselves. We would all benefit if we responded in a measured way in the first place. It's impossible to permit a child to behave badly and never respond in anger.

When we ignore unacceptable behavior, our child feels we have no faith in him and that we don't believe he can improve.

My daughter came home from a friend's house one day, frantic. She demanded that I speak with her friend's parents. I asked her what the problem was. She said with tears in her eyes, "My friend was saying bad words to her mother, and her mother didn't say anything; she just let her keep acting that way. How can she love her and not tell her to stop!" My daughter interpreted the lack of punishment as the mother giving up on her child.

If we abdicate our role as socializers of our children, who will teach them to behave? When they don't know how to respond to authority, will the authority figure kindly educate them? Probably not. "No" is a fact of life; they will hear it from peers in kindergarten, all the way through school and in the big bad world. Are we trying to shield them from the pain of discipline? It will hurt much more when a person who does not love them is left to discipline them.

When we shield by holding back disciplinary action, we hurt our children in the long run. They don't learn to socialize correctly. They become the tyrants in charge, and they are shocked and unprepared for society's behavioral demands put upon them by uncaring people.

Says Professor Jordan Peterson in his masterful work *Twelve Rules for Life* (another must-read),

Parents are the arbiters of society. They teach children how to behave so other people will be able to interact meaningfully and productively with them. **It is an act of responsibility to discipline a child. It is not anger at misbehavior. It is not revenge for misdeed. It is instead a careful combination of mercy and long-term judgement** (Random House Canada, 2018, 124; bolding added).

Whether we like the word punishment or not, we engage in it all the time, most often in a clumsy, ineffective way. Here are some of the mistakes we make. Find your style in this list. (I was a combination of 1 and 3.)

If discipline is so important, why don't we discipline at all, or discipline poorly?

1. **The patient one:** We hold back patiently, let the bad behavior slide, and finally, when we can't take it anymore, we blow up and give out a big punishment. Most often this punishment is impossible to enforce because it is too big, so we find ways to wiggle out of it. "You are not coming with us on the camping trip next week!" we declare in anger. Really? How are you going to work that one out without triggering a visit from social services? The outcome, of course, is that our child sees us as raving lunatics and can't trust our word. Also, since we have held back for so long, our explosion is ugly and mean, causing a major break in our relationship with our child.

2. **The warner:** We warn; we count to three; we tell them that next time it will be a huge punishment. Is there any method to our madness, or does the child have a good chance of getting away with his unwanted behavior indefinitely? If our children know that we will repeat ourselves hundreds of times, they know they can continue doing whatever it is they

are doing just a little bit longer. They also know that they have very nagging parents who never stop talking. Imagine us as flies that just won't leave our child alone; we keep circling and diving right at his nose. That's us! Zzzzzz, swat, zzzzzz, swat. They don't hear anything we say; they are just trying to get rid of us.

3.   **The explainer:** We see that our child has done something wrong, such as hitting another unsuspecting child in the park. We respond by putting the child in our lap and explaining to the child what he has done wrong and why he should not do that again. All the while, the victim is dusting herself off and wondering where the adults are.

4.   **The protector:** We feel so much compassion for our child; we assume he didn't understand. Maybe we were too harsh on him; maybe she was tired, hot, hungry. At all costs, we will continually find excuses for bad behavior rather than inflict any reproach or discomfort on our child. The results are a child with no moral compass, left alone at the ripe old age of five, trying to make sense of proper behavior. He learns early that he is never wrong; it is his parents or society imposing unfair pain on him.

5.   **The moral justifier:** We think, "Who am I to impose my will on this child? She has her own desires and will. She is smart enough to figure out what she needs to know. She should have the right to choose her own behavior." The result is an abandoned child who does not yet have the wisdom or skills to intuit what society demands of her. We would never let our child decide to drive a car and teach herself the rules of the road at the age of seven. We are sure to teach a child how to cross the street before allowing her to cross on her own. Why do we assume she has some internal compass that will guide her towards proper socialized behavior? Children are looking for guidance. If we don't fill the role, a very unforgiving world will take our place.

If all parents struggle with discipline, do the parents of Instant Gratification kid stand a chance at socializing their child? The job is more monumental, more vital, and more difficult for this child. Whereas other children can pick up some social norms from their surroundings, our child is resisting these lessons. He is looking for stronger responses from us and other kids; he loves novelty, so he might try and see what happens if he yells or touches or says no. He hates doing rote work, so cleaning up the toys will not appeal to him. He is allergic to routines, making bath time, bedtime, and homework a huge struggle. In short, he needs more discipline than any other child but is the most discipline resistant.

What are the drawbacks of punishment?

With all this talk of the importance of discipline and rule setting, we also must examine the drawbacks of punishment. Let's get a sense of where the pitfalls are.

1. Parents and teachers fall into the aggressive punishment trap. The punishment leads to cessation of bad behavior **temporarily**. Because of our initial success, when the behavior returns (which it inevitably does), we quickly turn again to aggressive punishment. Shouting or using other aggression towards children is the junk food of discipline. It feels good for a few minutes, making us feel full, but we always eat too much of it and regret it in the end. In response to our aggression, the child also becomes more aggressive.

2. Punishment teaches the child what not to do but does not tell him what he *should* do. If our child is only getting the "no" message, without knowing what to replace the behavior with, this will lead to great frustration for both parent and child.

3. Children adapt to punishment. As we up the punishment, our child learns to live with it because what she is doing is gratifying enough to her that she is willing to pay the price of punishment.

4. If we don't catch the unwanted behavior and punish immediately, the reward for the bad deed is motivation enough for a child to continue doing it. Say a kid eats all the chocolate without permission. We bumble along half an hour later, discover the mess, and only then respond with a punishment. Who was already rewarded for her sneaky behavior? The chocolate-faced kid.

5. Harsh punishment leads to a gap in the relationship between parent and child. We hope our children will want to confide in us and trust us, and the wrong kind of punishment drives them away.

There are many objective problems with punishment, but it is still a necessary part of our discipline plan. We must deliver a clear message that we know our child can make good choices, and therefore we will stop him and redirect him when he expects less of himself.

What are we punishing? Is any behavior we don't like eligible for a scolding? Not at all! Before we get to respectful discipline, we must set up the house rules.

What are the rules in your home?

This question makes parents squirm! "We don't have any rules," they declare. "If we knew how to set and enforce rules, why would we be meeting with you?" Or, "Do you mean the rules we set up that the kids totally ignore? Really, you want us to establish rules when we can't get him to pick his underwear up off the floor?"

I get it, but I am still going to ask the question.

1. What rules would you like to set up in your home?

2. What values are important to you, which you have not yet succeeded in communicating properly? What rules have you suggested to your kids that they flat-out disobey?

If we want to know which great behavior we will celebrate and which behavior we will help redirect, we must start with clear communication.

Try this for fun with your kids. Ask them about the rules in your home. None of them will say, "We have none," but you may be surprised to hear their responses. Generally, they will list something as a rule if we repeat it a lot or they know we value it.

Establish between three and five rules—no more, please.

Here are the three rules in our home:

1. **Respect parents,** and listen to what they say. If kids don't have basic respect for their parents, it's not possible for them to foster respect for siblings, friends, other adults, or property. Parents come first. This includes responding when parents speak, speaking respectfully without curses or rough words, no raising voices, and listening right away.

2. **Respect siblings.** This includes no hitting, no touching them if they don't want to be touched, no taking their things without permission, talking with respect, no cursing, and no making fun of them. Anything less than this would be us sending a message to our child that we don't believe she can behave well and allowing our weaker children to be constant victims.

3. **No putting yourself or others in danger.**

What are your rules? Write them down for yourselves. Do not post them on the wall; this is not a classroom. You will communicate these rules by stating them and by rewarding children with an enthusiastic compliment for following the rules.

Little kids love to play (for more on older kids, keep reading). They especially enjoy playing with their parents. We can strengthen our rules by playing games with them. We can play "house" with dolls: have one of the dolls follow or break a rule, and play the scenarios out with your children, showing them the positive and negative consequences of their choices.

Allow your child to lead, and see how much kids need structure. She will probably be much stricter with the rules than you ever intended to be. You can also role-play with your child. Be the child and allow her to be the parent. Play out some scenarios that can happen at home and have her decide what the proper response should be. Make sure the focus is not on punishment but on the praise you each lavish on the other for following the house rule.

You can also bring up scenarios at dinnertime and allow your child to play "judge." Give him a scenario in which a child does something dangerous but does not know it is dangerous. Ask your child how he, as the judge, would rule on the case. In the case of not knowing, we would probably let the child off with a warning, but would your "judge" do the same?

Here is my most important rule for us parents, before we begin disciplining our children:

Parents may only punish if they have given their children the ability to choose to behave well.

An Instant Gratification child will choose to behave well if he lives in a home that is infused with positive attention and feedback. Before permitting ourselves to use the punishment tool, we must be experienced at positive feedback.

Here's how respectful punishment is carried out:

Punishment/Correction #1: The Cookie Punishment

When a child makes a bad decision to break a rule, he could have chosen better. Our responsibility is to help him stop the behavior and turn it around. How is this done?

Here's a perspective on this punishment. Imagine you were in a bad mood one day and mouthed off at your neighbor. Oops! You could have done better, but no one's perfect. You can call her and apologize; that would be a good place to start. But you can take it up a notch so that you **actively** try to repair the damage you caused. Would you like to bake her some cookies? She may not need them, but you have corrected the situation by *doing* something. *When we act rather than just apologize verbally, we become more thoughtful people.*

The most respectful punishment is one in which you allow the child to "do something" to correct the situation.

Imagine a child speaks disrespectfully to his father. This behavior is against the rules and values of your home. You say, "Tyron, speaking disrespectfully is not allowed in our home. Please fold that load of laundry to correct the mistake you made."

Hold on! Are we using household chores that we want our kids to do in order to punish them? Not only that, but there is no connection between what he did and the punishment given. How will Tyron learn to speak respectfully? Furthermore, what are the chances he will follow through with the punishment? This will be one more cause for a fight. "Don't give me more work!"

Good questions.

Why would we use household chores to discipline kids? We want them to like chores.

The goal of this punishment is to stop a child in his tracks and remind him that he can do better. The chore is just a means to an end. If you can be clear that this is a way for your child to choose to do better, the chore is inconsequential. No one likes to do them, but if the chore must be done, your child can get through it without too much struggle.

Our other goal is to give as much respect in punishment as possible. We are letting our child know that through his actions, he caused damage to our home environment. No one is perfect, so now he can correct the damage by doing a positive deed.

Allowing children to "do something" and then thanking them for doing a great job is a way for them to see punishment not as painful but as corrective.

Here is an adult example: A husband gets very angry and shouts at his wife. He realizes soon after that he was too aggressive, and she did not deserve that behavior. He wants to apologize. With his apology he also says, "You relax this evening; I will get dinner going and bathe the kids."

His gesture has nothing to do with shouting at her. If we are looking for the punishment to match the crime, the wife should now shout at him. That would lead to more chaos and misery. Making dinner and bathing the kids are chores, but the husband is offering to be extra available, going beyond the normal routine so that he can **actively** express his apology.

Kids can distinguish between a chore done to help out in the house and one done to remedy a mistake. They can also understand that both household help and a punishment chore make the home a better place to live in.

How will he learn to speak respectfully by folding the laundry or washing a window?

He will not learn to speak respectfully directly through the chore he is doing, no matter what the chore. What he will learn quickly is that it's a poor choice to speak disrespectfully. *Only by catching your child speaking respectfully and complimenting his behavior will he learn to speak with respect.* Punishment serves the purpose of stopping an unwanted behavior. Enforcing good behavior comes from consistent positive feedback and modeling the desired behavior.

There is no chance my child will be told to wash the dishes as a punishment and say, "Sure, Dad!" and just do it. I can't get her to do anything. Why are you setting me up for more battles?

The reason we deliver this punishment first is because it is the most respectful way to help our children improve their behavior. She will be given a choice, and she can either choose to respond to the correction request or refuse to do the chore; we can't control that. If she refuses, which is her choice, we move to punishment option number two. When you launch this program in your home, your child will probably not opt for the chore option first, but as time goes by and she realizes that you are consistently respectful and calm and that you have faith in her, she will come around.

Here are some cookie punishment chore ideas:

- Organizing a bookshelf
- Giving a snack or drink to a sibling she just hit or making her bed
- Washing a few dishes
- Picking up the garbage that blew into the front yard
- Folding a few items of laundry
- Organizing the junk drawer (we all have one)
- Unloading the dishwasher

- Washing down a sticky shelf
- Organizing a shelf in the pantry
- Cleaning a window
- Polishing silver
- Voluntary time-out.

Punishment/Correction #2: Taking Matters Into Our Own Hands

Every new system involves adjustment time. Right now, your child is not listening nicely. She is bothering siblings, throwing tantrums, or refusing to help out at home. She can overcome all these behaviors and *must* overcome them so that she can become a fully functioning member of society. The cookie punishment may take some time to implement as she's not quite ready to make the mature choice you are offering. Don't lose hope; she will get there. Until then, we can use punishment option two.

This is how it goes:

Your child hit his younger brother and then grabbed his toy away. Now it's your turn. First, the victim must be protected at all costs. Next, you say to your child, "Jesse, in this house, we do not hit and grab things. Now you have to clean up the building blocks."

"No way! He started; he took my toy first!"

"I see that you are having trouble doing the chore I gave you. Now I will have to take away the trucks you are playing with for fifteen minutes."

What is the rule? If your child rejects the chore (cookie) option, which you always offer first, *you then either take an item or a privilege away from him.* The goal is a swift but small message delivered very consistently. Slight discomfort, immediately following unwanted behavior, is more powerful than a big and painful punishment delivered sporadically.

Here are some "taking matters into your own hands" punishment ideas:

- Taking away a toy the child is playing with now
- Taking away the first ten minutes of a movie the children are sitting down to watch
- If a treat is being given out, she gets half or none
- Not coming to the supermarket with a parent
- Going to bed a few minutes early
- Reading a shorter story at bedtime
- Less allowance.

The punishment should be delivered as close to the unwanted behavior as possible. If you are not home, you can either let the child know that this is the punishment she will get at home or have some punishments ready to use. An example would be not getting popcorn at the movies, sitting on the park bench for a few minutes, or sitting in the back seat in the car.

We often ask our children to say they are sorry, and that's fine, but the punishment stands.

The family piled into the car, all excited to head to the beach. The day was beautiful; the ocean water beckoned. Lo and behold, the kids started to fight in the back seat. They were arguing over who got to sit next to the window. Mom tried to reason with them but was making no headway. And then Ariel took matters into her own hands and smacked her brother right over the head.

Mom proclaimed, "Ariel, in our family, we are not allowed to hit. When we get to the beach, you will sit on the sand with me for fifteen minutes and then you can go in the water."

Ariel was upset but took it well.

Dad, on the other hand, started shifting in his seat. "Ariel, say sorry to Mom. Say sorry to your brother, please, sweetie."

Out came an apology, and Dad felt good. He then turned to Mom with a hopeful look. "She apologized . . ." Dad thought maybe the punishment was too harsh. If he used his connections with Mom, maybe she would cancel the punishment. Nope! Ariel sat, and she sat nicely.

"Good job, Ariel," Mom said. "You took responsibility for your actions."

What have we learned?

- **Keep your word:** When a parent declares that there should be a punishment, she must keep her word. A child can only trust a parent who trusts herself. Never give a punishment that is too painful for *you* to carry through. If you are feeling bad for your child, you will not follow through. Think of small punishments you can stomach.

- **The punishment stands:** Apologies are welcome. They are not as impactful as having a child actively repair his behavior with a cookie punishment, but they may help your child be more civilized and reflect on his actions. The power of the punishment is in its immediate delivery and consistent carry-through.

- **Stay positive:** Complimenting a child for behaving well during a punishment or after it is concluded is a welcome response from a parent.

Be careful. Do not step on these punishment land mines:

1. **Don't punish in anger:** Never punish when you are angry as the punishment will be too punitive and out of proportion. If you cannot think clearly, wait until you are calm.

2. **The punishment should be quick and mild:** Choose a short chore, not more than fifteen minutes long. If you are taking away an item, let the child know when you will be returning it.

3. **Always reward the good behavior first:** If you are focused on reshaping a specific behavior, be sure to begin behavioral intervention by first catching your child doing the right thing and rewarding with a compliment. Only when you feel

comfortable that your behavioral reinforcement program is bearing fruit should punishment be introduced.

4. **Avoid punishing with something you are trying to enforce:** If you want your child to exercise, don't take away the bike.

5. **Never ever humiliate your child:** This leads to a desire on his part for revenge. A humiliation punishment never leads to corrective behavior.

6. **Carry through on punishments:** If you threatened a punishment, carry through. Respect your word.

7. **Don't remind the child about his misdeed:** Once a punishment is over, don't remind your child of his previous wrongdoing.

8. **Use punishment sparingly:** The ratio of praise to punishment should be 5:1. Punishment is an important skill but should be used with respect. Remember, punishment does not teach a child what to do right; it stops him from doing wrong. This skill can be used only as an add-on to our positive parenting program.

9. **Don't over-punish:** If you find yourself punishing for the same misdeed several times a day, it's time to reconsider the program. Maybe your child needs more positive reinforcement, or maybe the punishment is not the right one for him.

10. **Start small:** Because it can be overwhelming to punish for all misdeeds at once, choose one behavior to focus on consistently for the first month of intervention.

Are you still a little uneasy?

This was my fifth meeting with these parents. Two meetings before, we had discussed implementing a punishment program. I asked the parents how it was going. "Not really. It's not working at all."

These parents had chosen to focus on their child's frequent aggression towards his siblings. I asked them how often they had helped him correct himself for hitting this week. The mother was sure she had done it once on Sunday. Dad was batting zero. The parents were so uncomfortable with the concept of punishment that they were still using it as a last resort. So, what were they doing when the child hit? Going back to their old methods: begging him to stop, warning him that next time there would be a punishment, and finally, yelling, which Nate interpreted as haphazard, out of control, and punitive.

The takeaway for Nate? His parents couldn't keep it together. He was the one pulling all the strings while his parents merely responded, and his actions had little connection to the response. In other words, he either learned nothing or received a damaging message that he was responsible for his own discipline, and that made him feel unsafe.

What have we learned?

- **Focus on one behavior:** It can take time to get accustomed to this program, so choose one behavior to focus on, both by way of compliment and with punishment.

- **Use punishment as your first line of discipline:** Do not use this method as a last resort; this mode of punishment is the gift your child deserves. He benefits from you remaining calm and in control. You are sending a consistent message of faith in him, and you are letting him know he can depend on you. Your previous methods led to shouting and caused additional pain and harm to everyone.

- **Let your child face the consequences of his actions:** Too frequently we don't allow our children to face discomfort as a consequence of their poor behaviors. We coddle them too much for fear that we will break them. What is the consequence? Instead of giving a clear and loving message, we resort to our much more aggressive, less kind, less protective, and certainly less educational behavior. Our children are strong and resilient and want to behave well. Let's give them that choice. They only need protection from a raging parent who has not learned to punish in a calm, measured way.

What should a parent do when she punishes and the child's behavior escalates?

A child often ups his bad behavior in response to having been punished. No one likes to be scolded. If he is throwing things in rage and a parent steps in and says, "In our house, we do not throw things around and break them; we have to respect property," he gets angrier.

Obviously, the child is in no state to participate in a cookie punishment, so the parent says, "You will have to miss the first ten minutes of the movie this evening," The child's behavior escalates; now he's mad! His throwing-and-breaking tantrum picks up speed. Help! Can you stop him? In most cases, no.

Helping a child change a behavior takes time; there are no instant fixes. Do not get discouraged; this consistent process will eventually show great results. Removing a child forcefully is not a good approach. Touch should be reserved for positive feedback. The parent can tell her child that since he has continued and escalated his misbehavior, she will have to add an additional ten minutes to his punishment, and then *the parent must get away*.

That's right: **leave the room**. Get busy folding laundry. Call a friend. The behavior the child is exhibiting needs an audience as its oxygen to continue. Once we are gone, so is the oxygen.

Yes, the child might cause damage, but staying there to watch and yell and manhandle gives him too much negative attention and doesn't stop the behavior anyway. When he does calm down, which he will do shortly after you leave, you can let him know that he made a very good choice to calm down. Even so, the punishment stands. Punish without fear.

The punishment is a small step in the process of helping your child behave better. We start with directed compliments and use punishment sparingly and only when necessary. Now we must help our child dig up the emotional stress triggering this difficult behavior. Our child would choose to behave well if he could. If he has an emotional barrier, it will get in the way of his good choices. Emotional intervention is part of the next section of the book. Stay tuned.

What should a parent do if the child insists that the punishment is fun or that it doesn't even bother her?

This is not a problem.

I once told a parent of an eleven-year-old girl to use this method to punish her daughter for constantly disregarding her mother, ignoring her, and cursing at her. One evening the family had just returned from a two-day trip, and the suitcases were open all over the living room. The daughter began to yell at her mother, so her mother took a deep breath and told her daughter calmly to put away all of the clothing that had piled up on the couch as her punishment for being disrespectful.

The daughter looked at her mother in contempt and said, "That's a stupid punishment; it's totally no big deal. I can do it in a minute." The mother was deflated but instructed her daughter to continue clearing. As the daughter worked, she stated, "This is no big deal" repeatedly. At some point, the daughter burst into tears. From that point onward, the daughter began to improve in her communication with her mother. She finally trusted that her mother had faith in her.

Often a child will minimize the effect the punishment has on her to defend her honor. That is okay. The goal of the punishment is not to shame; it is to stop and redirect your child. If the punishment is "fun" for your child, don't worry. She is still doing it, and that's what we are aiming for. You have asked her to do something positive, to bake cookies to correct the damage she caused, and she is doing just that. Good for her.

Is this system right for older children? (ages 13–17)

As children get older, punishment gets harder. Getting a big kid to do a chore is nearly impossible. You must gauge your own child. If he would not be willing to participate in the higher-order punishment, move on to taking away a privilege or item. Again, this may be difficult. Taking a fifteen-year-old child's phone away for an afternoon could result in a physical response, and we don't ever want to get into a physical altercation with a child. Docking part of an allowance or moving up a curfew can be used.

An older child needs to get the message, just like a younger child, that we know he can behave better and can make better choices. Just because your child is now taller than you does not mean he should be allowed to hurt himself by behaving in socially unacceptable ways.

Be careful here. As children get older, our responses can cause shame. Be very respectful. In many cases the best response to unwanted behavior in an older child is an emotional intervention, which will be discussed in chapter seven, rather than a punishment.

If a child this age is testing boundaries consistently, she is calling out for help. Involving a mentor or therapist to help uncover emotional stress or promote better communication between you and your older child may be of great value. Children this age still need us. They are more independent now, which is excellent. But they must still know that we care and believe in them and their ability to make good choices. We will be by their side to help them when they are struggling with those choices.

Building the punishment treasure chest

Because punishment allows us to love our children better and to respond calmly and predictably in difficult situations, it gives our children a feeling of safety. This system is indeed a treasure.

Look at it this way.

You have decided that you eat too much junk food, and you want to shed a few pounds. In the morning, the diet is easy: you grab an apple, some healthy nuts . . . excellent start! The afternoon is less simple. You drag yourself into the house with the kids and the groceries after a hard day's work. You're hungry, hot, and tired, and so are your kids. There's a cake on the counter, and you ate the last apple this morning.

What are the chances you will not down that cake? Zero? You need backup! There is no way to fight all these battles simultaneously and not slip up. It's impossible.

Now imagine . . . you prepared yourself a beautiful quinoa salad before you left to work, anticipating your stressful 4 p.m. return because you respect yourself and know how difficult it can be in the afternoon.

Can you resist the cake now? Do you feel stronger? I'll bet you do.

Punishable situations always occur at times of stress. Ten things are going on just when your child digs in. Your cortisol is surging, so you are going into fight or flight mode, and you will not make good choices because self-control has evaporated. Now what? If you have prepared your punishment list or your salad in the refrigerator, that's your treasure. It will calm you down.

When we know what to do under pressure, and we have all the tools, we can activate our thinking minds and behave like responsible adults. Our children need us to respond with calm leadership more than ever when they have lost control. Chop that salad. Don't leave yourself exposed to stress, unprepared. Download a quick-access "punishment treasure chest" list from my website, www.hyperhealing.org.

Instilling the concept of rules and their value without lecturing

The following is a natural way to instill the concept of rules and appropriate boundaries in your child. We all spend a lot of time with our kids in the car. I do not allow the kids to be on screens in the car (for reasons we will discuss later), so since we are trapped in a small space for a while, it's a great time to talk to kids about the road. We talk about the traffic light, the signs and signals, what a solid line or broken line on the road means, parking regulations, etc. As they get older, we discuss driving techniques. I test them on their road skills (even the little guys—who has the right of way? Why should that driver get a ticket? Why should I have just been booked?). They ask me questions; I tell them funny driving stories.

In this way, kids understand that we need rules and boundaries everywhere. They grasp that if we don't follow road rules, we can cause accidents. They learn that we must all agree to keep the rules as a community so that we can use the roads together safely. If one person decides to drive against traffic, we all suffer. They also learn that it makes no difference if your car is more expensive than mine or a different color; we all must follow rules and equally enjoy the benefits that the roads provide us.

Once they really understand that rules are for our benefit on the road, we can demonstrate that the same concept applies to our home. See if they can figure out what a double line in the house could be (maybe not entering the bathroom when someone is using it), or using blinkers (telling a parent or older sibling where you are or where you are going), or a red light (giving others a chance to speak at the dinner table), etc. As you develop the concept of rules and healthy boundaries, your child will begin to understand that every area of life is governed by rules, not just a house or classroom.

Action Plan

1. Think about the three to five rules you would like to establish in your home.

   ▫ When you choose rules, remember that they are meant to educate your children to be respectful and responsible people. Choose rules that will build their character, not just rules that will keep the house quiet and clean, although you can include those too.

2. Ask your child what she thinks the rules in your home are.

3. Choose one or more rules that you intend to begin implementing now. Don't shy away from the harder ones.

   ▫ Begin by catching your child following the rule and only afterward follow up with a punishment if the rule is broken.

4. It is critical to remain calm when giving a punishment. Therefore, prepare your punishment treasure chest.

   ▫ Make a list of cookie punishments, deeds your child can do to say he's sorry, and a second list of punishments that are not in his control, such as taking away a privilege or item.

   ▫ These lists are your salad; they will keep you calm.

5. Do not punish as a last resort because this will put you in danger of slipping into old, more aggressive habits.

   ▫ This process takes time, so stick with it. If you told a child she will be punished, carry through. If the child throws a tantrum or destroys property, up the punishment and leave for a few minutes.

   ▫ If you keep punishing for the same rule, check why the message is not getting across. Don't keep repeating a method that's not working.

Dear Parents,

We are doing great! We are now ready to invite our Instant Gratification child to be part of the program. He is a healthy and fully capable child whose environment clashes with his personality and needs. We cannot change his personality, nor do we want to. We also can't fully change his environment; he will still be expected to go to school, finish tasks, and get along with the people around him.

What we have accomplished in these few chapters is setting up the home environment to be a place where she can flourish. We did not create her challenges, but we have a lot of power to help her overcome them. She needs us to be healthy, strong, and in control. She needs us to be loving and consistent. This is a vital process for us parents, and every small step is a great accomplishment. Demanding perfection for yourself will just slow you down because no one can be perfect, and no one can change habits overnight.

Take it slowly, and be proud of every small change you make. Review the last few chapters before moving on to Part Two: Healthy Habit Formation.

Now it's our child's turn.

THE CHEAT SHEET

Chapter Five: The Respectful Discipline Intervention Program (punishment)

- ☛ Why do we punish ineffectively, aggressively, scarcely?

  - ◻ Society tells us our child is fragile.

  - ◻ We think only positive discipline is appropriate.

  - ◻ We need our children's love and admiration.

  - ◻ We are told we may not impose our beliefs and rules on our children.

  - ◻ We have no idea how it's done.

- ☛ Our children must know we believe they can make better choices; therefore, we are not waiting for "natural consequences." Rather, we are choosing to respond with a clear message.

- ☛ If we do not teach our children to be civilized, society will, but it will do so much less kindly.

- ☛ Here are some mistakes we make when we discipline:

  - ◻ We are over-patient.

  - ◻ We threaten and warn, but we do not act.

  - ◻ We resort to explanations rather than action.

  - ◻ We are over-compassionate and overprotective.

  - ◻ We morally justify not responding.

- ☛ Our Instant Gratification child thrives on strong feedback. We are responsible for providing safe, calm, and respectful responses, as well as leading with strong rules.

- ☛ Only punish behaviors that are in violation of the rules of the home.

☛ Establish three to five rules at home.

☛ Rules that are enforced provide clarity and safety.

☛ Parents may only punish a child if the child has been given the ability to choose to behave better. That means not yelling, always complimenting good behavior, and being consistently loving.

☛ There are two types of punishments.

  ▫ The cookie punishment: Have a child do community service (a chore in the home) to correct his poorly chosen misbehavior. This is a more respectful punishment.

  ▫ The taking matters into your own hands punishment: This comes into effect when the child rejects the first punishment. The parent takes away an item or privilege for a short amount of time.

☛ Our goal is a swift, small punishment that stops our child in her tracks and redirects her to a positive activity. The punishment must be delivered in a consistent manner. Choose punishments that are not too challenging for the parent to deliver.

☛ If parents threaten punishment, they must follow through.

☛ Apologies are wonderful, but the punishment still stands.

☛ Compliment your child after he has completed his punishment and invite him back warmly.

☛ When we give a punishment, we may NEVER:

  ▫ Punish in anger or with aggressive touch

  ▫ Give a long, drawn-out punishment, or punish with something we are trying to strengthen

  ▫ Humiliate.

☞ Punishment should be used sparingly. The bulk of the discipline program is positive communication and strong habit formation (next chapter), with punishment intended to help guide children to make better choices. If we continually punish for the same behavior, we must stop and reevaluate.

☞ Build a punishment treasure chest.

PART TWO

Healthy Habit Formation;
Now It's Our Child's Turn

CHAPTER SIX

It's All About the Habit

I NSTANT GRATIFICATION KID. We now know him well. We have learned to discipline him with kindness and love, building his strengths and respectfully reducing inappropriate behavior. We have broken our own unconscious behavior cycles, identified our curses, and stopped passing them forward.

Now we will tackle outward behavior, social stress, and internal emotional triggers. Once we have solidified an intervention program at home, we will share it with our child's teacher. It's also time to invite our child to be part of the program. He plays the leading role in his skill-gaining journey and therefore must get involved immediately. We waited this long because of our steadfast rule: **parents may not punish unless they have given their child the option to choose to behave well by using positive communication.** Now our child has a choice. We are ninja moms and dads, and he is getting fantastic feedback in a supportive environment.

Step up to the plate, dear child!

Instant Gratification kid is routine phobic, rule resistant, spontaneous (impulsive), and emotional. He stays up all night to read a book he can't put down; she is addicted to the screen and the constant stimulation it provides. He starts projects but rarely finishes them— they are no longer fun once he has to get into the details. She responds emotionally and without thinking through her response.

What is missing from a child's life that is fostering this difficult behavior?

Habits.

Forming habits is a lot of work. It requires repetitive behavior and consistent practice. Other kids may have figured out by now that they will have to get up every morning, that homework is an unpleasant yet necessary part of the afternoon, and that eating takes place at the table. Our little guy may understand these concepts in theory, but in practice, every day is packed full of possibilities, and these routines get in his way.

How do we help our child learn new habits? In this chapter we will unpack the obstacles to habit formation and gain skills in guiding Instant Gratification kid towards the habits she needs in order to excel. Has every chart you tried failed? We will create a behavior chart that is tailor-made for kids who don't like to be controlled. Then we will address the "chart resistant" kid as well. We will examine all the pitfalls in the program and help you be flexible and think on your toes.

Habit formation can be compared to forging a path in a thick jungle. Imagine you were challenged to traverse the jungle daily for a month. There are no paths. What would be the most strategic way to make this exercise more effective? You would want to cross the jungle every day in the same spot so that within a few days you begin to create a path. Once there is a path, the journey becomes simple and enjoyable.

What if this jungle is so interesting—full of beautiful flowers, scents, and sounds—that everything draws you in? You must get across, but along the way you hop to the left because of a rustling in the bushes. Could it be a jackal? And then to the right, what a magnificent rare flower! At the end of thirty days, how does the jungle look? Have you left your mark? No, it looks much the same; there is still no path.

Creating habits makes permanent changes in our brains (the jungle). According to Michael Merzenich in *The Brain That Changes Itself* (Penguin Books, 2007), practicing a new habit under the right conditions can potentially change billions of the connections between the nerve cells in our **neural pathways**. Donald Hebb's landmark discovery in 1949, "Neurons that fire together wire together," revealed that the more the brain does a specific task, the stronger the neural network will be. Each time the behavior is repeated, the process becomes more efficient (Wiley, 69–74).

If we repeat the same behavior daily for at least a month, we will create a new neural pathway in our brain. At that point, whatever we have practiced will become automatic, and simpler for us to do without too much thought. But if instant gratification is our engine, we will have a hard time forming habits because we are continually distracted by all the novelty along the way. Waking up in the morning feels like a new chore every day because we have no pathway, no habit.

Our kids are habit resistant because they are novelty seeking.

Life is hard without habits. Our kid needs our help to get him focused on the jungle path so he will not be led astray by the beautiful distractions along the way. He must create habits because his world (and ours) revolves around routines and responsibility. He can do it; we must just work with his personality to get him there.

Why have most programs failed to help your child form habits?

1. **The parent absorbs the full responsibility and pushes the uninterested child along.** The parent wants to change the behavior more than the kid does. So, even though this program is meant to empower the child to form new habits, the parent is still too involved in making sure the kid succeeds.

   To illustrate: *(true story) A doctor declares that her patient is dangerously overweight and orders the patient to begin an exercise program. The patient can barely move, so the doctor introduces her patient to an exercise therapist. The patient lies on a bed while the therapist moves her hands and legs for her. The program helps the patient begin to build some muscle mass; everyone is pleased. But the minute the program is over, the patient goes right back to sitting all day and does not even consider exercising.* Why? Because she never developed a habit; she remained passive while another person practiced the habit on her.

We do that with our kids all the time. We expect them to do something every day, but then we carry them through it. Think about how we get a child dressed or walk him to the bathroom and place his toothbrush in his hand. <u>The goal is not to get him up this morning (no matter how painful it is when he doesn't get up). The goal is that he eventually forms the habit of getting up independently.</u> We must stop wanting him to succeed *this* morning but rather want him to take responsibility for himself *every* morning.

2. **We want to improve everything right now.** The programs we set up are too complex, and we are mightily impatient. We have big dreams—indeed, too big. Don't we all want to exercise, be more organized, spend more time with our spouse, be better at quality time with the kids, entertain guests more . . . We all have a long list of things that need improvement. If we try to tackle all of them at once, there will be no progress at all. We give up when we are overwhelmed. <u>Let's not overwhelm our kids with too elaborate a program, but rather choose one behavior to tackle at a time.</u>

3. **We want to work on improvement all day so that our child really understands what to do.** We assume that more is better. But we will drop out of the program with exhaustion and resentment way before our child has developed his shiny new habit. <u>Less is better. An intervention program of one hour a day is more effective than a full-day program that can't be maintained.</u>

4. **We promise big prizes, which take too long to earn.** Our child thrives on instant feedback, so waiting for a prize for two weeks will not work for him. He needs the option of getting rewarded quickly. <u>We want to help him form a habit that is not natural for him. We must reward him in a way that will keep him treading on the same area of the jungle daily, so that he can form a pathway.</u>

The program outlined in this book (adapted from one developed by Kazdin) is tailor-made for your child. Together we will do this right. Follow these steps carefully.

1. Make a list of behaviors that your child frequently exhibits, which are impeding his social/emotional/behavioral development.

This list can include not getting up in the morning, often skipping teeth brushing, picking on siblings, cursing, homework noncompliance (assuming she understands the assignment), afternoon tantrums, disorganization. List it all—don't hold back.

2. Choose <u>one</u> of the items on your list to implement as your first project.

Helping a child create habits is a valuable process that takes time. We can't tackle all her challenges at once because we will overwhelm her and us.

My daughter's sixth grade teacher had the best of intentions. She wanted my child to get more organized, take out her books for every lesson, have a pencil handy, copy down her homework assignments, and actually do them. All worthy behaviors, I agreed. One day my daughter came home from school with an elegant chart. It was divided into seven lessons for five school days. My daughter could earn thirty-five points per day if she got a check for all five items in every class. Let's get to it!

My daughter was motivated; the prize was good. The first week she racked up lots of points. The second week she waited for her teacher to give her the new chart, but it seems the teacher forgot. Two days passed, so I called to inquire about the chart. "No problem," said the teacher. "I will give it to her tomorrow." The chart never materialized. Why not? The teacher had overwhelmed herself; she could not keep up with the thirty-five points, with marking the chart in every lesson, and with providing a new chart each week. Everyone lost out.

We must be good to ourselves and begin by tackling only one behavior. We will choose only one part of the day to implement the program, not all day. **The goal of this program is to help our child consistently repeat a behavior that he finds challenging (and boring)**

until it becomes a habit. There is more value in expecting improvement in fewer areas, and using the chart for less time per day, than shoving in lots of behaviors but collapsing under the weight of the demands on us. If a parent can't consistently pull off filling out the chart, the child cannot improve.

- Start with ten minutes of consistent follow-through.

- Choose a routine you know you can consistently stick with, even if it's fifteen minutes or less a day.

- Choose a time to focus on the chart when you have the most time and energy.

3. Phrase the challenging behavior in positive terms.

This is not just semantics. When we discussed punishment, we said that a child can't learn what is expected of him through a punishment; he can only learn to stop negative behavior. He learns to choose the right behavior when he is caught doing the right thing and complimented, or when we set up a deliberate positive behavior program. Since we are directing our child to choose the positive behavior, we must communicate this behavior in a positive way.

Negative behavior	Positive opposite behavior
Not getting out of bed in the morning	Waking up on time to get everything done calmly before leaving for school
Fighting with siblings	Treating siblings with respect and kindness
Being messy and disorganized and not being responsible for her things	Having a neat and clean room/backpack/putting things where they belong

4. Take the behavior you chose to help your child develop and divide it into four steps, then set up the behavior chart.

Extensive research has been done on working memory. Research has found that the working memory capacity of young adults is between three and five items (Cowan 2005). This means that if we want to set up a program that our child will succeed at, we should limit the steps required to no more than five. This way he can keep all his tasks in mind as he moves through the routine.

Let's think about this in adult terms for a moment. Say your kitchen is a complete mess, a likely scenario in most homes. The kids decided to make themselves an elaborate breakfast but did not clean up all the million ingredients and pots they took out. When you walk into the kitchen (after they already left for camp and you can't tell them to clean up), you are completely overwhelmed. Some of us are natural cleaners; we get straight to work. And then there are the rest of us. We start sending WhatsApps, calling a friend, basically anything to avoid the mess. It's just too large and too deep. If we add to the mess Instant Gratification personality, we are in for a disaster. We want it done already; the process is too long and involves too many steps.

How can Instant Gratification parent be helped through this torturous chore? By breaking it down into manageable steps. Start with just clearing the countertops. Can you do that? Sure, you do it ten times a day; no big deal. Now just the dishes. No problem. Can you sweep, but only sweep, right now?

Setting our kids up for similar success is vital. Asking children to clean their room or the toys is a frustrating experience! Either they flat out ignore us, or they begin the chore but fizzle out quickly. Is the job too big?

Teach them a life skill of **dividing** any *one* task into four parts:

1. Putting away laundry: Make piles of underclothing, shirts, pants, hanging things, and then put each pile away one at a time.

2. Cleaning room: Lift items from floor, clear off bed, clear dresser, make bed.

3. Cleaning up toys: Games, stuffed animals, LEGO, trucks.

Once you have introduced the dividing skill:

1. **Divide:** Help your child **divide** the different laundry piles.

2. **Train:** Get involved in the **training** by sitting with him and naming each category.

   This is the shirt pile. Here is the pants pile. Now we will make an underwear, undershirt, and socks pile, followed by hanging things, which will go in a separate pile.

3. **Find a home** for all the items (this skill is further explained on the following page).

4. **Compliment** him on putting his clothes away.

Remember to:

- Start by being very helpful and giving lots of instructions.

- Gradually become more hands-off and just give verbal cues.

- Finally, just observe and compliment.

The same system works for toys; assign the project, and help your child divide the chore into four categories. Be specific. Ask him to make groups and decide which one he would like to begin with.

Shedders

Are any of your kids **shedders**? A shedder is the term I use to describe kids (and adults) who drop things wherever they go. They walk in the house and their items just start to shed. One shoe near the front door, the other under the couch. A ponytail holder on the kitchen table. Backpack in the bathroom (yes, the bathroom!)

Why is she shedding? There are so many possible reasons; she has other more pressing things to do; the item in her hand is no longer useful or interesting; she has sensory overload and is trying to simplify. All this may be true, but it will do her no good to continue shedding. We can help a child break her shedding habit while we are doing room-and-toy organization training. We call it the **"find a home"** skill.

Find a Home

When your child is making piles by dividing the chore in four, she will pick up things she has no idea where they belong. Together you will find a home for every item she has. Ponytail holders go in the drawer in the bathroom. Great, we found a home for them. Now, anytime a ponytail holder is lying around, instead of getting frustrated, say "find a home" and hand it to her. Backpacks always go on this shelf.

Reward her each time she puts her belongings in their proper home, without being asked, with a very specific and enthusiastic compliment. Once she knows how to clean up and where to put everything, she has a very good chance of succeeding next time you ask her to tidy up.

Follow the same steps described earlier:

1. **Divide:** Help your child **divide** any cleaning or organizing chore into four segments.

2. **Train:** Get involved in the **training** by sitting with her and showing her how chores are divided and naming each category.

3. **Find a home** for all her items.

4. **Compliment** her on putting items in their home and use the term "find a home" as a trigger to remind her what you have practiced. Sometimes it's fun to use a timer when asking her to straighten up, to see if she can beat her previous record for cleaning up the toys. This routine, when repeated often, will strengthen her brain and get your home in order in no time.

Failure to launch

Many people struggle when trying to get started on any task, whether it be cleaning up or sitting down to do homework or signing up for an extracurricular program. We often call that procrastination, a fairly "fixed" word. What is really going on? Either the person has not managed to organize the task in his head and is therefore overwhelmed by the enormity of it, or the first step seems insurmountable for an emotional reason (often fear of failure or fear of appearing incapable), and a person gets stuck. A child who labels himself a procrastinator may shut down completely, which gives him an excuse for not getting anything done. Procrastinating is less painful and a better escape route than investigating the reason for the blockage and trying to divide it meaningfully to make it achievable. <u>When someone is procrastinating, we should be investigating why he is not doing what is expected rather than declaring who he is.</u>

Kiara was a thirty-year-old mother of two. She was very frustrated with life, couldn't get her home in order, was always being rescued by her parents or husband, and hated her job. She did not believe she could ever be satisfied in life; everything felt bland. I asked her if she had an image of a dream job. She replied that she would love to give children horseback-riding therapy. And then she added that she had already taken a course in horseback-riding therapy and that every time she was near horses, she felt a small thrill.

The obvious question was, if you are trained (but haven't yet practiced) and you get excited just thinking about the job, why not look for opportunities? She answered that she was just that person who doesn't get things started, that's why.

Sound like a curse? Why did she define herself as that person?

As a child, she was not expected to do any household chores because her more capable sister did everything better. When she was young, this seemed like a dream to Kiara—she got to watch movies and play with friends while her sister cooked and baked. Fast-forward twenty years and Kiara got the message: she was the one who couldn't get things done—the curse of low expectations. Due to that toxic message (from truly loving and well-meaning parents who mistakenly felt they should shield their daughter from the pain of being less capable), she was now that person who couldn't get anything done, the lazy procrastinator. Now she didn't dare make that first phone call to the stable because she had already failed before she began.

Together we lifted the curse for just a minute. We decided that for *just a fleeting moment she would not define herself but rather ask the question, "Why is <u>this</u> particular launch hard for me? Why am I not calling the stable?"*

We set one rule: The answer "I'm just that way" was forbidden. The new response became: "The owner of the stable intimidates me; I always have a feeling she doesn't like me." Now we were talking. By detecting what the blockage was, we could now identify the first manageable step in the process.

What did we learn?

- When we define ourselves as **being** a certain way, we short circuit any **process.**

- When a person is "procrastinating," it's because there is a first step that feels insurmountable.

- Asking "why" and "what" questions about procrastination will allow the person to separate the process and understand why he is not progressing. Declaring "I am a procrastinator" shuts down the process. Saying "Why am I stuck here?" opens the possibility of succeeding.

- Once the blockage to beginning a process is unclogged, the first step can be clearly defined and executed. When the process begins, the person has a high chance of finishing it.

Setting up a behavior chart

We have practiced dividing. We will now put it into practice in a habit-formation chart. Download a behavior chart from my website, www.hyperhealing.org. I know some parents are allergic to charts; the minute they see a chart, they recoil. Are you one of those? If so, that's quite all right. If the chart contradicts your entire personality, I will present another system following the chart segment. I encourage you to at least try the chart because it is simple and clear, progress can be followed, and most kids love the structure it provides.

Let's take "getting up on time and getting ready for school" as an example. This is how we would divide it:

	Getting out of bed at 7:00 a.m.	Brushing teeth and washing up by 7:15	Getting dressed by 7:45	Eating breakfast and being ready to leave by 8:00
Monday				
Tuesday				

This is just an example. Obviously, you would create the chart for the entire week. Also, you will tailor the chart for the needs of your child. If your child is struggling particularly with getting dressed, the chart would look more like this:

	Getting up at 7:00	Putting on undergarments until 7:15	Putting on shirt, pants, and socks until 7:30	Putting on shoes that are waiting at the door
Monday				

If your child is having trouble getting up, you may want to consider that he is not getting enough sleep, in which case the program would be more effective in the evening. This is how it would look:

	Shut off screens and other electronics by 7:00 p.m. (at least two hours before bed)	Shower and change into pajamas by 8:00	Brush teeth and read in bed (remember, no screens) until 9:00	Lights out at 9:00
Monday				

Adjust the expectations according to the age and ability of the child. Don't skip steps! If he is not yet ready to accomplish a goal, demanding that he comply will sink the program.

Here is another way to use the chart. The previous examples are more behavioral. We can also add an emotional element to the program by choosing behavior that involves other people. Another chart I have set up with much success is the "brotherly love" chart. This is for kids who fight in the afternoon when they come home from school. Here is how we would set it up:

	Brothers getting along with each other 4:00–4:15	Brothers getting along with each other 4:15–4:30	Brothers getting along with each other 4:30–4:45	Brothers getting along with each other 4:45–5:00
Monday				

Notice that we have divided this chart into segments of **time** instead of **behaviors**. Here are a few things to keep in mind:

1. First, if you are setting up a behavior/emotional chart, you, dear parent, must be up for the task. You will be checking on the kids every fifteen minutes for an hour, and this can be very demanding during a busy afternoon. If it's too much, reduce the time to half an hour; you will still be helping your child create a new habit and rewire his brain.

2. If one child is the instigator, make a chart only for her. If there are two or more children involved, make a group chart. The group behavior intervention program will require some sort of timer, which most of us have on our phones. A simple egg timer can also be used. You will then have to decide if the kids get points together or if each one gets points separately. Both are fine; it all depends on the dynamic in your home.

3. Finally, there are always emotional stressors causing unrest between siblings. Can we really chart away their fights? We can do some great work, but we will still have to address the emotional stress that is triggering the fights to begin with. Emotional intervention is discussed in chapter seven.

What behaviors can we chart? The rule is: **any behavior that your child should be able to do on his own can be charted** (keeping himself occupied in the afternoon, staying dry throughout the afternoon by age five, preparing her own food to take to school, cleaning his own room, being responsible for the dog, getting along with her siblings).

We must never accommodate! Our children will grow into the space we provide for them. We do them no favors when we continually take on the role of a one-person entertainment center, overflowing with ideas of how they can keep busy with friends, games, and projects. We are there to help our child generate ideas, and then set up a program where she gets to choose what she would like to do. Making a list of activities with her and then setting up an afternoon self-entertainment chart will empower her to fill her time successfully.

Children are disadvantaged if parents ignore the messy room because they define their child as just "that messy kid." Here's our chance to let him prove to himself that he CAN be neat. There is no gentler and kinder way to guide him than by helping him develop a new skill.

Notice that in the chart I have included the time a child is meant to finish each task, as well as a description of the task. Keeping time is generally less compelling to an Instant Gratification person. Novelty is his driving force. Therefore, we must introduce him to the value of time by including it on the chart and intensively sticking to the clock during each routine. Keeping time is so important; our children suffer when they do not develop this muscle.

4. Practice! We are setting our child up for success. This is how it looks on the chart:

	Task 1	Task 2	Task 3	Task 4	Practice
Monday					

Your child will get a point for practicing with you. Every day for at least the first week of the program, which will run for one month, you will either play a practice game with your child or have a short conversation with him. For example, if it's an evening chart for a younger child (age four to seven), you can play a short make-believe game. Move the clock to evening time and have the child act out what is expected of him. Don't practice during the hour set aside to implement the program; do that at another time during the day.

What are we accomplishing? We are getting our child used to doing what he is expected to do, with our assistance and positive feedback. We are also troubleshooting with him. We will ask him what part of the chart is challenging for him and how he can make it simpler. For example, if he is expected to get dressed by himself in the morning, we might discuss putting out clothing in the evening. If she is expected to keep herself entertained in the afternoon, we may suggest making a list of activities for her to choose from. We are also giving him the opportunity to reflect on his good behavior and plan for more.

When practicing with older children, invite the child to have a short strategizing conversation instead of playing a simulation game. We can initiate the conversation in three different ways, alternating our style frequently:

Discuss an occurrence from the day before that still needs improvement, and strategize ways of doing better. We are not preaching; this is a conversation. We must invite our child to be an active member and come up with ideas herself.

Invent a scenario that could arise (child not wanting to shut off the phone at the agreed-upon time, not being tired when he gets into bed, not being able to control her emotional response to her sister) and work through steps of overcoming the challenge.

Strategize how to be most efficient in earning points.

If the chart is strictly a behavior chart (going to bed, getting up, homework, keeping busy in the afternoon), one week of practice is enough. If the chart is an emotional/behavioral chart, two weeks or more would be very helpful, and in some cases, even more important than the behavior chart itself. During this conversation we will discuss the challenges of getting along from every angle. We will strategize about compromise, patience, letting go, how the child feels when fighting, and who she can turn to instead of hitting back. These conversations contribute dramatically to the success of the program.

5. Extra credit. This gives the child a chance to develop his character in a repetitive *and* competitive way. We address the "how" question here; how is he doing his tasks? Is he dragging his feet, or is there a hop in his step? Is she cutting it to the very last second or trying to work on giving herself ample time? Is she angry all evening or participating with a smile?

The more positively a child feels and behaves, the faster a habit will be formed. So, I add a "value," such as doing your assignment with a smile, doing it quickly, etc. Choosing "doing it quickly" is very effective because then we can play "beat the clock." If he gets to the breakfast table two minutes before the time written on the chart, he gets an extra point. You can decide if you want to give one point for the entire routine or one point for each successfully completed task. This part of the program is flexible.

This is how it looks:

	Task 1	Task 2	Task 3	Task 4	Practice	Extra credit Beating the clock or doing it with a smile (examples)
Monday						

6. The prize! You may have been thinking all this time—how are we going to get this kid to do something he has consistently not done until now? It's all about the prize. The most valuable prize is the compliment. While your child is moving from task to task, she should be hearing soul-nourishing compliments from you loudly and enthusiastically. Go back and review *The Art of the Compliment* before setting up the chart.

As for other prizes—write a list. Begin with a five-point prize and move up from there. Come up with a few ideas in each category and invite your children to give their own ideas. Before we get to the examples, let's discuss the two types of possible prizes: an item or an experience.

In a study conducted at San Francisco University and published in *The Journal of Positive Psychology*, the researchers found that people enjoy greater long-term well-being from enjoyable life experiences rather than from purchasing expensive items. They also consider the experiences a better use of their money. The pleasure generated from the purchase of an expensive item fades quickly, but people hold on to the memory created by experiences for a long time (Pchelin and Howell 2004).

I was surprised to see how true this finding was. I had the opportunity to visit with a family from my community, who I did not know well, for an event they were hosting. When I walked into the home, I was thrilled to see what a beautiful home they had. It was so tastefully decorated, I could tell they had put a lot of money, effort, and thought into designing their home. I gave my neighbor a compliment on the beauty of his home. This was his response: "Oh, we are already bored of it!" Was the experience of building the home more enjoyable than having the home itself?

Therefore, when creating a prize chart, we must consider experiential and physical prizes. Here are a few prize examples:

1. **5-point prize:** Getting an extra story at bedtime, a small chocolate bar, a dollar, a private walk with Mom

*   **10-point prize:** Choosing the dinner menu for tomorrow night, baking cookies, going out to the park with Dad, ice cream from the local grocery, getting baseball cards

*   **20-point prize:** Having a sleepover with a friend, sleeping at grandparents' house, going out to a café for a big dessert, buying a toy that the child has been wanting

*   **40-point prize:** Going to a movie with a parent or other relative, going to a sporting event or show, going out to dinner alone with a parent, purchasing a game.

The following chart-making rules will set your child up for success:

*   **Have the prize available:** Be sure you have the prizes you are offering available. If she chooses an outing as her prize, don't make your child wait too long before taking her out. The prize should directly follow the achievement, within reasonable limits.

*   **The points are like money:** We are building habits in an Instant Gratification child, which means he gets to choose how he uses his points. If he would like to cash in right away

and get a small prize for five points, that's great. If he wants to save his points for a few days and earn a bigger prize, he may do that as well. The points are his money; he should be allowed to "shop" when he chooses, although the store does not have to be open twenty-four-seven.

- **Do not punish by taking away points:** Never use the chart to punish! Do not take points off the chart for any reason.

- **Do not punish for a missed point:** If a child misses a point, just put a line through that section and move on. The only consequence is missing the point.

- **Don't beg your child to succeed:** Remind once, and then let her carry the responsibility. If you stand there and coax and beg, you are preventing the creation of a habit.

- **Stick to the chart; no points for anything else:** Points are only given for the designated routine, nothing else. You may not offer a point for good behavior at a different time during the day. Stick to the program.

- **Be prepared with many copies of the chart:** Be sure to print out a pile of charts so you are always ready for the new week. When we are not prepared, we often miss a few days, and our program can fall apart.

How do we introduce the program?

1. Invite your child for a conversation and tell her that you want to begin a program with her to help her create a new habit. Your child is smart, so tell her how she can make her brain stronger with each habit she forms.

2. Talk to her about the habits she already has and how useful they are to her. Tell her about the big jungle that is her brain, and how she can make new habit paths.

3. Show her your prize menu, with open spaces for her ideas. If she suggests a prize, add it to the menu at the price (amount of points) you feel it is worth.

4. Once you have discussed the prizes, show her the chart and have your first practice session. Give her a point right away for practicing, along with a compliment.

If the program is not working, consider the following:

- **Is my child capable** of doing the tasks I have put on the chart?

    □ Are the tasks too simple or too hard?

- **Am I being consistent?**

    □ Am I complimenting each task while my child is doing it?

    □ Am I filling in the chart as she moves through her routine?

    □ Do I have a chart ready at the beginning of each week?

    □ Is the chart hung somewhere where we can all see it?

    □ Am I over-reminding or letting him lead?

    □ Am I providing all the equipment my child needs to succeed, like a timer and watch?

    □ Did I make a program that is too hard for me to maintain, and I am therefore dodging it and hoping my child doesn't remember it's there?

A small, consistent program is far more valuable than an elaborate program that sucks the life out of the parent.

- **Is the prize right?**

    □ Is he excited about the prizes?

    □ Should I refresh the prizes, add more, make them exciting?

    □ Am I providing the prizes as he earns them?

- **Is the program getting monotonous?**
- We must get to a month, so if it's starting to feel old, mix it up. Give an extra point for every two consecutive days your child gets all her points.
- Add an extra challenge in the extra credit section.
- This is *your* chart; make it work for *your* child.

What do we do once the month is up?

Your child is getting the concept: he is waking up on time and has left for school on time for a few weeks now. How do we continue? We have a few choices. We can either expand the routine we are working on; we can switch to a new routine (related to homework or the evening); or we can fade out the program. Let's see how each one works:

Continuing and expanding the program

The first month:

	Waking up at 6:30	Brushing teeth and washing up by 6:45	Getting dressed by 7:00	Eating break-fast and leaving by 7:15	Practice	Extra credit: beating the clock
Monday						

The second month:

	Waking up at 6:30, brush-ing and washing, getting dressed (2 points)	Making bed	Packing lunch and snacks, or setting aside clothing in the evening	Eating break-fast and leaving by 7:15	Practice	Extra credit: getting the job done with a smile!
Monday						

We are reinforcing the progress from last month and expanding it. We do this for a child who has almost developed the new habit but can still use some more practice.

If you feel your child is ready for a new routine, go for it. Continue to compliment the first routine, but he will now only get points for the new routine. Go down the list of behaviors that you would like your child to develop a habit for and choose your next project.

If you feel your child has done great and does not need any more charts for now, transition out of the program by continuing to compliment the new habit; give points every two or three days, and then once a week, and then no points at all.

Will we be charting for the rest of their lives?

No, of course not. The good news is that once your child has a new routine, the next routines are easier to learn. Habits are contagious. Your list of missing habits may be long now, but once your child begins to organize his mind and environment, he will start developing habits on his own. I recommend you take breaks, give yourself holidays and summers off, and break between projects. You will find that after a few months of charts, you may not need to make any more charts for a while. After your chart vacation, you can either make a refresher chart or challenge your child to reach even higher.

We have two more issues to consider:

1. We are nurturing instant gratification behavior, but our child must learn to delay gratification. How do we help him with that?

2. What do we do with the chart-refuser and older children who are already too old for charts?

Strengthen the delayed gratification muscle by using a long-term chart

Kazdin offers a novel way to help stretch our children's gratification needs. You know the BIG prize your child always wants? A bicycle, a trip to Six Flags, a new phone . . . Set up an investment plan for your child. Every point that he earns each week will be worth two points at the end of the week. One set of points will be spent that week, the other is put into the "bank account." The bank account is his long-term chart. This is how it looks:

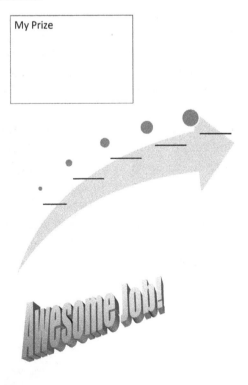

Put a picture of the big prize your child has chosen in the frame in the corner. Figure out how many points that item/experience would be worth. If it's a bicycle, you may want your child to earn eight hundred points for it. If she wants to go camping with her father for two days, five hundred points. How will she earn all those points?

At the end of each week, after your child has already used all his points, count the (already used) points again and put the points on the long-term chart. We have doubled his investment: he earns one point; we add the second. If she is earning points for the bicycle, and you have decided you want her to get the points in about two months, then you scale the long-term chart accordingly. If she earns in the range of twenty-five points per week, it will take an average of two weeks to amass fifty points and progress to the next step. After around eight weeks, she will have two hundred points and will have earned her big prize.

Calculate how many points your child will probably earn every week and determine the value of each step based on that calculation. Every big prize has a different value, which is why there are no numbers on the chart, and you must add them yourself. Write the value of each step next to the dot, and each week write down how much your child has climbed. If your child has chosen a smaller prize (like a large LEGO set), its value would be a hundred points. Each step would be worth twenty points, and the prize could be earned in two to three weeks.

Consider the age of your child and the size of the prize when deciding the value of the prize. Hang the short- and long-term charts side by side so your child can see how much closer he is getting to his big prize every week. He will continue to earn small prizes the entire time while he learns to delay gratification and work for his big prize. This second chart provides an extra layer of motivation to keep a child engaged in forming new habits. Download a long-term chart from my website, www.hyperhealing.org.

Chart-refusers and older kids

Now we must address the chart-refuser. This is the child who will not be controlled! He does not want his behavior charted and does not want you in charge of tracking his progress. Don't panic; you are in good company. Some of my favorite little people are chart-refusers. If the chart gets torn up into little bits and thrown directly in the garbage, your child may be telling you that this is not her style. You can try once more to set up a chart, but that's it; do not push it if this is the wrong method for your kid.

Instead of a chart, you can use an agreement. "Getting out of bed" will be our example because so many of our children (and their parents) struggle with it. Here's how it works:

The agreement is:

- Every time you get up in the morning on time, you will get X (think of a small reward with your child, such as extra time to read before bed or chocolate milk with breakfast).

- If you do *not* get up on time, you will have to (think of a small punishment, such as missing ten minutes of a movie in the afternoon or giving a dollar of his own money to charity).

- If you wake up on time three days in a row, you will earn a bigger prize; for a full week, the prize is even bigger.

Because we are not using the chart, the habit-forming program is a little weaker. Therefore, it requires the addition of a punishment with the reward, which we never have when using a chart. This system works well, but the chart is easier to implement, and helps us be more consistent. Be sure to compliment every success as you would with a chart. The agreement can be used for chart-refusers and older children. Money works really well as a reward for older kids.

Helping your child develop the habit of giving

Giving back is another habit that we often overlook, but it is of utmost importance. Children get so much more joy from giving than they do from receiving, but we get sucked into constantly caring for them, allowing them to become takers, and never give them the sweetest experience of giving and developing meaning and purpose in their own lives.

I was reminded of the power of giving and how it impacts our children recently when a group of friends and I took our children to a food-packing plant. This state-of-the-art plant was strictly for packaging dry goods to be distributed to the poor. The children ranged in age from three to fourteen years of age. This trip was organized instead of a trip to an amusement park. We mothers agreed that the children should give back to the community occasionally, instead of just being entertained during the long summer vacation.

We put on our aprons and hairnets and got working. The boys dumped the pasta in the machine; the girls filled the bags. The teens labeled the bags, and the moms sealed them. The kids filled thirty crates with bags of pasta, which were then loaded on trucks and distributed free of charge to the neediest members of our society. The work was hard; we were sweating. The kids (and their mothers) left the plant tired and fulfilled. I asked the kids how they felt as we drove away, and they all agreed that they had done great that day, and they were proud of themselves. They were happy. We are always happy when we do for others.

How can giving become a part of your child's life? Charity begins at home; we can start by expecting our children to do chores around the house. Here is how I have set up daily chore charts for the family:

- Each child is expected to ask me each day what her chore is, and then must do that chore for fifteen minutes.

- I include an extra credit point for doing the chore happily.

- I specifically do not write down the chore for each child in advance because I like my kids to be flexible and able to mix it up and do some fun chores and some less fun ones.

The goal is for them to understand that doing the chore is a contribution to our household; it is not being given so my child can have a fun time. If fun is a byproduct, that's great. The better the job they do, the more we will all enjoy living together. Every child, no matter her age, can learn to give and will love it right away.

In addition, besides planning fun outings for the children:

- Take them to volunteer. There are so many opportunities to give. You will be pleasantly surprised to see your child jump at the chance to help another child in need if you just provide that opportunity.

- Turn to your church, synagogue, mosque, or community center for suggestions.

- For the message that helping at home or helping others is giving, and giving makes for happier, more fulfilled people, we must be personal examples to our children.

- Step out of your comfort zone and look out for people in need. Visit a nursing home or hospital; help a sick neighbor or a woman after birth. Send your child to bring a cake over to a new neighbor.

The family that gives together sticks together.

Recently, a fire ravaged an apartment building in a neighborhood nearby. Thankfully, all of the residents escaped the flames safely, but they lost all their material belongings. A message circulated on social media that the homeless families needed everything. I told my children what had happened and asked them each to go through their clothes and see if there were garments they were willing to part with for the sake of these children who had no nice clothing to wear.

I was overwhelmed by my kids' response. Not only did they stuff some of their favorite clothing into bags to give away, but they went through their toys and games, handing over new, never-opened items. They could not stop giving. They went on a shopping spree in our home to make sure those kids would be taken care of.

Here's what our family chore chart looks like: (This chart can be downloaded from my website, www.hyperhealing.org.)

	Name of child	Name of child	Name of child	Name of child
Sunday	✓ Asking to do chore: ✓ Doing chore: ✓ Extra credit:	✓ Asking to do chore: ✓ Doing chore: ✓ Extra credit:	✓ Asking to do chore: ✓ Doing chore: ✓ Extra credit:	✓ Asking to do chore: ✓ Doing chore: ✓ Extra credit:
Monday	✓ Asking to do chore: ✓ Doing chore: ✓ Extra credit:	✓ Asking to do chore: ✓ Doing chore: ✓ Extra credit:	✓ Asking to do chore: ✓ Doing chore: ✓ Extra credit:	✓ Asking to do chore: ✓ Doing chore: ✓ Extra credit:

Creating a family habit

Every family has areas they need to strengthen when it comes to organization. In my family, it's the "Gimpel Double Exit" routine. We never leave the house once, ever! I can imagine the neighbors watching us pack all six kids in the car, strap the bags to the roof, shove in the dog, the picnic basket, and all other paraphernalia and drive down the street. By now they probably count to fifty, and as expected, we then come rumbling right back up the street. One kid jumps out frantically and runs back into the house to grab something really important that was forgotten—usually one shoe. Our smart neighbors only wave goodbye as we pull out the second time.

I'm sure this routine gives the neighbors some comic relief, and that's important. But since we never get this right, we must create a better exit routine. This involves observing what is most often forgotten and making ourselves a checklist. We could make an individual checklist for each member of the family or a family checklist. If we continually fall into the same trap, we must stop ourselves and ask what habit we have not yet developed and how, as a family, we can create a better routine. The more we pay attention, the more we can develop collective family habits and practice them every time the situation arises.

How can we create this family habit?

- First, pay attention to the negative family habits we have created.

- Next, brainstorm as a family about how we can improve.

- Finally, plan and practice! Remind each other of how we planned to do it better each time.

- Don't forget to catch one another practicing the new habit and give a specific compliment.

Before we know it, the neighbors will have to find another endearing thing about the Gimpel family to be entertained by. (Maybe our habit of playing touch football on the front lawn at six thirty in the morning before the school buses arrive.)

Making a daily schedule

One final habit that most of us lack, but which is worth developing, is making a daily schedule. As we know, the instant gratification personality is genetic, so some parents are not great at keeping a daily schedule. Our kids need order and predictability, and we, too, would benefit from a more organized schedule. We will work on two models— one for parents and older teens, and the other for younger kids. Kids have a built-in schedule for school days, so we will be addressing the weekends and longer vacations.

Here's a great system for adults and older kids, with a little bit of help from our smartphones (more on those dangerous little screens later):

1. Choose a quiet time at night to write down all your responsibilities for the next day, and **commit each**

responsibility to a time slot on Google calendar or another program you are using. Example: Shopping, 2:00–3:00. Kindergarten pickup, 3:15. Defrost chicken for dinner, 4:00.

2. **Set an alarm on your phone to ring three times daily**—in the morning, afternoon, and evening. When you hear the alarm, check your schedule and see if you are sticking with it.

3. If you are off course, don't panic; just **readjust**. Either remove the next activity on your schedule and reassign it to tomorrow or cut what you are doing short. If neither can be done, sweat it out; it's a great learning experience. Now you will get a better sense of how long things take and how much you can cram into a day. Readjust your expectations. Congratulate yourself on a lesson well learned. Self-flagellation is prohibited.

4. Our day is dynamic; appointments get canceled, and new responsibilities pop up on a regular basis. As soon as you get a phone call, text, or WhatsApp informing you of a schedule change, **freeze in place** and go directly to your schedule. Add the new piece of information to your schedule right away. If you just received an email invitation to a wedding, stop! Enter it into your schedule right now.

5. When you check your schedule in the evening, congratulate yourself on a day well spent, move chores that you haven't completed to a different day, and once again commit them to specific time slots.

6. If you are working on a big project, **divide the project into smaller parts** and commit to a specific hour and length of time you can work on the project this week. Add it to your calendar.

The schedule board for younger children

And now, for your younger child . . . do you like to do arts and crafts? Good, because a little cutting and pasting will be involved here.

1. Get a pack of colored paper. Use one paper as the base, and cut three other colors into strips. (You can obviously create the chart on the computer as well, or download from my website, www.hyperhealing.org, but it's less fun.)

2. Laminate the page.

3. Put a strip of Velcro on the center of each of the colored sections on the page.

4. Now take a picture of your child, laminate it, and cut it out.

5. Put a strip of the other side of the Velcro on the back of the picture.

You have created a **schedule board**. You can now use a whiteboard marker to divide any part of your child's day in four segments. Write down what you will be doing in each part of the day on a specific color, including the hours the color spans. It is useful to have the last segment of the chart be something the child enjoys doing.

Have your child move herself along the schedule so she has a better grip on what she has done and what to expect. Invite her to write down or draw her own schedule as well. Hang the schedule board at a height that she can access and interact with.

A great way to begin any day that does not offer its own built-in schedule is to plan a schedule together with your child. This activity makes her feel secure and in control and plants the seeds for future scheduling habits. It is also a way to teach your child flexibility. If there is a change in the schedule, which happens all the time, you can walk her to the board, have her erase what you had written, and add the change. This way, she does not feel confused by the change and can learn to handle glitches calmly.

In addition, if she is anticipating an activity she loves, while normally she would ask about it continually and even get hysterical that you are not providing it right now (Is it movie time yet? When are we watching the movie? But you SAID we were going to watch a movie today . . .), with the schedule board she can now see that the anticipated activity will take place when she advances to yellow, and she is now at blue. Moving along the board gives her the calm and confidence that the activity is on its way, and she is getting closer to it all the time.

A kindergarten teacher called to consult about Jane. Each morning, Jane would come into the classroom with a sweet smile, which would inevitably morph into a frown and then a tantrum. She would demand her cookies and juice all morning long. No matter how many times the teacher explained to Jane that cookies were given out at ten, Jane would not be consoled. The teacher showed Jane the beautiful daily schedule hung at eye level in the kindergarten, to no avail.

I suggested that the teacher make an individual schedule board for Jane, dividing the morning into four segments, the last being cookies. Jane's picture was placed on the board, and she was expected to move herself through the morning. The teacher would say, "Jane, we are now at green. What will we be doing now? How many more colors will you travel until you get to cookies?"

Jane calmed down. Because she was an Instant Gratification kid, she reset every morning. She assumed that today there would be an unpleasant surprise, everything would change, and all along, she had been terrified that the cookies would not arrive. Once she organized her time and clearly saw that her goal was in sight, she could enjoy the morning. She needed the schedule more than any other kid in the kindergarten. So do our kids.

The following are a few examples of how the schedule board can be used.

Example 1: Summer mornings

8:30–9:30 Waking up, washing up, and eating breakfast	9:30–10:00 Doing a morning chore	10:00–11:30 Going out to sprinkler park	11:30–12:30 Movie

Example 2: Dividing the time of a long car ride to help children behave calmly throughout the journey:

10:00–10:30 Leaving house	10:30–11:00 Half-an-hour drive	11:00–11:30 Half-an-hour drive	11:30–12:00 Half-an-hour drive

As you move your child or children across the chart, reward them with the agreed-upon prize, plus compliment them for every half hour they behaved well. Be specific about what you will expect in the car, and let them know what their reward will be in advance. Have them think of ways to occupy themselves in the car. One reward idea is giving children a sum of money for each successful stretch of time in the car, which they can spend on a small toy or treat when you arrive at your destination.

The more we assist our children in approaching their day in a structured way, the more we will be helping them be calm, flexible, and organized. Begin when they are young, and they will develop the organization skill early.

To illustrate:

We had been charting at home for some time, but still had not tackled the challenges inherent in packing lots of kids into the car. Each time we got in the car, the kids would begin to argue about who sat where. It was unpleasant, to say the least; it took all the joy out of the journey. One day I climbed into the car, and the kids were happily getting along. I thought I had sat in the wrong car; this could not be my family. But it was!

My older son had internalized the chart concept and realized that anything that was not working out could be readjusted by creating clear structure. That is exactly what he did. He got out a pen and paper and made a seating rotation chart with the kids. He put the chart in the glove compartment without even mentioning it to me. From that fabulous moment on, the kids consulted with the chart every time they got in the car and sat in their assigned seats. They just needed someone to create order so they did not have to feel the stress of not knowing if or when they would get the coveted seat. Once they knew they would get there, they were calm and flexible and able to share the seat without fighting. I gave them the method, and they then taught me a thing or two.

_____| Action Plan |_____

1. Write a list of challenging behaviors that can be turned into positive habits.

2. Write the description of the positive opposite, so the behavior can be charted.

3. Choose one behavior routine to launch the program with.

4. Divide the routine into four steps.

5. Decide on an extra credit "value" you would like to add to the chart.

6. Make a menu of prizes from five to forty points.

7. Introduce the program to your child

    ▫   Present the list of prizes and then the chart. Invite him to add prizes.

8. Get started!

    ▫   Hang the chart where you can all see it.

    ▫   Compliment every success.

    ▫   Be calm about missed points and mark down points as soon as they are earned.

    ▫   Be consistent! If you are not keeping up, reduce the program to fit your lifestyle. Any consistent program, even for ten minutes a day, is of great value.

9. Set up a long-term chart. This step is optional.

10. If the chart is not working, first find out from your child why he doesn't like it, then try once again. If your second attempt doesn't take, move to an agreement.

11. Get your child doing chores at home; giving to others brings us joy.

12. Go out and give! Find people less fortunate than you and roll your sleeves up and get involved in helping others as a family. There are many lonely, elderly, ill, or poor people who are waiting for you and your child to bring light to their day.

13. How's your daily schedule? It may need an upgrade. If so, follow the schedule steps and start using your time well.

14. Make a schedule board for your younger child so you can begin enjoying weekends and summer days together.

THE CHEAT SHEET

Chapter Six: The Habit-Formation Behavior Program

☛ Now it's time for our child to step up to the plate and take responsibility for his behavior.

☛ Our children are healthy and capable and missing important habits. Why is this?

☛ Forming a habit is like making a path through a jungle. Making the path requires repetitive clearing of one area. A person can be persistent and focus on the job or get distracted (instant gratification) by the lovely jungle. Creating the path (habit) makes a path in our brain.

☛ We must repeat behaviors for at least a month to solidify them.

☛ Why do behavior programs often fail?

  ◌ Parents need their child to succeed more than the child cares about his own success.

  ◌ The program is too complex; we try to fix everything at once.

  ◌ We try to create a program that runs all day, burning everyone out.

  ◌ The prize takes too long to earn for our Instant Gratification child to wait for.

☛ Building the ideal behavior program for your child:

  1. Make a list of your child's behaviors that need improvement.

  2. Choose one project and determine what hour of the day the chart will be implemented.

3. Reword the negative behaviors in positive language.

4. Divide the behavior routine you chose into four parts. Practice! If someone has "failure to launch" problems, meaning he procrastinates, find out why and what is standing in his way. Any behavior that a child should be able to do on his own can be charted.

5. Practice! Have a short conversation about the program during the day or play a make-believe game to practice the new routine and troubleshoot.

6. Extra-credit points. Address "how" a child is doing a chore rather than only *what* he is doing.

7. The prize! Make a menu of prizes from five to forty points. Make prize suggestions, and allow your child to suggest prizes. The prize should be readily available. Do not punish by taking away points. Don't push for your child's success more than he wants it. The points are her money. Give points only for what is designated on the chart.

☛ Introducing the program to your child: Begin by discussing the prizes and then introduce the concept of creating a habit. Explain everything.

☛ If the chart is not working, check if you are being consistent, if the chore is too hard or simple for your child, if the prize is exciting enough to generate motivation.

☛ Set up a long-term chart to help your child delay gratification. Use the points from the weekly chart twice.

☛ Help your child develop the habit of giving to others.

☛ When children can give to those who are needy, they feel fulfilled and happy.

☛ Lead by example: show your kids that small contributions to those in need go a long way.

☛ Do you have an organized daily schedule? Both you and your child thrive when you know what to expect. Use Google calendar to start organizing yourself. Take each chore, commit it to a time slot, and check your schedule three times daily. When new information comes in, enter it into your calendar.

☛ Make a daily schedule with your child for weekends, holidays, and the summer.

CHAPTER SEVEN

Behind Every Challenging Behavior Lies an Even Stronger Emotion

K ATIE CAME HOME *from school in a black mood. The minute she spotted her little sister sitting peacefully drawing at the kitchen table, she went into overdrive. She yelled at her sister, "Why are you looking at me!"*

"You just walked in. I wanted to see who came home," was her little sister's timid reply.

"Mom, she's bothering me!" yelled the agitated older sister.

Mom was caught by surprise. This was some out-of-control behavior.

Before Mom could pull herself together to respond, or perhaps she was stalling because she had no idea how to respond, the angry girl grabbed the crayons and threw them at the little girl and all over the room.

Mom swept up the victim and said, "Katie, in our house we can't behave that way toward siblings. This evening you will be missing ten minutes of your computer time. Now I'm going to my room to organize my clothing with your sister. You can join us when you calm down,"

Mom and the younger child went upstairs and began organizing clothing. A few minutes later there was a pitter-patter on the steps. Someone was coming up to see what was going on. When Mom heard Katie at the door to her bedroom, she said out loud, "I'm going to go through my clothing to decide what no longer fits and put it aside to donate to charity. I usually have a hard time deciding what looks good on me. Maybe there is someone who has great taste and can help me out here."

In walked Katie. "Mom, step aside. I know what's in style. You wear your clothing forever; I'll help you," And she did. Mom had very little left in her closet at the end, someone benefited from a large bag of her donated clothing, and Katie was calm and feeling better.

Whew! That could have been a disaster, but it went well. Let's move on . . .

Absolutely not! We are not going anywhere. Why did Katie behave that way? Is she just an explosive, unpredictable kid? Do we have to hold our breath and hope it will blow over quickly? The punishment was important. Good job, Mom, for giving a clear message that siblings must be respected, but we are not done here. Katie would have behaved well if she could have. Something is bothering her, and simply managing the symptoms of her emotional stress will not make the stress go away.

In this chapter we will discuss difficult behavior and how it is triggered by emotional stress. We will discover that our children's actions are rooted in one of two sources: either they have not yet developed vital emotional skills to cope with the demands of their environment, or they are dealing with suppressed emotional trauma. We will learn that we can help our child develop these skills, not by punishing harshly, but by taking an emotional "collaborative conversation" journey.

We will first identify what skills are missing and then understand why our child is missing them. Then we will roll out a program to help our children become more emotionally savvy. We will also address serious emotional trauma that our child may be experiencing, learn to identify behaviors that indicate that the child is being victimized, and help alleviate the isolation and suffering our child may be experiencing.

Remember the habit cycle we spoke about earlier? Katie has been triggered by an emotional cue, and neither she nor her mother know what it is. It is vital to figure out what is triggering Katie, because she will be triggered again, and once again will behave very poorly because she simply does not have the emotional skill to contain her distress. Our job is **not** to solve her problem for her, nor to come down hard on her with a terrible punishment; it is to help her become a problem solver herself.

Dr. Ross W. Greene, PhD, author of *The Explosive Child* (Harper, 1998), a must-read for all parents of children with ADHD symptoms, explains that challenging behavior occurs when the demands and expectations being placed on a child exceed the child's capacity to respond adaptively.

Why does our child lack the capacity to respond appropriately? She is missing the emotional skills to work through the problem and align her behavior with social demands.

We have behavioral expectations for every child, according to age. We expect our children to act in a socially appropriate way, but if our child is being overloaded and is missing the skill needed to behave in the way we would like, no punishment or behavior chart can fix his problem.

Consider an absurd situation in which a parent demanded that her child respond to all questions asked of him in French but had not yet taught her son the language. French is a beautiful language, and it would be fantastic if he spoke French, wouldn't it? Now imagine that Mom so desires that her son speak French that she sets up a behavior program for him. Every time her son responds in French, he will get a dollar, and when he replies in English, he will lose computer time. Can this child succeed? He is highly motivated; he just does not have the skill required to succeed! This is what responding to emotional outbursts with a strict punishment looks like.

We will not be focusing on the challenging behavior itself, because this behavior is a child's call for help, telling us he is unable to meet our expectations. Instead, we will focus on the skill our child is missing that is the root cause of him not being able to solve his emotional problems, and we will give him the skill to solve these problems. This process will be accomplished through a **collaborative conversation**, a partnership between adult and child.

The first two things we need to identify are the **skills** our child is missing and the **environment, conditions, or situation** in which the behavior is accruing. This may seem like an enormous task, but situations tend to repeat themselves, and if we pay attention, we can figure out what is triggering the clash between a difficult situation and lack of necessary skills.

What skills is our child missing?

A. **Executive functioning skills**

- Trouble with transitions

- Trouble sticking with a task that requires sustained attention

- Does tasks out of order

- Has trouble relating to or keeping time

- Can't assess how long a task will take

- Has trouble blocking out irrelevant noise to focus on a task

- Does not think before responding.

B. **Language processing skills**

- Struggles to express needs, thoughts, or concerns in words

- Gets confused with verbal instructions

- Does not follow conversation.

C. **Emotional regulation skills**

- Does not think rationally when frustrated or manage irritability in an age-appropriate way

- Struggles with dealing with disappointment.

D. **Cognitive flexibility skills**

- Sees situations in black and white; does not see shades of gray

◻ Can't envision other possibilities to solve a problem

◻ Gets confused when there is a deviation from schedule, rules, or routine

◻ Experiences stress with changes in plans, ambiguity, or unpredictability

◻ Generalizes and personalizes situations with words like "always" and "never"

◻ Labels himself or others based on one experience (I'm stupid; he hates me).

E. **Social skills**

◻ Does not interpret nonverbal social cues like facial expression and tone of voice

◻ Does not know how to start a conversation or enter a conversation with peers

◻ Seeks inappropriate attention from peers

◻ Does not understand how she is perceived by peers.

Why is our child with ADHD symptoms often missing these skills?

1. He responds impulsively in an instant gratification way. Each event is a stand-alone experience, and therefore does not lend itself to internalizing the problem and developing skills to solve it.

2. Every time she is triggered, she experiences it as a deep and painful experience, unrelated to any experience she has had before. This is because she has not learned to identify the triggering patterns.

3. When he has been triggered emotionally, he is less able to sort out his emotions and becomes overwhelmed and struggles to verbally express what he is experiencing.

4. She tends to view emotional stress in an egocentric way, blaming others for her pain rather than searching inside for solutions.

We may have spent a good few years either delegitimizing his emotional confusion because it is accompanied by such difficult behavior and what seems like untruthful reporting of events, or we have tried to soothe and fix the expression of pain quickly because the outbursts are too difficult to bear. We are not listening; we are shutting down the behavior and missing the emotional stress, thereby not helping our child develop emotional skills.

Our child explodes, and we are angry and worried. Will she ever be normal? Will he ever express himself without breaking things or using his fists? The answer is a resounding yes, but as in all worthwhile processes, this one takes some time, patience, and skill. Let us remember some of the skills we have developed so far:

- We have learned to de-escalate ourselves.

- We have learned to identify our own triggers. Very often those triggers are feelings that we are incapable of dealing with our child's tantrums. We have found a way to calm ourselves and change our own habit loops.

- We have learned to establish rules in our home. We know how to follow through with positive feedback for respecting rules and punishment for disregarding them.

- We have created a daily schedule to help our child be more in control and a behavior chart to start developing new habits.

So far, we are doing great. Our child needs emotional and physical order, and that is what we are providing. He must know he has a strong parent who is in charge and will care for him and love him, no matter what. He feels competent knowing that he is capable of mastering new skills. She feels safe knowing she is not the one in charge of the rules and aware that we will be by her side to help her choose to do well.

Yet he still tantrums; she still ignores us; he continually picks on siblings; she gets into fights at school. This is because we have more work to do. We still have not helped our child identify and resolve the emotional stress that is causing the difficult behavior.

Collaborative and Proactive Solutions, also referred to as Collaborative Problem Solving, is an excellent method, developed by Dr. Greene, in which a parent, teacher, or other responsible adult opens a dialogue to help the child build emotional skills and become an emotional problem solver.

How are Collaborative and Proactive Solutions accomplished?

Warm-up: Understand that our child wants to do well and will do well as soon as we work together with her in a collaborative fashion to help her develop missing skills. We can begin **by inviting our child to participate in an open conversation**, in which she is an equal participant.

It's important to stress that we cannot invite our child for a conversation when we are angry at her. We also can't be truly honest in conversation when we have already diagnosed the problem and chosen a solution. A truly collaborative conversation is a fact-finding mission, and it requires curiosity. It also requires quiet time and a scoop of ice cream or hot cocoa.

What behaviors will we choose to focus on?

1. We are looking for patterns, not stand-alone, challenging events that could easily have been triggered by exhaustion or hunger. Missing emotional skills will never be a one-time occurrence; the missing skill will be obvious in many social situations.

2. Any behavior that demonstrates that your child is suffering socially or emotionally. Examples include:

   ◻ Alienating peers

   ◻ Causing fights at home

◻   Being disrespectful to adults

◻   Behaving in an age-inappropriate way

◻   Frequently tantrumming or shutting down

◻   An allergy to hearing the word "no."

Some of these behaviors will demand your attention because your child is very loudly struggling (tantrums, fights with siblings) and the behavior can't be ignored. In these cases, your child is "inviting" you to a Collaborative and Proactive Solutions conversation. In other cases, your child will be struggling more quietly (trouble-making friends, difficulty interpreting social interactions, shutting down when overloaded). In these cases, we as parents must initiate the conversation. We begin the conversation in the same way whether we are initiating, or our child is, by finding a quiet time to sit down and talk. Don't forget the ice cream.

These are the steps to take:

1. **Show empathy:** This is the beginning of the conversation— the fact-gathering stage. We are trying to investigate what skill is missing. We are here to listen, to figure out what our child's concern is, how he feels about an unsolved problem. This step takes time. You may initiate this step a few times before your child responds.

What are some pitfalls you may discover when approaching the empathy step?

*   **Our child does not want to talk:** He feels you never listen to him and does not trust that you will really hear him this time. Don't worry; it takes all parents a few tries before getting it right. Make the invitation to the conversation. Set out the ice cream. Discuss how proud you are of your child for something specific. Begin the conversation gently. If he does not want to talk, that's okay; no one has failed. Ask him when he would like to talk. Give him a few choices of times. Do not be forceful; remember, this is a collaborative conversation.

Both you and he are equal partners and should have a desire to participate.

- **Our child starts making up stories**: You know, the kind you always feel you must correct? He says his brother started, but you saw the whole thing. It's a trap! Don't fall into it. Listen to what he is saying and mirror his words. Don't disagree, because that will end the conversation. The goal is to understand what emotional challenge your child is dealing with, not to present the facts before a judge and jury. He is building a wall to divert you, but you can jump right over it. He says Andre started; you respond with, "You feel Andre started? And what else is bothering you?" I admit it's hard. Untruths make us angry, but if we let *our* emotions carry us away, how can we help our child develop *his* emotions?

- **Our child feels defensive and does not want to reveal that she is jealous or hateful or ashamed**: It makes her feel petty or bad. We must be very clear that all emotions are valid. We must learn how to respond to our strong emotions, not punish ourselves for having them. A great way to help our children with feeling freer to share emotions is by telling personal stories. *When Dad was young, he got into fights with his brother all the time. He once threw his brother's McDonald's meal right out the car window because he felt jealous that his brother got dessert.* Share with your kids the funny stories, the challenging stories, anything that is appropriate for their ages.

- **Our child is not used to sharing emotions**: He's the strong, silent type. We must be the example. When we are processing emotional stress, do it out loud. A woman yells at you in a parking lot? Let your child know how that felt and how you wanted to respond (leaving out the profanities). Ask your child to help you process. Ask her how she would have felt in the same situation. While we do not want to invite our child to weigh in with an opinion when we punish, now's our chance to engage our child in meaningful conversation and clue her in to our emotional process.

What are we trying to achieve in this step?

We want to identify the emotion our child is feeling that is not allowing her to respond well to the situation. Through questions, stories, mirroring, and validating, we want to conclude the empathy step by understanding what caused our child to respond so poorly in any situation. In the case of the child throwing the crayons at her sister, consider the following:

Mom sat with Katie that evening for a conversation. Since Mom read a story to Katie as part of their nightly routine, this was a great time to talk.

"Katie, it seems you had a hard day in school today," began Mom.

"Nope, great day."

Mom could really skid off the tracks here, saying, "But Katie, that can't be true; you came home in such a bad mood!" But this mom is holding it together. She says, "Great to hear. Did someone bother you at recess?"

"No, I played ball."

"How about in the classroom? Did you get along with your teacher today?"

"She's so mean! I hate her!"

This is great! Katie is talking.

The story unfolds. Mom is listening, asking gentle questions, and affirming.

Katie stood up to get her notebook and passed a boy on the way back from her cubby. The boy moved his chair back, pushing Katie into the desk behind her and hurting her. Katie got mad and hit her classmate. At that moment the teacher took notice and blamed the incident on Katie. She asked Katie to stand in the corner of the classroom until recess. All the other kids stared at her for the rest of the lesson (from Katie's perspective).

"Wow, that's really rough, Katie. How did that make you feel?"

"Like I wanted to kill the teacher. I hate her; she's the worst teacher

EVER!" Here she is identifying her emotion as hatred. But that's not really what blocked her from making good behavior choices. More investigating is necessary.

"You are so mad at your teacher! I wonder how I would feel if I was in the same situation. I think I might have felt so embarrassed!"

"Yeah, all the kids were staring at me like I was a bad kid. And you know what else makes me so mad? She didn't even punish Bob; he just got to smash me and then stay in his seat. He kept smiling at me, and I wanted to bash his face!"

"It sounds like you were embarrassed and felt like it wasn't fair, like there was no justice."

"Yeah. So in the next lesson, right when the teacher came into the room, I got up on my chair and yelled, 'No one listen to the teacher! Only listen to me!'"

Oh goodness, this story has taken a twist. The teacher will be calling soon. But Mom has done some good investigative work. She has determined that embarrassment or shame, mixed with a feeling of not being treated fairly, was too much for Katie to process. She was not treated fairly by Bob or by the teacher and responded with poor or no communication to both. Is this a repeating trend? Does Katie respond to injustice and shame this way often? Are these emotions triggers for Katie? Thinking back, Mom can say there is very likely a pattern here.

"Katie, that was a very painful day for you. You felt ashamed and that things were not fair. Is it correct to say that it is very hard for you when you feel embarrassed and when you feel something wasn't fair? Both Bob and the teacher were not fair to you."

"Mom, this was the worst day ever!"

Step one has been completed very successfully.

Katie has shared her distress; Mom has not corrected her, only mirrored and questioned: and the outcome was the revelation that the two emotions of shame and need for justice were driving Katie's distressed behavior. What do we do about the double chair episode and attacking the younger sister? Moving on to step two.

2. **Define the problem from the parent's perspective**: Now it's
    our turn to express our concern and the problems we face
    due to our child's behavior.

Why do we have to inject ourselves into the process? Isn't this
about our child? It sure is, and an important skill our child must learn
is how her behavior affects others. When Katie attacks her sister,
how does her sister feel? How does her behavior clash with the rules
carefully set up in the home? Her behavior is often egocentric; she is
only seeing her own pain and discomfort. If we try to shield her from
hearing how her behavior affects others, we are denying her a very safe
way to practice and learn to see others. This is a skill she will need her
entire life.

We do a child no favors when we focus strictly on her emotional
stress and do not allow her to see the larger picture and the other people.
Our message, which we must continually reiterate, is that "every feeling
must be respected and understood. We must identify your feeling
and figure out together how to respond in a socially appropriate and
respectful way to your strong emotions."

Here is a continuation of the prior conversation:

"Katie, I see that feeling ashamed and feeling not listened to has
caused you to feel so bad that you behave in ways that are problematic
to others."

"I don't care. If the teacher doesn't listen to me, no one should listen to
her. If Bob pushes me, I should hit him back."

"We have some important rules about respecting classmates, teachers,
and sisters. Even when we are very sad and mad, we have to think about
those rules. You were too upset to choose another way to behave. Your
feelings were correct, but we have to come up with another way to respond
so that you don't hurt your sister or disrespect your teacher."

"My sister was looking at me like the kids in the class. She deserved it."

"Do you think that there could be a better way to talk to her if you had
a rough day and don't want her to look at you? In our house we have a
rule that children must respect each other. Your sister didn't know you
were having a hard day. We have to come up with a way that you can
share how you feel without disrespecting or hurting other people."

"I don't know how to do that."

"We are going to figure it out. I know that, together, we can help you share what you are feeling and learn how to let others know in a respectful way. I'm so proud of you for sharing your feelings with me. It's okay not to know things; we just have to work together and find out."

Sometimes our child will reject step two and insist that she is right, and she doesn't care how others feel. Take your time. Take a deep breath. As you repeat this process, she will start to understand that you are not angry with her, and she will be more willing to hear the other side.

Now that we understand our child's emotional triggers and we have identified the problem, it's time to search for appropriate solutions to the clash between the emotional feeling and the behavioral response. This clash is due to missing skills.

What skills is Katie missing?

- **Emotional regulation** – Katie had a very hard time thinking rationally when she got frustrated by being pushed. Her response was hitting back. This snowballed into being disrespectful to the teacher in retaliation for her unfair punishment. She had been treated unjustly and was not able to process and respond to the injustice.

- **Cognitive inflexibility** – She saw no other solution to the problem other than striking out at the teacher and her sister.

- **Social skills** – Katie could only interpret her classmates or sister looking at her as an obvious slight to her honor. Once she felt internal embarrassment, she viewed all others as scorning her.

When we search for a solution, we must consider these skills and how we will help Katie strengthen them.

3. **The child and adult find a solution to the problem together:** The adult and child brainstorm different solutions to the problem and resolve it in a way that addresses both the

concerns of the child and the adult. The concern of the child is the stress caused by the injustice and humiliation and the challenge of being unable to express her emotions or choose a more socially appropriate and respectful way to respond. If her problem is not resolved with a solution she can apply to other challenging experiences, she will continue to respond poorly and continue to absorb negative feedback from her environment.

How about the parent? What problems does she need addressed? The important house rule—respecting a sibling—has been violated. And basic respect for teachers and other adults is not firmly understood by her daughter. Both concerns must be addressed in the solution.

Time to brainstorm.

We begin by repeating the child and the adult's concerns.

"Katie, we talked about the very hard time you had in school when you got pushed and then you hit back because you felt the teacher was not hearing the truth and you felt embarrassed by her punishment, right?"

"Yes, we did. I just hate that teacher."

"You sure are angry at her. I also said that I had a few problems. Do you remember them?"

"No, not really."

"My problem, Katie, is that because you were so ashamed, you behaved disrespectfully to your sister and your teacher. You also made a choice to shove Bob instead of talking to him or the teacher. We must come up with a plan that helps you deal with your feelings and helps you make better choices even when you are upset. Do you have any ideas of how to solve this problem?"

"Okay, I won't go to school anymore, then I won't have to see the stinky teacher."

"Thanks for that suggestion. I'm glad you're thinking. Since you have to go to school, let's think of some other ideas."

"Can I tell the teacher how mad she made me? Can you tell her she has to listen to all the kids and not just guess who's wrong?"

"Katie, I love your idea! You want to have a conversation with the teacher? How will that help you feel calmer about being listened to?"

"Maybe if I can tell her that I need her to also listen to me and not just other kids, I will feel calmer. Maybe if I know she will listen, then I won't hit. Maybe I can tell her how embarrassed I was."

"You have some great suggestions. You are holding difficult feelings in your heart; how can we work together to help you share your feelings in words and not lash out at others or cross lines of respect?"

"I don't know. Do you have an idea?"

"I'm thinking that we can come up with a secret code that you can say to me when you feel bad inside, and then I will know that I have to stop and listen to you, and we can figure out together how to work through your feelings."

"Okay, how about 'explosion'? Can we try that? I will say it when I feel like I am going to explode."

"Fantastic! I have one more concern on my mind. Let's say you are so upset, and you begin getting frustrated with someone in the family. But you don't realize that you are upset about something that happened that you are carrying in your heart. You start to make bad choices, but you did not say 'explosion' to me. What should I do? Is there a way I can help you calm down and talk to me?"

"So, we need another plan. Maybe you can touch my shoulder when you think I am getting mad."

"I love it! What a great plan. This is what we will do. We will call your teacher to talk with her. We can discuss with her the feelings you were having, and you can apologize for being disrespectful. Does that sound good so far?"

"No. Why do I have to apologize to her if she didn't listen to me and embarrassed me?"

"Great question. You are right that she did not listen to you the way you wanted her to. But we have rules about how we have to respect adults, especially teachers. Even if she made you feel very hurt, you had a choice to communicate that pain in a respectful way. Can you think of a better way to tell your teacher that you feel she is being unfair?"

"I can tell her when we meet with her. I can tell her it's hard for me *when all the kids look at me, that I feel embarrassed. I can ask her to listen to me before she decides that I did something wrong."*

"And can you tell her that you will do your best to be respectful to her even if you are upset?"

"I can try."

"That's fantastic! What a pleasure talking with you. I think we found out a lot of important things about your feelings and how you can understand and tell your teacher or me how you feel, and that can help you calm your behavior. I really like the secret codes. Let's check in next week and see how our plan is working."

Now wasn't that easy? Just kidding. It's a challenging yet worthwhile process. Let me give you a few more examples so you get the hang of it. Keep in mind that, most often, a Collaborative and Proactive Solutions conversation does not run so smoothly and in one sitting. Frequently, you will begin one evening and conclude a few days later. Alternatively, you will spend many hours just on empathy before you identify the emotion your child is grappling with. Also, in the case above (based on a true story), the child was able to offer solutions, but in many cases, your child will not have ready solutions, and you will have to suggest some of your own.

The solutions should involve skill-building, such as developing self-awareness, awareness of others, self-control, understanding of expectations, and flexibility, to name a few. Our goal is not to plug up the problem that occurred today. We want to use the event to strengthen long-term skills. Explosive or negative behaviors are big, loud signs for us from our child that she is overloaded and is missing the skills to make better choices. These behaviors are not failures; they are opportunities for self-development.

Here are a few more examples of problems that are the result of missing skills:

The Attention Drain: *Every time Mom sits down with one of her children to do homework or give any other type of concentrated attention, Sara shows up. Not the quiet kind of showing up; no, Sara lets herself be heard and felt. Sometimes she picks on the child being attended to; sometimes she demands help from Mom. It takes Mom some time to notice the pattern because the behavior is so disruptive, she* *feels too depleted to connect the dots. Until now her strategy for dealing with the constant disruptions has been to accommodate, yell, punish, or try to ignore the disruptive behavior for as long as possible. All have backfired! When she moved on to the next ill-conceived strategy of trying to offer a reward for time that Sara grants her to spend with other siblings, that was not a great success there either. The other children resented the reward, and Sara continued to disrupt, but a little more quietly.*

What could be triggering Sara?

Time for a conversation. Mom has a sneaking suspicion that Sara needs abundant attention and is jealous about having to share it with her siblings.

1. **Show empathy:** First, Sara denies that she behaves that way. Mom brings a few examples, to which Sara declares that Mom gives EVERYONE more attention than she gets. Breathe, Mom, you know that nothing is further from the truth and that in reality, Sara sucks up more oxygen than all the children in the house, and possibly the neighborhood, put together. This is not the time to correct her, though, so mirror her words. "Sara, you feel like you don't get enough attention, and everyone gets more than you?"

   Great! Let's move forward; you were not tripped up by the need to correct. Maybe it's time for a little story. Can you tell Sara about how when you were a child, you felt jealous of your brother who was younger than you and Mom did everything for him? How about the kid who sat next to you in class and seemed to get good grades without studying? When she hears from you that everyone feels jealous sometimes, even adults and even her mother, she may be less ashamed to share her feelings. Ask her if she feels jealous. Tell her it's okay. Sometimes offering a menu of feelings allows a child to think through her experience. She may not be able to pinpoint the emotion without some help. Sara agrees that she does have a hard time when her mother spends time with other kids.

2. **Put the parents' problems on the table:** Sara's mother's problem is not that it's bad for a child to be jealous, nor does she expect Sara to be happy when others get attention. Not at all! Her mother wants to tell Sara that jealousy is a very real emotion that hurts, and it is perfectly legitimate to be jealous. Sara's mother's problem is that Sara is having a hard time expressing her feeling of jealousy in a clear and helpful way and is therefore behaving very disrespectfully towards her siblings. She is also not allowing others to get the attention they deserve. She is demanding attention by force, thereby hijacking the peaceful environment. Her mother has a problem with the choice Sara is making to disrupt rather than communicate.

3. **Find a solution:** Half of the problem has already been solved by identifying why Sara demands attention. Now that we understand that she is jealous and is having trouble expressing her need, we can focus on a solution to the problem. Sara has no solution ideas. Here's Mom's suggestion: "How about when you are feeling jealous, like you really need attention, you come over to me and tell me quietly, 'Mommy, can you please give me some attention?'"

Have we fully solved the problem? Not yet. Mom can't always drop everything and give Sara attention on demand. Also, the others need attention as well. How is this solution helpful? Mom tells Sara that she cannot always give Sara attention on demand, but she can let Sara know when she will be available. She can say, "Sara, I am so proud of you for understanding what you need and asking for it. You have helped us keep a calm and respectful environment! That was very mature. I'm helping your brother with his math homework for the next ten minutes, and then you and I can prepare dinner together." She can also tell Sara that she will not be available for a while, and they can discuss for a minute what Sara can do while she waits.

Sara is now calmer because she knows how to communicate in

a way in which she will be heard. She is not perceived as a bad kid who is always bothering people, and she has a way to get the attention she so dearly needs. She also understands that all people feel jealous sometimes, and she can share that feeling without shame. As always, the final step is setting up a time in the very near future to revisit how the plan is working.

The "No" Explosion: *Every time Jason hears the word "no," he explodes. When he is told he must come right away when called, he has the same response. Obviously, we can't hermetically seal Jason's environment from demands or limitations. This would be sending a message to Jason that he is fragile and that we have low expectations of him. But this has been the approach in his home for the last year or two. His parents describe it as walking on eggshells. They word requests carefully and try not to say "no" too often. This has led to Jason getting his way a lot, and as we know, kids cannot be expected to be responsible for deciding what's right and wrong; they make terrible decisions. The parents have stepped out of the picture, and now both parents and child are suffering. Since this behavior is a pattern, it demands a Collaborative and Proactive Solutions intervention.*

The parents suspect that Jason is struggling with feeling controlled. He may also be transition phobic due to his fear of being told to stop one behavior with no promise that the next one will offer any pleasure. This looks like instant gratification clashing with real life.

1. **Show empathy:** Mom and Dad (or the parent who can communicate more calmly with Jason) sit him down for a talk. At first, Jason is not interested. He would rather watch a movie. The parents decide that the conversation would be more effective if rescheduled to the car ride on the way to soccer practice. Jason is usually chatty then. They tell him that they have noticed that he has a hard time being told "no." He sure does, because according to Jason's recollection, they always say "no" to him; he is not allowed to do anything. Obviously, Jason is running the show, but this is not the time to point it out.

"So, Jason, you feel like we always say no to you. That must be difficult. How does it make you feel?"

"Like you are controlling me, like you're building a wall. I feel like I can't make any decisions myself."

"Do you think, Jason, that parents should help children make decisions?"

"Yeah, but I always have to do things; I can't just play. You make me stop playing on my iPad to take a shower. And you say I must come right away. I hate it!"

"It can be quite difficult to be forced to stop doing something fun."

The parents can conclude with Jason that it's hard to make transitions, and if they understand Jason correctly, he feels that he is not in control of his time and he is always being forced to do things that are not fun. He feels trapped and controlled.

2. **Put the parents' problem on the table:** Jason's parents have a few problems. Firstly, they must help Jason understand that parents have to make rules so that children can grow up in a safe home and become good people. They must communicate with Jason the challenges of an instant gratification personality, and also its advantages. Right now, Jason is only suffering from the challenges. His parents can discuss this by giving personal examples of how transitions and feeling controlled have been hard in their own lives. But they must help Jason understand that although it is difficult to feel controlled, parents must set rules and teach their children how to behave. His feelings are legitimate, but his response of tantrumming or ignoring his parents cannot be tolerated.

3. **Find a solution:** Rules cannot be eliminated, as Jason is suggesting. He does have one excellent idea though. He says

that since he feels controlled when his parents tell him to come when called right away, maybe they can let him know a few minutes in advance so he can prepare for the transition. What a fantastic suggestion! This can work in most situations, but when the entire family is in their coats, hats, boots, gloves, and scarves and holding all their sledding gear and Jason is reading a book, for example, there must be another, more flexible solution. His parents must make clear that this is a great new approach, but there are some situations in which Jason will still have to get moving right away. Is this still a good plan? Jason says yes.

What about his response to transitions and being told no? How can this be resolved? First, Jason needs to truly understand why he struggles so much with transitions. His parents must explain his fear of being pulled away from something he is enjoying to some unknown activity or some obviously inferior one. Giving examples or telling a personal story would be helpful and will help Jason feel validated. Now that he understands better, how about setting up an afternoon behavior chart with Jason, focused on one hour of making nice transitions? Dad promises to remind Jason each time that there is about to be a transition so Jason can mentally prepare for it.

We still have "no" to deal with. There are a few possible acceptable responses to "no." "Sure" is obviously the best! "Why" is a runner-up. "Can we compromise?" can work as well. "Tantrum" has been kicked off the list. Let's add Jason's response to "no" or "you must" to the practice part of the chart. This way Jason can earn a point for discussing different scenarios in which hearing "no" would be difficult and practice a good response. And then, during the afternoon hour where we are working on transitions, we can also work on responses.

How should his parents respond the rest of the day? They can clarify the rules in the home and praise Jason for his good listening while giving a small punishment for tantrums. This will only work if Jason understands the rules, knows that he can ask for a compromise, and is practicing his good behavior every afternoon.

Here is Jason's chart:

	Responding calmly to "no" (either by listening right away, asking for clarification, or making a compromise) **Half an hour**	Responding calmly to "no" (either by listening right away, asking for clarification, or making a compromise) **Half an hour**	Being prepared for a transition **Half an hour**	Being prepared for a transition **Half an hour**	Practice: Discussing situations in which a parent has to say "no" or demand something and learning to respond
Sunday					
Monday					

The following are additional examples of missing emotional skills that can be addressed with Collaborative and Proactive Solutions:

1. **Sensory sensitivity:** *A child may be suffering from sensory sensitivity but not understanding his challenge and feeling that everyone is out to hurt him.* A good solution could be helping him understand his stress from the sensory overload and learning to tell a parent that he is having sensory overload, instead of demanding that everyone in the house acquiesce to his demand for total silence. This way a parent or older sibling can help the child find a quieter place to spend some time.

2. **Tactless comments:** *A child is saying tactless comments, which invite very angry responses from others.* Does she understand what a tactless comment is and why it is so? Take some time to discuss it. Share some funny or embarrassing stories of

your own. See how she feels when those comments are made to her. Practice with her.

Now, for the plan: She is not a bad child for asking someone if they're pregnant, but she still has to learn what is socially acceptable and what is not. Can she and her parent make a secret code, maybe a gesture from the parent (snap, clap, wave) to let her know that what she is saying should be stopped and reevaluated? Can they spend a few minutes a day (or have a once-a-week conversation alone with a fun snack) reviewing what should be said and what should not, and most importantly, why?

The "compliment game" may be useful in this situation. The way it works is that any time a parent and child enter a new social situation, they race to give a compliment or say something nice about a person or place they have just encountered. It is not a game with a prize; it's just a fun contest where the child can hear many appropriate comments from her parent and practice them herself. Because it is an unthreatening interaction and the child is directing her comments at her parent and not a stranger, she will not feel criticized and will be able to learn the tricks of the tact trade in a stress-free way.

3. **Making friends:** *A child is struggling with making friends.* First, allow her to share her difficult feelings of being rejected, seen as strange or different or never knowing what to say. Let her know that making friends is a skill like any other, and she needs to practice relating to people to get it right. Plan to have strategy conversations where she can report on what happened in school during the day and figure out better ways to interact or discuss new social skills with her. Plan to invite friends over in the afternoon and be present to help provide fun activities and coaching if necessary.

4. **Homework refusal:** *A child is refusing to do schoolwork.* Is the work too hard? Is he stuck in a fixed mentality? Would he rather play than work? Discover with your child why he is not engaging. Does he need a tutor? Does he need an understanding of fixed mentality—the need to be the perfect or smart kid—and a shift to growth mentality? If a child is making a poor choice and playing around, a behavior chart and follow-through on rules and consequences may be in order.

5. **Unpleasant habits:** *A child has a habit that others find disgusting and hard to live with.* He probably feels rejected and can't understand how that sound or behavior would bother someone. He may enjoy the attention he gets when he makes a loud slurp. He might think it's funny to drink seltzer quickly and let out a huge burp (are you sensing I may have some experience here?). Either way, the message he is getting is that he is disgusting, and no one wants him around. Take the time to let him know you understand his feeling and that it is painful to feel rejected. Help your child understand that everyone has to feel comfortable in the home, and if one person is causing others to get nauseous, that is inappropriate. Ask him about the things that make his own skin crawl. One solution is to have him give you a high five every time he wanted to burp/spit/slurp but controlled himself.

6. **Lying or stealing:** *A child is not telling the truth (making up stories) or is taking things that don't belong to him.* Why does he feel the need to represent facts differently than they occurred? Does he experience things through his own vivid imagination? Is he impulsive? Is he looking for attention? Is he unaware that it is wrong to misrepresent?

    We parents tend to panic when our kids lie or steal. We assume that this kid is clearly headed for a life of crime. But he is not going to become a criminal based on his ten-year-old behavior! Before inviting your child to discuss these behaviors, try to reduce the fear. Some of my favorite kids have treated their friends to snacks on their parents' credit line at the local supermarket, running up hefty bills before being caught. You would be blown away by these kids' sharp cognitive functioning today, and they are most definitely upstanding non-criminals. The following may make you feel better:

There is strong evidence that the ability to lie is positively related to the development of cognitive skills such as theory of mind and executive functioning (Evans et al. 2011; Polak and Harris 1999; Talwar, Gordon, and Lee 2007; Talwar and Lee 2008). So, if your child is lying, you know he is developing higher cognitive skills.

But still, he must not lie, or steal. Approach this conversation in the same way you would approach any other, with curiosity. Identify why your child feels the need to conceal or misrepresent or take things without permission. Let your child know that lying and stealing are big problems for you because they break trust, are disrespectful to the victims and make the child a less trustworthy person. Use examples. Ask how he would feel if someone took something of his or told him a lie. What is the solution? That depends on why your child is behaving this way.

In each of these cases, the problem was repetitive, the child was suffering, and there were one or more emotional skills missing. Your child would have chosen to do better had he been able to. Once you help him identify the weak missing skill and make a plan to strengthen it, working as a team to develop the new skill will become a pleasure. We must, however, also be aware of other potential causes of outbursts or academic, emotional, and behavioral stress: trauma.

The final step in the Collaborative and Proactive Solutions program:

7. **Checking in:** We choose a solution with our child, but sometimes the solution just doesn't work out. As such, we must set up a time to review progress, check the solution, and make changes as necessary.

The above program will help children understand and develop missing emotional skills. We now move into a very heavy topic of helping a child who has suffered from any form of abuse.

Another source of terrible emotional stress in children, which leads directly to academic and behavioral struggles and all the telltale signs of ADHD symptoms, is childhood trauma caused by emotional, physical or sexual abuse, and neglect. The impact of trauma on children can manifest in difficulties in the areas of self-regulating, focusing and trusting others, and can lead to academic and social failure. If we discover that a child is suffering from emotional trauma, our first intervention must be giving our child full emotional support. Only then can we add other interventions.

A mother of five came in to consult about her son, who had been a strong student, but of late, his grades had begun to drop. He was twelve years old, just at the cutoff for an ADHD diagnosis according to the DSM-5. The mother described a child who had previously been happy and energetic, loved to learn, and was very curious. His grades began to tank at the beginning of sixth grade. She suggested that maybe the classwork had finally become too challenging for him and he was drowning. If only he had a boost from Ritalin, he would be able to catch up again.

Although it's possible for a student to suddenly become overwhelmed, the more likely explanation in this situation was that something was going on in this child's life that was knocking him off-kilter. After I asked my usual hundred questions, the mother reluctantly spilled her sad story. There were two boys in the class that were picking on her son and most likely sexually assaulting him. The boy was seeing a therapist to help him cope with the difficult situation, but all three children were still in the same class, and the principal and guidance counselor had still not been informed. Why not? I asked. She did not want to humiliate her son by being perceived as weak, nor did she want to cause problems in a school that had been very difficult to get accepted to.

The mother insisted that even though her child was indeed suffering "socially" as she called it, he might also have ADHD that needed to be addressed. I explained that when a child is clearly suffering trauma, it would be irresponsible to peg him with a diagnosis and mask his call for help with medication. I then contacted the appropriate authorities and prayed that this sweet child got the help he was begging for.

This is a tragic and perhaps atypical story. Healthy parents respond protectively if they are aware that their child is suffering abuse. Often, our children do not let us know they have been victimized right away and carry the burden of shame and anxiety on their own for years. While they are holding their abuse close to their heart, they are shouting out loud, expressing how much they are suffering through their actions. This behavior looks just like ADHD symptoms, so it often lands children with an ADHD diagnosis and subsequent medication. We can implement the entire program set out in this book, but our children will continue to rage until we address their inner turmoil.

As a parent, it is frightening to know that we send our child out into the world and cannot always be right there to protect her. Children are exposed to predators from within the family and outside, as well as bullies at school. According to a study for the National Center for Post-Traumatic Stress Disorder, 90 percent of children who have been sexually abused knew their abuser (Whealin 2007). In the many cases of abuse within the family or neighborhood, children are even more reluctant to speak up. They are either protecting the perpetrator, are fearful of that person, or worry that their parents will not believe them. Sometimes, especially when sexual abuse occurs inside a family, a child is not even sure he is being abused; he only senses it in the pit of his stomach. Children may also be shrouded in a cloud of shame that keeps them from exposing the abuse.

Although we cannot be at our child's side every minute of every day, nor are we to blame in most cases if our child falls prey to abuse, we must look out for signs that our child has been victimized. We must also speak of abuse very openly in our home, so that our child is more equipped to know when to speak. Our child must be told continually that she will always be heard, that we will always take his side no matter what.

Our message should be crystal clear. If our child ever feels endangered by anyone, she should get out right away and not worry that she is offending or insulting someone. If the person she feared turned out to be harmless, we will be there to defend her anyway and be proud of her quick thinking and self-protective reflex.

My daughter's school had a wonderful parent/child "Say NO" day to educate about sexual abuse and how children can learn to protect themselves. They ran an experiment as part of the presentation. A child was invited on stage. She was told that she would be approached by different people, and she had to put one hand out in front of her when she felt the person was coming too close and two hands up when she wanted the person to stop. This was an exercise in becoming aware of our personal space and reading our inner voice that tells us our space is being violated. One child after another was able to sense the difference between being approached by someone familiar (a teacher), someone from the outside (her friend's dad), and someone who could approach and give her a hug (her parent).

I have repeated this exercise many times with my children. I tell them that as soon as they feel they would like to put one hand up, they should start listening to that inner voice. It may be time to look for help or get going. When they feel the need to put two hands up, way before they have been touched, children should know that they have every right to get away. We are built with a "personal space" radar. Give your kids instructions on how to use it, and remind them they always have permission to listen to it.

Children who have been traumatized by abuse are often diagnosed with ADHD.

Nicole M. Brown, attending physician at the children's hospital at Montefiore and assistant professor of pediatrics at Albert Einstein College of Medicine, was looking at signs of abuse and noticed a trend when treating patients diagnosed with ADHD. "Despite our best efforts in referring them to behavioral therapy and starting them on stimulants, it was hard to get the symptoms under control," she said of treating her patients according to guidelines for ADHD. "I began hypothesizing that perhaps a lot of what we were seeing was more externalizing behavior as a result of family dysfunction or other traumatic experience." She noticed that much of the behavior described as ADHD originated in childhood trauma.

Brown found that children diagnosed with ADHD also experienced higher levels of violence, divorce, substance abuse, and poverty. The children who suffered four or more adverse childhood events (ACEs) were three times more likely to be prescribed ADHD medications (Brown 2017).

Dr. Heather Forkey, a pediatrician at the University of Massachusetts Memorial Medical Center, has been trying to spread the word to doctors that hyperactivity and inattention symptoms do not have one neat diagnosis. These symptoms have many different causes, just like chest pain can be attributed to many conditions. Therefore, before diagnosing ADHD, physicians must consider the child's background and possible trauma as the source of the symptoms (Ruiz 2014).

Another trailblazer, bringing attention to the confusion around symptoms that are being called ADHD but that in reality are rooted in childhood trauma, is Cealan Kuban. She is a trauma and loss consultant and offers training courses to practitioners, teachers, and doctors. Kuban describes how traumatized children find it difficult to control their behavior and shift from one mood to the next quickly. They might drift into a dissociative state while reliving a horrifying memory or lose focus while anticipating the next violation of their safety. To a well-meaning teacher or clinician, this behavior can be quickly diagnosed as ADHD (Ruiz 2014).

How common is child sexual abuse?

According to David Finkelhor, director of the Crimes Against Children Research Center, one in five girls and one in twenty boys will be victims of sexual abuse. Too many children are carrying a burden heavier than they can bear. It is not someone else's problem; it is right here, in our community, in *every* community. Let's look at some of the symptoms we may see in our children.

Symptoms we may see in children who are suffering from sexual abuse:

- Nightmares, fear of the dark, or other sleeping problems

- Extreme fear of monsters

- Spacing out at odd times

- Sudden mood swings: rage, fear, anger or withdrawal

- An older child behaving like a younger child, such as bed-wetting or thumb sucking

- Fear of certain people or places (e.g., a child may not want to be left alone with a baby-sitter, a friend, a relative, or some other child or adult; or a child who is usually talkative and cheery may become quiet and distant when around a certain person)

- Refusing to talk about a secret he/she has with an adult or older child

- New words for private body parts

- Talking about a new older friend

- Suddenly having money

- Stomach illness all the time with no identifiable reason

- Loss of appetite, or trouble eating or swallowing

- Pain in or around the genital area

- Unexplained bruises or redness around the anus or mouth

(How to Identify Child Abuse Ages 6–12, November 24, 2018, The Whole Child)

If you see these behaviors, the first step is to sit your child down for a warm, loving, accepting, and most importantly, patient Collaborative and Proactive Solutions conversation. Listen well without interrupting; reassure your child that she has done nothing wrong and that she is very brave for sharing her story. Let her know that you will always believe her. If such conversations are practiced in your home on a regular basis, your child will feel less intimidated to share, knowing that she has a parent who can listen without correcting and who always accepts her word.

Even in a warm and supportive home, a child may still not be willing to talk. Inviting a therapist to join your team is often necessary and highly recommended. We need trained professionals to support our child and our family in the case of abuse.

The above list of symptoms is not proof that your child has been abused. If you see any of the symptoms listed above, investigate immediately. Remain calm and let your child talk because hysterical or fearful assumptions will shut her down.

Bullying as another form of abuse our child may face

Another form of abuse our children can be exposed to is bullying, which is defined by the CDC as unwanted aggressive behavior, observed or perceived power imbalance, and repetition of behaviors or high likelihood of repetition. Bullying, whether it be in person or online, has powerful and unfortunate repercussions for our children.

According to the federally run website *stopbullying.gov*, kids who are bullied can experience mental health issues as well as physical problems. The following is a list of possible symptoms a child may exhibit if he is being bullied:

- Depression and anxiety

- Increased feelings of sadness and loneliness

- Changes in sleep and eating patterns

- Loss of interest in activities the child used to enjoy. These issues may persist into adulthood.

- Health complaints

- Decreased academic achievement—GPA and standardized test scores—and school participation.

- More likely to miss, skip, or drop out of school.

How can we create a space in which our child can naturally share his experiences of school or a visit to a friend's house? When our child comes home from school in the afternoon, we tend to ask blandly how school was. The response, often just as bland as the question, is "fine." There the conversation ends.

School is your child's profession; he spends most of his waking hours there. "Fine" can't be the only feeling he has about a long and multifaceted day, just as it is probably never the feeling you have after your long day's work. Try asking a few questions, but do not interrogate! I like to ask about recess. "Did you stay in the classroom or go out to play soccer? Who were the children you spent the most time with?" If you have a school schedule at home, you can also ask about specific classes. "Which class was interesting today? None? Okay, so which ones were terrible? Was the teacher yelling?"

Ease into conversation by sharing a little about your day. Let your child know how you felt when you got to the bank only to discover that it was closed due to a holiday. Share an interaction you had that elicited a strong emotion from you. The more you show interest and availability, the more your child will share. He loves talking with you; he only needs a caring and curious invitation.

One warning here: do not correct him or tell him what he should have said or done in a school interaction. It will reduce his confidence in his ability to navigate the social environment. Just reflect with him, share your story, and ask questions.

Action Plan
---

1. Make a list of behaviors your child exhibits that are not resolved through clear and loving communication and discipline or by behavior intervention. These behaviors have an underlying emotional trigger due to lack of skill.

2. Choose one behavior to tackle.

3. Before inviting your child for a Collaborative and Proactive Solutions discussion, see if you can identify possible emotional triggers to the behavior. Remember to remain open to being surprised; this is a fact-finding mission and requires much curiosity.

4. Begin the conversation at a calm time, making sure to give your child your complete attention. Shut off your smartphone and put it away! Take out a nice treat and create a warm environment by telling your child how special she is.

5. Engage in the three steps: **empathy, putting your concern on the table, and finding a solution** calmly and lovingly.

   ◻ Give fun personal examples

   ◻ Do not be critical, don't correct, and don't take what your child is saying personally. She is trying to figure out how the world works and is using you as a sounding board, so be that for her.

   ◻ If you do not succeed in completing the entire intervention in one sitting, don't despair! Most of us need a few conversations to fully understand how to help our child gain new emotional skills. Your success lies in your invitation to talk and your willingness to listen attentively.

6. At the conclusion of the conversation, be sure to set a time to check in later and see how the collaborative solution is working.

7. Use Collaborative and Proactive Solutions any time you see a pattern of behavior that is harming your child, or as a follow-up to particularly difficult behavior. As you engage in collaborative and proactive solutions, they will become a natural part of conversation in your home, and you will be surprised to find your children engaging their own struggles this way.

8. Keep an eye out for signs of possible abuse or bullying and invite a therapist to help your child and family in the case of suspected abuse.

9. Put your phone down for ten minutes when your child comes home from school and talk with him. Ask curious questions and share experiences from your day.

THE CHEAT SHEET

Chapter Seven: The Emotional Intervention Program for Children Lacking Social Skills or Suffering from Emotional, Sexual, Physical Abuse, or Bullying.

- A child will behave well if given the opportunity. A child lacking social skills or experiencing abuse will exhibit symptoms of ADHD but will not be able to adjust his behavior.

- We must not solve our child's problems; we must give her the skills to become a problem solver.

- Our child is missing the skills to work through emotional/ social problems.

- Punishing or medicating a child for responding poorly to emotional situations is counterproductive because the child has not yet developed a specific emotional or social skill set.

- What skills are our children missing?

  - **Executive function** – Transitions, sticking with a task, organization, keeping time, blocking out background noise

  - **Language processing** – Expressing needs in words, confusion with verbal instructions, trouble following conversation.

  - **Emotional regulation skills** – Poor frustration management, doesn't handle disappointment well

  - **Cognitive flexibility** – Black and white thinking, gets stressed from changing plans.

  - **Social skills** – Doesn't know how to start conversation.

- How do Collaborative and Proactive Solutions build these skills?

  ◦ Start with the warm-up. Invite your child for a conversation.

  ◦ Never invite when angry. This is a fact-finding mission, so approach it with curiosity, not conclusions.

  ◦ Set the stage. Make it warm and fun to talk.

- What behavior will we focus on? Any behavior that repeats itself often and that indicates social or emotional stress.

- Four steps to follow:

  1. Empathy – Just listen to your child, ask questions, and mirror. Give examples, suggestions of emotions, and never judge.

     ◦ **Pitfalls:** A child may not want to talk, makes up stories, gets defensive, or is not used to sharing. Keep at it until you understand the emotion your child is struggling with.

  2. Define the problem from the parent's perspective – Show a child that his behavior affects others.

     ◦ "Every feeling is legitimate; your *feelings* must be respected and understood. We must understand and help you adjust your *response* to that strong emotion" is our message.

  3. Find a solution – Work together; respect every suggestion.

     ◦ Be prepared with your own suggestions.

     ◦ Brainstorm together. A good solution is one where both sides are respected.

  4. Check in to see if the solution was good and if progress is being made.

- Childhood trauma is often diagnosed as ADHD because the child exhibits all the symptoms.

- We must pay close attention to our children and look for signs of potential abuse. Most children are abused by someone they know, so they will not tell on the perpetrator for many reasons. A child must always hear that she will be listened to and trusted no matter what. If we practice Collaborative and Proactive Solutions regularly, our child will feel more comfortable speaking with us.

- Bullying is another type of trauma our child may be grappling with.

- When your child comes home, take the time to find out how his day was. Share your story and ask curious questions. The more we talk with our children, the safer they will feel in letting us know when they are struggling or hurting.

- Get help if your child has been abused. Parents cannot carry this burden alone.

CHAPTER EIGHT

Making Friends is Hard to Do

*B*RANDON CAME TO *school with a sparkle in his eye and a brand-new ball. He was excited about the new game he had invented and wanted to share it with his buddies. He was sure the boys in his class would love the game, and he was right. They happily joined in, and a great time was had by all until . . . Brandon got out in his own game and refused to accept the ruling of his friends. He grabbed his ball, threw it in the garbage, and sat on the garbage pail. Game over! And so are all the potential friendships Brandon may have formed during this game and many others.*

Brandon is a gregarious kid, a real leader. The kids love to play with him; he has so many good ideas. Unfortunately, slowly but surely, after similar repeated incidents, they begin to mistrust him and his ability to play fairly.

What's wrong with Brandon? Is he a kid who just can't make friends? Why is he behaving this way? His parents are worried!

Stella is quiet. She has an imaginary friend she likes to speak to, sometimes even during class. She looks out the window a lot, imagining that she is floating on the elephant-shaped cloud that's drifting by. Stella wants more than anything to make friends. She gets teased a lot because of her strange whispering to herself (she insists it's not herself she is speaking to, which doesn't strengthen her case). When she tries to start conversations, the girls look at her strangely and move away. She is never sure if she is butting in or if she is welcome in any social interaction. She's all alone and in pain. Why doesn't anyone like her?

Can you feel Stella's pain? Is she your daughter? If so, there may be many hours of sobbing at home and begging not to go to school.

In this chapter we will explore why children diagnosed with ADHD struggle socially, the consequences of the isolation they experience, and how we can create a system to help our child learn the skills he is missing. We will borrow some skills we have already begun developing from previous chapters and develop new social skills programs as well.

Solutions offered to help socially struggling children: Do they work?

- **Stimulant medication:** Brandon and Stella's diagnosis of ADHD, which is supposed to explain why they struggle socially, gives us no useful information about the struggles these children face or how to treat them. Stimulant medication is recommended in some cases to "slow down" and "focus" the children so they're less impulsive and don't say or do socially inappropriate things.

  The problem, of course, is that stimulant medication simply cannot help a child socialize better. Stimulants reduce a child's curiosity about his environment, thereby allowing him to hyper-focus on the task at hand without distraction. This may be a great intervention for math or science class, but socializing requires a desire to engage. When a child is medicated, he withdraws socially and often no longer has that desire. Is he less lonely? No way! Is he gaining much-needed skills through social interactions? None at all. Ritalin cannot help a child gain social and emotional skills. The school of life is the only way to go.

- **Guided social skills training groups:** The other common recommendation for a socially struggling child is to enroll him in a social skills group. While some kids learn skills in these groups, there are two problems. Firstly, the groups are packed with children who are fumbling socially, so there is no one to copy and learn the right kind of behavior from. We don't want these kids sharing their underdeveloped social abilities with one another. Also, the best way to learn any new skill is by practicing it in real time, like learning a new language.

- **Throwing her into the deep end and assuming she will figure it out:** A third solution is letting a child learn to socialize on her own. This has some benefits. The child may make a mistake and be pushed back enough times that she figures out the right responses. Most often, though, the reason the child is not getting it is because she is missing skills. She would do well if she could. We would never throw a child into the deep end of a swimming pool before teaching her to swim.

Why do children with ADHD symptoms struggle socially?

Usually the reason our child is struggling socially is because he is missing all the skills listed in the previous chapter. Initiating a Collaborative and Proactive Solutions conversation with your child is a good way to identify what skill he is missing. You can identify together that there is indeed a problem, empathize with your child's struggles, and agree together that there are ways to learn new social skills. Once we understand what emotional stress and missing skills may be blocking good communication, we can begin implementing and practicing new skills.

Here are some underlying challenges that you can discuss with your child as the trigger to the missing skills.

- **Instant gratification personality:** Our child is an Instant Gratification kid. He wants things fun, fast, and immediate. He may not be processing how others perceive his behavior, and in some cases has not even become aware of the importance of focusing on others yet. He struggles with boring follow-through, which is a requirement in forming relationships. He will jump from one friendship to the next yet will not take the time to develop more intense friendships. This behavior is described as egocentric and childish, which are accurate descriptions but do not lead us to a resolution.

- **Trouble with follow-through:** When a child is seeking stimulation and fun, he is not very dependable. He may be very involved and caring while there is high stimulation but will not be there for his friends in times of need.

- **Inflexible thinking:** Our child with ADHD symptoms is a novelty seeker and develops habits slowly, so he is not paying attention to patterns, nor is he reading the social map well. He relates to social interactions very impulsively. When he is insulted or rejected, he cannot identify the cause of the problem. He makes a leap directly to "he hates me," "he thinks I'm stupid," or "he's a bad kid," He does not yet have the mental discipline to analyze the nuance of the interaction to understand what went wrong and how to improve the situation.

- **Fixed mentality:** He might also be a fixed mindset child. He may be protecting an image and not want anyone too close lest it be discovered that he is "dumb" or "incapable." Children with learning challenges feel defensive and ashamed, two feelings that do not allow for smooth relationship development.

- **More emotionally sensitive:** Some children experience life in a more emotionally vibrant way. Everything affects them strongly. They feel joy more deeply and hurt feelings can often be devastating to them. This "condition" has its very own name and list of symptoms. It is called Rejection Sensitive Dysphoria (RSD). Feeling so deeply can be painful. These children are more sensitive to criticism, always feel as though they are being rejected by loved ones, and have a perception of constant failure. If a parent says, "I am disappointed in your behavior," it may be interpreted by the child as an abusive comment and a complete rejection of the child. A small disagreement with a sibling can feel like a slap in the face that she has no skills to interpret.

It's quite hard to understand a child who experiences emotions so strongly, because her perception of reality is vastly divorced from our intentions and what is really occurring. She may feel unloved and uncared for even in a caring home. She must not be dismissed as the crazy oversensitive one, but rather we must respectfully understand that every person is more sensitive in one area or another (physically and emotionally), and emotions are this child's most sensitive spot. We must consider that this child may be sensitive due to trauma triggers, in which case she needs a very sensitive, loving, and fully focused response. Learning not to take her interpretations to heart is difficult, to say the least, but absolutely necessary. Once we can distance ourselves from our child's scathing feedback and extreme emotional interpretations, we can get a better grip on the pain she is experiencing. We can then begin to help her gain skills to align her emotional interpretations and suffering with her environment so she can begin to enjoy healthy interactions.

- **A history of bad social experiences**: Children can be quite vicious to each other; that's why they need the adults in their lives to set the parameters of respectful social conduct. Unfortunately, when a child seems different, such as being a little more energetic or a dreamer, children see an opportunity to pounce on the victim and tease him relentlessly. When any child is bullied, teased, or sidelined, it is very hard to overcome the trauma and build trusting friendships. When our child experiences this behavior, his instant gratification thought process does not allow him to draw helpful conclusions. He may choose to be more aggressive or retreat, but rarely will he be able to communicate his despair effectively.

Every child needs friends! What happens to a socially isolated or rejected child?

The pain of loneliness or being misunderstood is unbearable. Your child is suffering. In conversation with your child, you can discuss the intense stress her lack of healthy socializing is causing, and explain that there are ways to learn these skills. Here are some of the risks of allowing social isolation to fester.

- The child does not get a chance to develop and practice skills, thereby further regressing socially.

- Children with ADHD symptoms are not born with low self-image. As a matter of fact, they think they are quite wonderful (which they are), just like any other child. Constant social rejection takes a toll on our kids. They develop self-doubt, and eventually, low self-esteem.

- They lose faith in themselves and self-define as less capable or undesirable. As a result, they shy away from taking positive risks like attempting leadership positions. The fear of failure is too frightening for a child who lacks strong social standing. Bold leadership requires the kind of confidence which comes from positive social feedback and friendship.

- Isolated children take more negative risks and turn to more dangerous behaviors and activities. This may be because they are desperately seeking friendship in the wrong places or they do not have good peer role models to spend positive time with. Because of this, they may turn to drugs, alcohol, or dangerous sexual activity to drown out their sorrow.

- Loneliness leads to feelings of deep sadness, depression, and anxiety.

You can help your child make friends.

What blocks us from jumping in to help our socially struggling child as we would if she were struggling with any other skill? Our thinking gets clouded by fear ("will she ever be normal?") or resentment of other children ("why is everyone so mean to my child?") or anger at our child for not just "pulling it together." We all need the helpful reminder that our child would choose to do well if she could. She wants friends more than anything in the world. She is not self-sabotaging on purpose. She just does not know how to proceed.

Let's get into some hands-on strategies that you can discuss with your child as approaches to the problem. The first intervention is a plan you will construct with your child to *anticipate social problems that may occur in the near future*. The second helps us *"clean up" after a difficult social interaction* and learn skills that can be applied the next time your child finds himself in a similar situation.

Approach Number One: Preemptive Social Intervention – The Four Rs of Social Development

In his book *It's So Much Work to be Your Friend* (Simon and Schuster, 2005), Richard Lavoie, a brilliant educator and lecturer, presents a simple yet effective way to help a socially struggling child gain missing skills.

These are Lavoie's four Rs of Social Development:

1. **Reason**: provide a reason for the rule

2. **Rule**: state the rule

3. **Reminder**: provide the child with a hint or memory trigger of some kind

4. **Reinforce**: recognize and praise.

Here are examples of how this approach works:

*Every time you invite friends for dinner, just the thought of your child's likely behavior at the table spoils your appetite. Will he be friendly to your guests' children? Will he allow them to play with his toys? Will he speak really loudly and dominate the conversation, not allowing for others to contribute? Lots can go wrong; it may not be worth socializing. Or perhaps you can apply the four Rs **before** the event, thereby giving your child new skills and direction.*

First, anticipate what will go wrong and why, meaning the reason for your stomachache. Establish a small social rule and explain why this is an important rule to follow.

> *"Brandon, you know how we enjoy having friends over. Their son Jeremy loves to play with you. Sometimes it's hard for you to share your toys, but if Jeremy doesn't have a friend and some fun games and toys to play with, he will not want to come over and see us. Just like Mom and Dad share their home and food with friends, we need you to share as well. Think about what toys you would like to share and put them aside for Jeremy's visit. This is how we treat our friends kindly."*

The **rule** is that the child must share toys with friends.

The **reason** for the rule is that sharing with friends is kind and helps them enjoy time with us.

The **reminder** can be a specific pile of games and toys ready for the playdate, which helps Brandon remember that he chose those items and will be kind and friendly when using those toys while playing with Jeremy. Mom or Dad can point to the pile discreetly if Brandon forgets the sharing rule. Take note that the reminder should be planned in advance.

Finally, the good behavior needs **reinforcement**. Remember, catching your child doing the right thing is the best way to reinforce his good behavior. When you catch Brandon sharing his toys, quickly compliment his efforts.

Let's look at another example.

How can we help Stella with her social isolation using the four Rs? Establish a small social rule and explain why this is an important rule to follow: *"Stella, you have a special friend that you like to speak with in your imagination. I'm so glad you can tell her everything. But other children are confused when you speak to your friend because they don't see her and think you are talking to yourself. When you speak to your special friend in school, it makes it much harder for others to understand you. Let's decide that you will speak to your friend at home and not in school. That is an important rule because then you will be able to have more time to make friends. You can take a jump rope and some cards to school and invite children to play with you instead of speaking with your imaginary friend."*

The **reason** is that it is socially confusing for other kids when Stella looks like she is talking to herself.

The **rule** is that she speaks to her imaginary friend at home and plays with real friends in school.

The **reminder** is a little notebook that Stella can use to write a quick note of what she will discuss with her imaginary friend when she gets home.

Reinforcement is practiced with loud praise when Stella comes home and shares a notebook or tells you how she controlled herself and invited a child to play a card game with her.

One more example.

Barry likes to be a funny kid. He makes lots of noises, facial expressions, and jokes during class. He also likes to learn and can do well in school. His teachers are constantly complaining about his ADHD despite his high grades. They don't know how to get him to stop disrupting and start paying attention to school rules. They say Barry should understand the rules by now and know not to disturb during lessons. But he doesn't, and it's not because he wants to get in trouble constantly. He wants friends; he wants social approval; and he is quite unaware that he is hurting himself daily. How can you, his parent, help the school better understand him and implement the four Rs?

Explain the **reason** for the rule to Barry: *"The reason we are meeting (parent, teacher, and student) is to discuss some school rules and break them down for you. (Give examples of school rules that Barry is either understanding too literally, trying to cut corners on, or does not notice altogether.) Sometimes you do not fully understand what is expected of you, so you make mistakes like disrupting in class or bothering another student. This is because it's hard for you to grasp social expectations. Once you begin asking what the rule is and have a conversation about what is expected of you, you can begin feeling proud of your own behavior."*

The **rule** is that when Barry sees that someone, such as a teacher, is frustrated with his behavior and that person tells him he has done something wrong, Barry should ask what rule he broke and inquire how he can fix it. He should make sure to get all the details of that rule so he can follow it more closely in the future.

The **reminder** is an agreed-upon gesture or gentle touch on the shoulder when the teacher or parent sees that Barry is either taking a rule too literally or is missing it altogether. Once Barry sees or feels the reminder, he can gather his thoughts and ask which rule he broke, all the details about the rule, and how he can do better next time.

Barry will be **reinforced** with enthusiastic compliments from parent and teacher, notes home about followed rules, and a call home on days when Barry has stopped, asked, and found out what is expected of him.

We can use the 4 Rs method for a child who stands too close, speaks too loudly, or touches too much for the socially accepted norms, as well as any other social conflict. Your child is not trying to bother you, so don't get angry! Try to anticipate what behavior may be exhibited in a social setting and plan the four Rs in advance.

Some warnings from Lavoie:

- Don't discourage your child from developing a friendship with a child younger than him.

- Don't punish a child for making a social mistake. Rather, assume he did not understand his behavior.

- Don't force a child to participate in large group activities if he is not willing or ready.

- Don't place your child in highly charged competitive settings.

- Don't assume your child understood your social instructions just because he didn't ask a question. Ask him to repeat the directions.

- Don't scold your child when he shares stories about social confrontations or difficulties he is experiencing. This will shut him down from sharing in the future. Instead, use these stories as cues to yourself that a new social rule should be discussed.

- Don't teach social skills at a time of high stress. Practice social interactions well in advance of the event.

- Don't rely solely on praise. Showing genuine interest in what your child is involved in is also positive reinforcement.

Life is messy.

We cannot always anticipate what social mistakes might happen in advance. Sometimes we are caught responding rather than planning. Again, your child is not trying to destroy your life; she did not understand how to behave. We must internalize that we are not just trying to teach a child to survive the uncomfortable situation; we are trying to teach social skills.

Often when I tell parents about my work with people with ADHD symptoms, they respond by suggesting that I am trying to help parents "cope" with the challenges their children present. No, we are not developing coping mechanisms. Quite the contrary! We are thriving, not surviving. We are developing missing skills. If we have a survival mindset, it suggests that we don't believe our child can improve. He can, so long as we fully engage in guiding him. He will fumble and make many mistakes until we teach him the correct social language. Lavoie gives us guidance for responding to events that have already occurred.

Approach Number Two: The "Clean-Up" Social Skills Autopsy

The clean-up autopsy concept is based on a medical autopsy. Think of that sinking feeling you have right after your daughter points to a complete stranger and declares loudly, "He has a bigger nose than our whole family put together!" How about when the school calls to tell you that your son had a temper tantrum on a school trip and had to be restrained by the principal? The event is over. The body is "dead." Social suicide was committed, and now it's our job to determine the cause of death. We must identify the error, determine the cause, assess the extent of the damage, and try to prevent it in the future.

There are five steps in the autopsy:

1. **Ask the child to explain what happened**. Try to get the complete story. Let him do the talking. Don't judge, and don't interrupt.

2. **Ask the child to identify the mistake he made**. Children often struggle to identify the mistake they made.

3. **Help the child identify his error**. Don't tell the child what he *should* have done; rather, discuss what he *could* have done.

4. **Create a new scenario** where the basic principle or moral understanding can be applied. Fabricate a short story that may occur in a different context and ask how your child would respond in that scenario.

5. **Give some homework**. Ask the child to report back to you if he was able to practice his new skill this week. Make sure you follow up with him on his homework.

If the autopsy is done right, children enjoy the process and do not feel reprimanded. Lavoie reports that children request an autopsy when they realize they have made a mistake but cannot figure out what they did wrong.

Example one:

1. Ask your child to explain what happened. Get the complete story, but don't judge.

Laura comes home from school in tears. She had a fight with her best friend (for this week) and the girl refused to sit next to her on the school bus coming home. Laura comes in, throws her backpack on the floor, and goes directly to her bed to cry. Laura often struggles with this particular girl. There is always a story, and the stories repeat themselves. Time for an autopsy.

Mom goes to visit Laura in her room. Poor Laura has buried her tear-streaked face in her soggy pillow. Mom strokes her back and asks what happened. Laura begins her heart-wrenching story. "I was playing with Sam at recess. We were having a good time, and suddenly she got so angry at me and told me that she doesn't want me to be bossy and she doesn't want to play with me."

Not much information there. *"Okay, Laura, Sam got upset because you were bossy?"*

"But Mom, I wasn't being bossy at all! I was just trying to help her."

"How were you trying to help?"

"We were playing in the classroom and she took a pencil that was not hers from another desk and I told her that it was not nice to touch other people's things. She said I shouldn't tell her what to do, so I said she didn't have permission to touch the pencil and should put it back right away. I said we would continue playing after she put it back. Then, instead of listening to me, she said she doesn't want to be my friend."

A fresh torrent of tears rolls down Laura's cheeks.

2. Ask your child to identify the mistake she made.

"Laura, what do you think your mistake was when you were playing with Sam?"

"That I told her I would not play with her if she didn't return the pencil?"

"No, the problem was something else. Can you figure it out?"

"Maybe that I was butting into her business and telling her what to do with something that had nothing to do with me?"

"Excellent! You got it. Sam probably did not like that you were telling her how to behave instead of letting her decide how she would like to deal with the pencil and the child it belongs to."

3. Discuss the error with your child. Don't tell her what she should have done, rather what she could have done.

"What could you have done differently in the situation with Sam?"

"I could have told her that the pencil was not hers but let her decide what she wanted to do with it?"

"You could have done that; that would have been very good. Could you also do something else?"

"*I could just not tell her about the pencil and let her do what she wants and just play with her?*"

"*That sounds like a very good idea. Do you think Sam can figure out on her own how to treat others' property? She seems to really enjoy playing with you but very much does not enjoy it when you tell her how to behave. Could you see that she touched the pencil but continue playing with her and enjoy the game without judging her?*"

"*I think I can do that.*"

4. Create a new scenario where the same principle can be applied.

"*Let's say you are sitting next to Patrick in class and you look over and notice he made a very big spelling mistake in his essay, so you want to help him correct it. It bothers you that he made a mistake, and you know a way to help him fix it. What should you do?*"

"*Ooh, that would be hard! It makes me crazy when people do the wrong thing and I know what's right. But I should probably leave him alone and let the teacher make the correction unless he asks for my help.*"

"*You understood that very well! I see you get that looking around to correct your friends is not a great idea. They don't enjoy it and then don't want to play with you.*"

5. Give some homework that you will then follow up on.

"*This is what I want you to do, Laura. Next time your friend makes a mistake that doesn't involve you, I want you to come home and tell me that you minded your own business and trusted your friend to make the right decision and continued to play. See how much she likes playing with you when you only focus on enjoying her and the game and don't check that she is doing the right thing.*"

Since the autopsy requires some focus and practice, let's run one more scenario.

Example two:

Candice goes to visit her friend Susan after school one day. Susan takes out the photo albums to show Candice. It's exciting to see old pictures;

they are both sharing a great time. The mood tanks when Susan takes out her parents' wedding album. Susan thinks the pictures are dreamy and beautiful and is looking forward to sharing them with her friend.

Candice scans the photos and, in her blunt way, blurts out, "Your mother looks so eighties! We would never wear dresses or get hairdos like that, right? Look at all these funny-looking people."

Susan slams the album shut and is no longer in the mood to play. What went wrong? Candice wonders. When Mom comes to pick Candice up from the playdate, she can sense that something is not right. Susan enthusiastically waves goodbye as the car pulls away.

It's time for an autopsy.

1. Ask your child to explain what happened. Get the complete story but don't judge:

"Candice, what happened with Susan? It seems the playdate did not go so great."

"Susan was showing me pictures. We were having a great time. We were laughing about all the old-fashioned people, and then Susan got upset and slammed the wedding album shut."

"Was Susan also laughing at the pictures?" Perhaps this question will help Candice zoom in on her error.

2. Ask your child to identify the mistake she made.

"What do you think your mistake was, Candice?"

"Maybe we looked at the pictures for too long, so Susan got bored and upset when we got to the wedding album?"

"That is probably not why she got upset because she took out the album herself. Can you think of something you may have done or said that could have upset Susan? Was Susan proud of the album? Why do you think she wanted to share it?"

"She said she thought her mother looked so beautiful. I laughed because the gown and hairdo were so eighties. I couldn't believe anyone would like a dress with those puffy sleeves and the big hair. Susan didn't think it was funny."

"Can you try to think now about what would have upset her?"

"She thought the album was beautiful, and I was laughing and giving my opinion. I don't think she liked to hear that I thought they looked weird. She probably wanted me to say her parents were beautiful."

3. Discuss the error with your child. Don't tell her what she should have done, rather what she could have done.

"What could you have done differently?"

"I could have seen that she really loved the pictures and let her enjoy showing them to me without giving my opinion. I could have looked at the photos and found a nice thing to say about them, and just not said the not-so-nice comments."

"So, you could have seen that your friend was enjoying sharing something that was special to her, and you could have been complimentary and not shared every thought about what you were seeing?"

"That's it. I could have done that; I could have let Susan show me the album and let her know I liked it too."

4. Create a new scenario where the same principle can be applied.

"Imagine you see a friend at school. She is wearing a skirt she just bought in the secondhand store. She feels great in her new skirt. You know that this skirt is not really new; it was in style five years ago. You bought it at the Gap then. You could easily say, 'Nice skirt. I remember when it was in style.' What will you choose to do?"

"She feels pretty in her clothing, and it's new to her. I can just compliment her and not say every thought I have about her skirt."

"Excellent! You really understood that when someone is enjoying something they have, we should enjoy with them, without adding comments that will probably make them feel bad (even if they are true) and make them unhappy with what they have."

5. Give some homework that you will then follow up on.

"Ready for a little bit of homework, Candice? We notice lots of things about other people all the time, but not everything needs to be pointed out. Friends don't like when we make comments about how they look, if their hair dye is fading, or they gained weight. We especially don't

want to point things out if the person can't change or fix the 'flaw' we noticed, like a run in her stockings or the wrong kind of jewelry when she is already out.

"All these observations may be true, but they do not help us be a better friend; it just makes our friend feel sad. Next time you notice something that may be true about another person (and it's great that you notice so many details) but will not make her happy to hear, or it's something she can't change, just focus on what is nice and give a compliment. Then come right home and tell me what a great job you did."

This method is so helpful for children who struggle to understand tactful behavior. They need direction in order to examine the mistakes they have made. Using a nonthreatening learning process to truly understand what is socially acceptable and why will bring your child one step closer to building lasting friendships. One day she will laugh with her friends about the blunt comments she used to make. But right now it's not funny and requires our full nonjudgmental attention.

Here are other proactive strategies I have developed to help a child make and keep friends.

- **Be a fly on the wall in your child's school.** Go on a school trip or get involved in an after-school activity involving your child's class. Take noncritical mental notes of where your child is struggling. Be careful not to compare him to other students, remembering every person has his own challenges. With new social information, you can begin setting new social rules with the four Rs.

- **Help your child make a playdate.** Plan it carefully so that your child does not feel intimidated by the intensity of the encounter. Be present to suggest games to play or activities to do. Make sure your home is an attractive and fun place for children to come to visit. After a playdate, review with your child his successes and consider doing a social skills autopsy to make the next playdate even more successful. Let your child know that making mistakes is part of learning and that he is not expected to be perfect; he is just expected to try his best and have fun.

- **Get information from your child's teacher**. Get a layout of the students in the class and find out from the teacher which kids can be potential friends. See if your child can be placed next to other kids who would be easier for him to get along with. Ask the teacher to fill you in on what social missteps your child is committing so you can help him practice better choices at home.

- **Get your child involved in after-school activities**. Sports, dance, or martial arts are great choices. These are structured activities and provide a lot of social interactions. Sometimes sports are overwhelming; there are too many kids to socialize with and too many potential mistakes to be made. Take it slowly. A small swimming group or art class may be a better first choice. Figure out what your child loves to do and help him do it after school with other kids.

- **Strategize together at home**. Get rid of the stigma surrounding social challenges. Socializing is a skill we can learn, and the more we present it this way, the more progress we will make. To illustrate, when my older daughter was starting college, she was tense about navigating a whole new social environment with new rules and expectations. She brought up her fears at the dinner table. Her sage youngest sister had some advice for her. "Just be very friendly and look around for ways to be helpful to others," she declared. Two weeks later, big sister checked in to tell us that the advice was working great. She had already made a bunch of new connections.

  If social strategy is a family topic, as it should be because we all are tested frequently with new social scenarios, everyone can share openly and help one another. Establishing and practicing new social rules is very helpful. The **rule** my little girl established was, "When you are helpful to others, they will probably want to be your friend." Also, "Be open and friendly to everyone; you never know who is open for friendship."

- **Practice specific skills.** Skills can include asking for help, waiting your turn, giving compliments, listening, admitting to mistakes, sharing, disagreeing politely, and accepting others with all their differences. Each of these skills can be highlighted and practiced. Make a family flash-card game where you write down these social skills and others and have a child choose a card and either act out not understanding or totally nailing the skill. Have the rest of the family guess what skill he is practicing.

  Obviously, for this game, the family would need the prior habit of eating dinner together at least a few times a week. Get that going! Some of the best learning and bonding happens at dinnertime. We just have to set the stage. Dinner can be scrambled eggs; just get the gang together without phones for even half an hour. It makes a world of difference.

- **Practice asking questions.** People love to talk about themselves. Help your child begin conversations by practicing asking open-ended questions. Help her use her natural curiosity to find out more about people, and make sure to practice reciprocating questions others ask of her. Even making a mental list of questions people like to answer (about family, hobbies, trips, funny or challenging experiences, camp, etc.) is helpful. It feels contrived at first, but the more we practice, the more naturally we converse.

- **Set small goals** with your child such as, "Today I will ask one child to jump rope with me" or "Today I will bring my ball to school and invite a few kids to play football" or "Today I will go out to the yard during recess instead of staying inside with a book." Discuss progress and troubleshoot what didn't go as planned. Don't set big goals that are intimidating and unachievable.

- **Study body language.** Here's a fun one: together as a family watch YouTube videos or TED talks that analyze and explain body language. Discuss how body language affects behavior and vice versa. Practice sitting in a confident manner. Do you feel more confident? Put on a warm, welcoming smile and lean forward a little. Is that more connecting? Practice understanding personal space and see how it feels when that space is invaded.

- **Praise and reinforce any positive social interactions** you observe or hear about. Help your child see how much progress she is making.

- **Pay attention to your own behavior.** When we over sympathize and take on our child's social burden, we run the risk of giving the message that this is a permanent situation that cannot be resolved. We unknowingly cause our child to feel powerless. "Fitting in" can be a painful process indeed, and it's rough to see our child struggling, but struggle he must. The only way she will overcome the challenge is by taking it on. If a child hears from you that making friends is a process that takes time and hard work, and he can do it, we give him power. When she knows that challenges strengthen us and build our emotional muscles for the next big challenges, she is more likely to dive in. Finally, when our child knows that mistakes are part of the process and not a hugely disappointing setback, she will take more chances.

I like to tell kids that they have a magical power called "overcoming challenges." The child and I imagine that we are sprinkling the child with "[fill in name of child] magic" to go out and face any challenge, knowing that he will be stronger just by getting out there to try. If we present the social challenge not as suffering but as a way to become stronger and develop magical "overcoming challenges" dragon-slaying powers, our child will feel more prepared to engage.

Action Plan

1. Identify the stress your child's lack of social skills is causing you.

2. Figure out your trigger and examine if your response is coming from a deep, painful emotion inside of you.

3. Is your behavior toward your child when he messes up socially more aggressive or disappointed then it need be due to your own skeletons?

4. Remind yourself that learning to be socially appropriate is a skill like any other. If your child were struggling with memorizing the multiplication tables, you would probably roll up your sleeves and help him gain the skill. The same approach is required when building social skills.

5. What social skills is your child missing?

6. Identify them and make a list so you can help her tackle them one by one.

7. Invite your child to a Collaborative and Proactive Solutions conversation to begin to understand his stress from social failures.

8. Make a plan to begin helping your child develop the skills. Together, plan how to proceed.

9. Using the four Rs to start setting social rules may be a good place to begin.

10. Introduce the social skills autopsy. Use it on yourself as well in order to model making a social faux pas and identifying the source of the mistake.

11. Choose a project from the list of proactive strategies to begin making small steps towards great success.

12. If you see that your child's social stress is isolating him or that he is showing signs of depression or anxiety, get help. Consult with a child psychologist who can add a fresh perspective and be a safe place for your child to share his pain. It's hard to grow up! Get all the help you can when supporting your child as she navigates the social minefields of elementary school and high school.

THE CHEAT SHEET

Chapter Eight: The Social Skills Development Program

☞ Problematic solutions often offered to children struggling socially:

- Stimulant medication: This can't solve social struggles because stimulants make children withdraw and reduce curiosity. This medicated focus may be good for math or science class but not for learning from the "school of life" how to socialize.

- Social skills groups: All the children in the group are struggling; there are no role models to copy.

- Throw the child in at the deep end: The child is missing skills, so she is more likely to sink than swim.

☞ Why do ADHD-symptom kids often struggle socially?

- The instant gratification personality causes many impulsive social mistakes.

- Kids with impulsivity struggle with follow-through, checking on a friend, being thoughtful.

- Inflexible thinking does not allow for fluid relationships.

- "Fixed" mentality gets in the way of honest and vulnerable relationships. The child is defensive and self-protective.

- Children with ADHD symptoms can be more emotionally sensitive.

- Children with a difficult social history avoid interacting so as not to be hurt again.

☞ What happens to a socially isolated child?

- He does not practice socializing and falls behind.

- The lack of positive social encounters harms self-esteem.

- The child blames himself for social failures

- The child sees herself as less desirable—she shies away from leadership and volunteering; he takes negative risks; she develops depression and anxiety symptoms.

☞ Preemptive social intervention plan: The 4Rs of Social Development

- **Reason** – Explain the reason for a social rule (your friend will feel bossed around)

- **Rule** – State the social rule clearly (we don't point out things others do wrong)

- **Reminder** – Set up a reminder for the rule (tap on shoulder)

- **Reinforce** – Compliment the child for following the rule in a specific way.

☞ Warnings to parents:

- Allow your child to be friends with younger kids

- Never punish for social mistakes

- Never push a child to socialize until he's ready

- Ask a child to repeat instructions

- Don't scold when a child is sharing a story where she made a major social mistake.

☞ Social intervention after the mistake already occurred: The social autopsy

  a. Ask the child to explain what happened

  b. Ask the child to identify his mistake

  c. Help the child identify his error

    d. Create a new scenario where the lesson can be learned

    e. Give some homework

☛ More proactive solutions for children struggling with appropriate social interactions:

    a. Be a fly on the wall in your child's life, school trips, and after-school activities to identify social problems.

    b. Help your child make safe and organized playdates.

    c. Get information from your child's teacher.

    d. Get your child involved in after-school activities.

    e. Practice specific social skills as a family at home, such as asking meaningful questions.

    f. Set small goals and stay positive and complimentary.

    g. Help your child study and understand body language.

CHAPTER NINE

Building a HyperHealing Team

*J*ACK LIKES TO *learn. He reads books nonstop, shares all the great information he finds with anyone who is willing to listen, and asks lots of thoughtful questions. One would assume that Jack would be the ideal student. One would be wrong! Jack spends his school days strategizing how to skip class without getting caught. When he's trapped in class, he does what he can to be as uninvolved as possible. Day after day, he comes home with a disheveled backpack with none of the relevant books inside to do homework. Even when he calls a friend to get the homework, he can't remember what he learned that day and therefore can't complete the assignment. Mom and Dad know this kid can learn; they have seen it with their own eyes.*

Jack's major obstacles to success are his extreme disorganization and his time spent either dreaming or with his head in a book. It doesn't help that it's more fun to cut class than attend, especially if he can get away with it. It's a big, noisy class, and the teacher is young and gaining experience on the job.

Jack's parents get called in for a meeting with the homeroom teacher, guidance counselor, and the principal. After the teacher describes Jack's dismal behavior, grades, and lack of class participation, both the principal and guidance counselor are alert. Has this kid been diagnosed yet, they both want to know? Of course he has, reassure the parents. The obvious next question is, "Maybe he needs his dose adjusted. Have you made an appointment with the doctor?" To the shock and dismay of all participants, the parents say they have chosen not to medicate but rather to use other interventions to help get Jack back on his feet.

"He is losing precious time; he will fall way behind the rest of the class and suffer with a poor school record if this matter is not attended to at once," says the principal, with genuine concern.

The parents suggest that perhaps what Jack needs is a little more structure, guidance, and assistance with organization, consequences for cutting class (right now he has nothing to lose and much to gain by not showing up to lessons), and a chart to get him motivated.

This is a progressive school; they are willing to try a new program. The principal declares that they will meet in a month and until then each person will be assigned a job. The teacher will make a chart; the parents will help Jack organize his backpack; and the guidance counselor will meet with Jack to discuss how important it is to go to class.

The month flies by for Jack. He spends most of it poring through books in the school library, and as one can imagine, the follow-up meeting is depressing. The teacher can point to no progress. Jack is as inattentive as he was a month before. The guidance counselor says that all interventions have been explored, and it is now time to consider medication.

In this chapter we will discuss the dilemma parents face when their child is not flourishing in school. As we will see, it is most often the teacher who is the first to refer a child for ADHD evaluation, and the parent who feels pressured to comply. Why is this? What are the obstacles to smooth, respectful communication between parent and teacher? Once we understand why we are clashing, we can build a dream team to help our precious child flourish. We will conclude with classroom suggestions that will give your child the boost he needs to start learning well.

Just reading about Jack's experience can make any parent scream with frustration. We have all sat in those meetings. I will never forget the meeting for one of my children where the guidance counselor glared directly into my eyes and said, "Why would you not medicate your child? You are hurting her. Don't you know that medication works?!" While it may be clear to us that our healthy child needs a little more help, better structure, and a different discipline program, what the school sees is a labeled child who they would very much like to help, but they have very few tools in their ADHD kit to do so.

The teacher is the most important adult in your child's life besides you, so she should be a natural partner to help your child gain missing skills and flourish in school. In many classrooms, though, this is not the case. Parents feel defensive and adversarial towards the teacher and vice versa. While all involved have the best interest of the child at heart, we are often not all on the same page.

There are multiple problems that contribute to miscommunication between teacher and parent, and the child pays the price. Please note that there are many situations in which the teacher is not available at all to partner with you. Do not despair! Obviously, having the teacher on our team is ideal, but this chapter will empower you to give your child a boost in school, even without such assistance.

What are the obstacles to productive communication between parents and teachers of a child diagnosed with ADHD?

1. **We are not there!** We, the parents, can't help the teacher understand our child better. We have our hands tied when it comes to discipline, organization, homework, etc., and have to rely on the teacher's interpretation of our child, his abilities, and his behavior. While at home we may have started helping our child take responsibility for his belongings, our child is still likely to come home without his homework written down or the books he needs to do said homework or the ability to locate either in his jungle of a backpack. It will forever remain a mystery to me how the entire pencil case gets emptied every day. We can't implement the same program in school because we are not in charge there.

   When we ask a teacher to help our child write down homework or pack his bag with the books he needs, the teacher is likely to respond by saying, "Fifth graders are expected to be responsible for their homework on their own." She's right, for most students. Our child is missing a skill, which he is fully capable of gaining if only we can set up a habit-formation program. The teacher may assume we are trying to get him to baby our child and do his work for him. Again, he is not wrong. As a teacher, I would not agree to help my student do his work if I knew he was looking for a free ride.

This is a typical misunderstanding between the teacher and parent. We are not asking for him to baby our child; we are asking the teacher to acknowledge that in specific tasks, our child has weaker muscles right now. In order to build those muscles, we must not skip steps. We must see what the student is capable of now and build from there.

We want the teacher to be our teammate in strengthening our child. Can we explain this? We can't be there to set up a chart with our child, so can we effectively communicate what our child needs from his teacher without setting up shop in the hallway (thereby guaranteeing our little one will never make friends)?

Can we help with discipline when we never get the full story, just our child's creative interpretation of the facts and calls from the teacher? Our frustration lies in our inability to implement what we know works best. School is our child's full-time job. We need the teacher on our side.

2. **The teacher believes that our child should be medicated.** I am honored to be a lecturer in a teacher's college, a job I cherish. My students are highly experienced teachers who have often been in the classroom for many years. They are fed up with ADHD kids. They begin the semester with preconceived notions about ADHD and frustration with the stubborn unscientific parents of those children.

I begin my course with a "detox," meaning the introduction, where we examine the science behind ADHD. This is undoubtedly an eye-opening yet disturbing experience for my students. My students get angry. They want to know why they have never heard any of these scientific facts in any other lectures and have only heard the opposite. Once they have understood that ADHD is not a neurological disorder but a clash between personality and environment (and in some cases, the symptoms are caused by environment alone), teachers have a new perspective on educating kids diagnosed with ADHD and see our children in a healthy new light.

Not all teachers get this in-depth perspective. Teacher education is often informed by interested parties such as pharmaceutical companies. There is a likely chance that your child was first "diagnosed" by her teacher, and studies suggest that teachers have a bias towards believing that ADHD is a neurological condition that requires "fixing" through medication (Sax and Kautz 2003).

Teachers are bombarded with continuing education materials provided by pharmaceutical companies, masquerading as educational content websites. School workshops are offered to teachers and school personnel, including nurses, so the staff is well versed in identifying and referring students for ADHD evaluation. Since these courses are sponsored by industry, very little information is provided to teachers about classroom programs for unmedicated children with ADHD symptoms.

Therefore, many teachers believe that the best treatment for ADHD is medication, and they have little sympathy for the parents who choose an alternative treatment plan. They may even see those parents as neglectful for allowing their children to struggle for no good reason. It is clear to many teachers that medication is the optimal treatment for ADHD; therefore they neglect the art of implementing behavioral, academic, and organizational tools to help our child flourish in the classroom. Instead, they depend heavily on medication to do the trick.

3. **Our child is making the teacher's life difficult**. The teacher has already expended her entire storehouse of patience for our child in the first few weeks of the year and probably doesn't want to hear our fabulous suggestions. My mother-

in-law shared how the PTA meeting for her wonderful son went in the third grade. Before my mother-in-law could open her mouth, the teacher stated, "Your son devours 50 percent of the energy I have for the whole class. I have to divide the other 50 percent among the other twenty-five students!" If only that teacher could see my husband now. Was this teacher open to parental recommendations? I think not.

4. **The teacher may have the will but not the way.** Your child may have a great homeroom teacher, but the teacher is limited in two things that are beyond her control. She is not your child's private tutor, and she has very little extra time to devote to your child and his needs. Additionally, she rarely has a well-developed intervention plan due to the sheer amount of information she would need in order to develop such a program.

Getting past these obstacles is imperative because our child depends on both parents and teachers supporting him for his success. We must respectfully work together. We are on the same team; we are all invested in this child and his progress.

How can we overcome the obstacles to smooth and cooperative communication between parents and teachers?

1. **Step one: Respect!** Your child's teacher has signed up for a very challenging task and is your partner in every way. You must listen carefully to what the teacher has to say. This requires some humility, which can be in short supply when we feel we know best and don't welcome the teacher's contribution. Parents can also be quite defensive, feeling their children have been wronged, misunderstood, and mistreated. This is our precious child, and someone is judging him. Not an easy feeling.

2. **Step two: Addressing the elephant in the room … medication.** You may have decided you would like to medicate your child, in which case, move on to step three.

The parents who have rejected medication treatment for now and are swimming against the tide have some challenges ahead. Once again, begin by respecting the teacher and listening to her perspective. Don't argue. Listen and discuss. And never say never! Don't say you will never medicate, just that you want to consider all other treatment options first. Agree that your child is struggling and needs help, and place yourself and your child's teacher squarely on the same team.

How can you present your perspective? Begin with information. According to studies, teachers often automatically associate diagnosis with medication (Wienen et at. 2019), despite the fact that those teachers actually receive very scant education about medication (Snider et al. 2003). Their optimism for medicating students is often based on misinformation or no information at all. The teacher may not be married to her perspective on medication and may be open to hearing an educated perspective. If that is not the case, agree to disagree after a respectful sharing of ideas. For more information, see my book *HyperHealing: Show Me the Science,* to be published by Gatekeeper Press in 2021.

3. **Step three: Take the lead!** As I mentioned above, your child's teacher is not his personal tutor. She is juggling a lot all at once, all day, every day. I spent many years on the other side of the desk. Teaching is hard work. Every student has different needs. There are academic, social, and emotional dynamics to navigate, and all those must be navigated before a teacher gets to her actual job—teaching information and skills. Her plate is full, but if we can provide the plan, the teacher may be open and willing to participate.

Here are some guidelines for an effective plan:

1. The time we ask the teacher to expend on our program must be limited to a few minutes per day.

2. The responsibility for the program, including building it, consistently managing it, and providing all rewards, is on our child and us.

3. The program must promote smooth and helpful communication between teacher and parent.

4. The program must help our child develop missing skills. We will not make a program based on where the child ought to be, but rather what his skills are right now. If we start at the beginning and build steadily, he will catch up. If we begin in the middle (for example, expecting him to do homework at a fifth-grade level when he still has not mastered the skill of writing the homework down and bringing home the correct books), our child will drop out of our program in frustration.

Creating the "bridge" between school and home

The bridge between school and home is:

a. A simple chart

b. A daily general discipline program

c. Setting the student up for success

The chart is very similar to the chart you have already developed with your child at home. Note that a child may have a school chart and home chart at the same time, but not two home charts or two school charts. This is important as we don't want to overwhelm our child in any environment.

The following is an example of a school chart. I will explain all the nuances afterward. This chart is available to be downloaded from my website, www.hyperhealing.org.

Key:
0 points: The student did not fulfill the requirement.
1 point: The student fulfilled the requirement partially.
2 points: Grand success! The student completed his responsibility.

	Assignment 1: _____	Assignment 2: _____	Assignment 3: _____	Teacher signature:
Monday	0 1 2	0 1 2	0 1 2	
Tuesday	0 1 2	0 1 2	0 1 2	
Wednesday	0 1 2	0 1 2	0 1 2	
Thursday	0 1 2	0 1 2	0 1 2	
Friday	0 1 2	0 1 2	0 1 2	

Dear Teacher,

We would like to work with you to develop a classroom program to help our child improve his skills as a student. With your guidance, we have chosen three assignments for our child to work on improving in **one lesson per day.** Our child will be expected to present this chart to you every day. We ask that you rate his performance on these three assignments and add your signature to the chart daily. We take full responsibility of keeping track of points earned and will reward our child accordingly.

Thank you for your participation.

Let's understand this "bridge" step by step:

Transportation points

The chart must get to the teacher every day for the designated lesson. This means that your child will be expected to give the chart to the teacher daily and then bring it home to you. Okay, you're looking at this and thinking, "Has she forgotten who my child is? How does she expect him to give a chart to a teacher and get it back home every day?"

Let me explain. Your child will want to earn points, right? As part of the points your child will earn for fulfilling his assignments, there will be two "transportation points." He will be rewarded for transporting his chart to his teacher's desk and then back to his parents' hands.

This program has two parts:

1. Specific skill development, which will last for at least one
    month and take place in one lesson per day.

2. General discipline for the rest of the school day.

Specific skill development

- Get your child a small notebook and photocopy the chart
  above several times. Paste at least four charts on four pages in
  the notebook. Write the date of the beginning of each week
  on each page with a chart on it. The program must run at
  least one month in order to effectively help a child develop a
  new skill.

- Set up a meeting with your child's teacher to discuss what
  skill(s) you will be tackling first, and what lesson during the
  day she will use the chart. You have two choices when it
  comes to selecting the skill-development daily task.

  1. The first option is to **choose three separate skills** to
      practice in one lesson per day. This chart can be used to
      help a student develop any missing skill in the classroom.

  2. The second option is **taking one skill** and checking that
      the student is practicing that skill three times during the
      lesson.

**The rule is that if the child is not participating in class as he should
be, he is either missing the skill required to accomplish that task or is
being blocked in some other way.** We will examine possible blockages
later in the chapter.

Here are a few examples of dividing the skills-development chart:

1. **Skills for a child who is uninvolved in the lesson:** Sitting
    quietly without getting up during the lesson, asking one
    question, answering one question.

2. **Skills for a child who needs a jump-start in getting homework done**: Copying down the homework, taking yesterday's books out of the backpack, putting the correct books into the backpack in order to get the homework done.

3. **Skills for a child who is disorganized**: Clearing the desk completely, putting only the textbook and notebook on the desk for that class, along with a fully loaded pencil case (this requires a pencil case checklist at home with ample school supplies to replenish missing items).

4. **Skills for a child who disrupts the lesson by making lots of noise and shouting out answers**: Raising a hand and waiting to be called on before speaking, sitting quietly in the lesson, writing in a small notebook thoughts or questions that a child is not permitted to say during class and sharing it with the teacher afterward.

5. **Skills for a child who does not get started on his assignments and misses half the class while finding the book or opening it**: Open the workbook/notebook as soon as the teacher instructs, begin doing the assignment right away, work on the assignment for ten minutes. (This is just an example. We must ascertain how long your child can focus right now. As the program progresses, we will slowly extend the time he is expected to stay on task.)

6. **Skills for a child who is aggressive towards other students in the class**: Keeping hands to self throughout the lesson (no touching anyone), using only words that are acceptable in the classroom (be specific), asking and answering questions during the lesson.

Example:

	Assignment 1: Keeping hands to self	Assignment 2: Using acceptable words	Assignment 3: Asking and answering a question	Teacher signature:
Monday 1st lesson	0 1 2	0 1 2	0 1 2	
Tuesday 1st lesson	0 1 2	0 1 2	0 1 2	
Wednesday 1st lesson	0 1 2	0 1 2	0 1 2	
Thursday 1st lesson	0 1 2	0 1 2	0 1 2	
Friday 1st lesson	0 1 2	0 1 2	0 1 2	

We can also **choose one skill** to be practiced throughout the entire lesson. If a child has one problem that needs to be focused on, such as talking nonstop, touching other students, shouting out answers, not getting his in-class assignment completed, or getting up and wandering around the classroom, we will focus on that skill for the entire lesson. In the case of a single-skill development chart, we write down the skill three times on the chart, as all three assignments.

For example, you would write down "staying in your seat" three times because that is the only skill being practiced. Ask the teacher to divide the lesson into three parts, fifteen minutes each, and have her rate your child's behavior three times during the lesson. It is helpful to provide the teacher with an egg timer or its more technological equivalent so that she can track your child's performance without extra effort.

Ask the teacher to signal to your child as he moves from one quarter hour to the next. We divide the time so that a child will have more workable units, and so that if he fails during the first segment of the chart, he can still get points on the other parts.

Example:

	Assignment 1: Staying on task for 10 minutes 9:00–9:10 (break 5 minutes)	Assignment 2: Staying on task for 10 minutes 9:15–9:25 (break 5 minutes)	Assignment 3: Staying on task for 10 minutes 9:30–9:40 (break until recess)	Teacher signature:
Monday	0 1 2	0 1 2	0 1 2	
Tuesday	0 1 2	0 1 2	0 1 2	
Wednesday	0 1 2	0 1 2	0 1 2	
Thursday	0 1 2	0 1 2	0 1 2	
Friday	0 1 2	0 1 2	0 1 2	

Although teachers agree to participate in the skills-development program, they are often concerned about discipline problems and disorganization during the rest of the school day.

The skills-development program is only half of the plan. We will now progress to the second part of the bridge, the overall discipline plan. It is quite like the discipline program you have already set up at home, and therefore will be simple for you to help the teacher get started. Note that if a child is getting consistent discipline messages both at home and in school, it works best.

The overall discipline program

Find out from the teacher what her classroom rules are. She should have the rules prominently posted for all the students to see. If this is not the case, prepare a list of rules for your child to tape to the corner of his desk. Make sure he understands every rule.

1. **Reword the classroom rules and tape them on your child's desk**: Teachers are taught to write rules in positive language. I understand the concept, but it just doesn't work for our kids. Imagine a rule such as, "Be respectful to all students." Sounds nice, right? Now climb into your kid's head. How is

he interpreting this rule? "If Jimmy is looking at me like I'm stupid, then the most respectful way to treat him would be to punch him in the face" may be one interpretation. We could rewrite the rule so it is more clear: "No touching, hitting, kicking, or cursing at other students."

Discuss a positive feedback motivational program for the entire school day: Once we know that our child understands the rules, we need to help the teacher "catch" him doing the right thing. There are two ways to do this:

a. A teacher can reward our child with specific compliments when he follows the classroom rules. Remember, the compliment must be enthusiastic, immediate, specific, and with no added negative comments. In my experience, many teachers respond that they don't have time to stop and compliment all the time. They may be right, but it takes much longer and exhausts much more energy to discipline a child who is testing his limits. This strategy saves time and builds a healthy, strong relationship between student and teacher. Also invite the teacher to send compliments home.

b. We can also upgrade the positive feedback program with the teacher's permission (no stepping on toes here; respect the teacher and the system she has in place, only offering your idea if she has not yet implemented a positive feedback program or is looking for suggestions). How is this done? We can purchase a roll of prize tickets, the kind kids win at the arcades, and the teacher can distribute these tickets to the entire class throughout the day to students who have followed the rules.

For example, if there is a rule to be prepared for every lesson by having a clear desk with only the textbook, notebook, and pencil case on the desk, as soon as the teacher tells the students to prepare for math class, she can verbally and physically reward the first five students who are ready. As our child sees that he will be rewarded for his good behavior, he will be more likely to jump on the positive behavior bandwagon.

What should the teacher do with all of the prize tickets? I had my students glue an envelope in their homework journal so that the tickets did not get lost, and once a month, we had a "sale." The students could purchase all sorts of prizes.

Here are a few prize examples:

a. Student is provided one question to the upcoming test in any subject

b. Dictating the spelling test on Friday

c. One homework-free night

d. Purchasing an extra five minutes of recess for the class

e. Purchasing a story hour for the class (students can pool their tickets)

f. Playing a baseball game with the teacher

g. Watching an educational movie.

All these examples are experiential prizes, the best kind of prize. If the teacher prefers a physical reward, the school and parents can participate in purchasing these prizes.

Once there is a positive environment in the classroom where good behavior is celebrated, our child will be more likely to participate.

Our child has the will, but does she have the way?

When a student is not doing what is expected of her, she is either missing a skill, or there is some other barrier stopping her from succeeding. When we ask a child to have the correct books on the desk, and only those books, can she pull off that task? Well, that depends on a few factors.

• Does she still have the book, or has she misplaced it?

• Is her cubby a mess?

• Is her pencil case fully equipped?

- Does she get up to get her book only to get lost along the way and end up talking to a friend or forgetting what she was going to get?

Before we initiate any program, we must make sure that our child has a chance of succeeding.

- Ensure that she has all her books and notebooks, with her name on each one.
- Help her set up her notebooks in a way that she is less likely to misplace them.
- Ask the school for an additional set of textbooks to keep at home so your child is less likely to misplace them in transit.
- Reward your child once a week for having all her notebooks and a fully equipped pencil case.
- Make sure you have ample and easily accessible school supplies at home to replenish her stock.
- Instead of scolding her for losing them, reward her for responsibly asking to replace lost scissors.
- If she gets lost going to her cubby, place an office box either under or near her desk to store her books, instead of in the cubby, so she doesn't have to walk past all her friends.
- If disorganization is her main struggle, set up the skills development chart and completely focus it on organization.
- Ask her what she feels is getting in the way of her focus in class. Is she daydreaming? Is the class boring? Does she understand the material? Address each obstacle seriously and plan with your child and the teacher to reduce barriers to success. Set your child up for success by ensuring she has the tools to succeed. If the teacher detects emotional stress, refer to a therapist for help.

The negative discipline program

Now that we have a positive discipline program (teacher's compliment and ticket program, removing barriers to success), it must be followed up with a punishment plan. Implementing a punishment plan before the positive discipline program is a mistake. The child must have the ability to choose to behave well, and this only happens when he is being rewarded for good behavior. Punishment is very unpopular, and teachers dislike punishing, but this step may not be skipped. Go back to chapter five, "Punishment Is Not a Dirty Word," to remind yourself how vital this step is in our program.

What punishments are we never going to use?

1. Calling a parent or sending a WhatsApp are not good punishments. The punishment must immediately follow the misbehavior to be effective.

2. Taking away recess is out of the question! Children must run around in order to think and learn.

3. We will not ask a student to write anything one thousand times because we are trying to strengthen writing skills, not extinguish any desire the child has to write.

4. Humiliating a student is unforgivable.

Use "community service" as the preferred punishment program. Here are a few ideas of small punishments that improve the classroom environment, which any student can respectfully implement:

a. Putting the chairs on the tables at the end of the day

b. Organizing the classroom library

c. Reading a short paragraph and answering two questions

d. Creating a poster about the topic being learned

e. Reading a story and writing the lesson the student understood from it

f. Helping set up for a school assembly.

Some of these "community service" punishments may not feel serious enough to the teacher. She may say the child is having too much fun doing it, so she feels she is rewarding him. Here is a quick reminder: The goal of the punishment is not to cause the student to suffer or to feel ashamed. It is to stop a student from making a poor choice and redirect him to make a better, more productive, and helpful choice. If this punishment is delivered consistently, the student feels respected and becomes more responsible. Eventually, he will not want to get "community service"; he will prefer to make a good decision and follow the classroom rule.

If our child refuses to participate in the punishment, the teacher must have a plan B. Plan B is taking away a school or classroom privilege. The teacher must not take away something that is helping the student learn better, such as a calculator or electronic dictionary. Instead, the teacher may exclude the student from part of a class project or outing. She may not take away recess but can have the child sit in class for an extra minute or two of recess and then send him to join his class.

We must remember two things. First, we will only use this punishment if the child refuses "community service." Second, parent and teacher should make a "punishment treasure chest" together. Think of uncomfortable yet not punitive punishments that can be delivered swiftly and for a short duration of time.

The program is structured as follows:

- We begin our parent-teacher coordination program by meeting with the teacher to determine what skills our child has to focus on and to decide in what lesson this new skill will be practiced every day.

- We prepare the chart at home, and either the parents or teacher introduce the chart to the child. The parent is responsible for the rewards and keeping track of points.

- In the same meeting, we will discuss the classroom rules with the teacher. If we feel the rule is too vague for a child, we will rewrite the rule more clearly and have our child tape the rule to his desk.

- Since the skills development program is reserved for one class per day, we will then discuss the positive discipline program.

- We will create a punishment treasure chest with the teacher, making sure we are on the same page and both confident with the community service punishment, as well as taking away a classroom or school privilege.

- We will keep open communication in order to decide on the next skill to tackle, and to set our child up for success by eliminating any barriers such as missing books, disorganization, social tension, learning challenges, or fear of failure. It is helpful to set up telephone meetings once a month for a few minutes to check in with the teacher and verify progress.

Some tips a parent can pass on to the teacher (from a teacher)

There are a few little tricks that can go a long way towards creating a positive and enjoyable learning environment. The following are tips I have either developed or gathered from master teachers over the years. I have tried them all in my own classrooms and found them invaluable.

- **Privilege with responsibility:** Sometimes a student has ants in his pants and learns better standing or moving around a little. Obviously, this can be a very disruptive activity in a classroom, and it makes teachers crazy. What if a student learns better if she goes out of the classroom for a few minutes to take a break, run up and down some stairs, and come back? Is this something that can be permitted? How will she know to come back? Will she come back? Will she enter the classroom quietly? There is also the student who learns better when he can drink some water or nibble on a healthy snack. This is usually a big no-no in most classrooms. But we have kids who may learn more quietly and with more focus if they were able to stand, take a break, or eat and drink. Does the teacher have options?

A teacher can make a "privilege with responsibility" agreement with her student. She can place a small podium in the corner of the classroom. If a student chooses to stand, he must go quietly with his school supplies and books to the podium at the back of the classroom and continue to participate in the lesson. His **privilege** is to stand during the lesson. His **responsibility** is to participate quietly in the entire lesson. If he does not fulfill his responsibility, he loses his privilege for the next lesson or until the end of the day.

The same is true for leaving the classroom, playing with a fidget toy, drinking, or eating. The teacher allows the privilege if the student fulfills her responsibility. If a student is permitted to leave the classroom for five minutes, she must return on time. If she returns late, she will not be permitted to go out during the next lesson.

- **Making comic strips:** Doing any tedious chore is always easier if we can simultaneously engage in something we enjoy. Think of folding the laundry; it's a boring task! Now add music you love, or an interesting podcast, and the laundry gets folded in no time. How can we use this idea in the classroom? If the student is sitting in a class where she is expected to take notes (history, government) but struggles to concentrate, allow her to illustrate the lesson. At the end of the lesson, the teacher will know if the student understood based on her drawings. The student will remember the information better and will be engaged throughout the class. A teacher can also allow a student to use clay to create a personality from the lesson. Allowing students to have a doodle pad to scribble in while listening to a lecture can be helpful as well.

- **Setting up an enrichment corner:** A classroom is a dynamic and challenging place. The only unifying factor between the students is their age, and even that has a full year spread. Learning ability, personality, and emotional maturity vary. As a result, teachers find themselves in a bind when they give assignments. Some students finish the assignment in a few minutes, while others need two lessons to complete the task. What is a teacher to do?

Many years ago, I heard a lecture from the principal of a large and successful school. This was a man worth paying attention to. His lecture was engaging, and jam-packed with useful information. And then he said the strangest thing. He asked us what the best reward for a completed task was. Members of the audience were throwing out answers all related to prizes and vacations. The principal shook his head vigorously at each suggestion. And then he cleared his throat and said, "The best reward for work well done is more work."

What? As a young teacher, I just assumed he must be out of touch. But his confidence compelled me to give it a try.

I set up an enrichment corner in my classroom. I purchased a cardboard file holder with many cubicles to store papers. Office managers often have them on their desk. I photocopied different activities and worksheets related to different topics. I had math challenges, science experiments, English essays, etc. I told my students that the minute they finished the work required for that lesson, they were welcome to get a worksheet from the enrichment corner. I offered no rewards, only the opportunity to do more work.

The results were stunning! My students were racing through their work, asking me to review it, and then sprinting to the enrichment corner. They couldn't get enough of the sheets. Some focused strictly on science, others on math. My classroom became a busy little factory with sweet little students racing around doing as much work as they could. The slower students worked faster so they could be rewarded with a trip to the corner. The students with dyslexia begged to do fewer examples of the required work (which I happily granted) so they, too, could merit extra enrichment.

Get that enrichment corner going. It works best from first through sixth grade.

- **Get the students moving, but not by sending them out of the classroom:** We will spend some time discussing the value of exercise in brain development and focus in chapter thirteen. For now, I would like to recommend three different ways to get your students, who sit way too much, to start moving.

  a. **The figure eight:** Use paint or tape to make a big figure eight in the back or on the side of the classroom, wherever there is more space. When a student starts to get jittery, allow her to walk the figure eight quietly. She could hop it, walk it, dance it, or even walk it backward, using a mirror that you have hanging on the wall next to the eight. This keeps your students in the classroom while allowing them to get up and move in a controlled way. This is a "privilege with responsibility" activity, so a student earns the figure eight if she walks it quietly and quickly returns to her seat.

  b. **Deskercise:** No one should sit for more than forty-five minutes, including adults. When there are two lessons in a row, students are expected to sit for way longer than is healthy for them. Take five minutes at the beginning of the second lesson to deskercise. Do exercise with your students, but without moving desks or chairs.

A talented occupational therapist gave me a fantastic suggestion. She said that the teacher should write a "menu" of different exercises (push-ups, jumping jacks, touching toes, handstands, etc.) and hang the list in the classroom. Each day, invite one student to be the coach and choose four exercises from the list and lead the routine for his classmates. Conclude the five-minute deskercise session with a few moments of deep breathing and then get started with the lesson. The class is rewarded with more deskercise sessions if they can start learning right after exercising.

  c. **Invite students to stand up to ask or answer a question.** When one student stands up, other students focus more on her comment, and the standing student gets time to stretch. In a dynamic classroom where students are encouraged to participate, students get significant exercise while asking and answering questions, and also receive stimulation for their minds.

d. **Situate students who are just starting to flex their concentration muscle in a location in the classroom that allows for optimal focus.** Every student is different. Some kids with ADHD symptoms prefer the front center seat. Others like to sit at the end of the row, so they are not bombarded by sensory distractions. Tailor your student's location to his needs.

e. **When giving instructions for any task, write it down, say it verbally, and confirm that the student understood by asking her to repeat what she heard.** This will not be required all year because the teacher is building a listening skill, and the student will acquire it midway through the year. Once the student sees she is expected to fully pay attention to instructions and be responsible for repeating them back to the teacher, she will become a better listener.

f. **If a student is frequently off task, invite him for a conversation where you agree upon a secret code, which will remind him to get back to his work.** Reward the return to task with either a compliment, prize ticket, or both. When this strategy is used consistently, it is habit-forming.

g. **Never communicate with parents through the child's personal homework journal.** Find other ways to communicate with parents. A child should not be forced to incriminate herself. Write compliments freely in the journal for the student to bring home and show her family. Spread the compliment and turn it into the gift that keeps on giving.

The following are some classroom discipline programs that have worked wonders in my classroom over the years.

- **The time-out ribbon:** Each child wears a red ribbon around his neck. While the child is wearing the ribbon, he is fully involved in the rich classroom environment, full of praise and feedback, receives ample attention, and can participate with questions and answers. When he misbehaves, he removes the ribbon for a few minutes and does not participate during that time. When his time out is over, he is welcomed back to full participation. No reminder of his previous behavior is necessary. This strategy only works in a positive, complimenting environment (Foxx and Shapiro 1978).

- **The group program:** If a large group, such as a class, is having trouble with a specific behavior (homework, coming in on time...), establish a group program whereby when 75 percent of the kids accomplish the set assignment, the entire class is rewarded. After a few weeks, raise the expectation to 90 percent achievement, with a class reward to follow. Finally, expect 100 percent achievement, rewarding the class for their unified achievement. This plan allows students who need some time to develop the habit a window of growth and gives the students the responsibility of encouraging each other.

What if the teacher will not participate? Are we stuck?

No! We can still help our child succeed in school from home. Here are a few ideas of home-fueled programs:

1. The note-taking program

- Get your child's weekly schedule either from your child or from his teacher.
- Print the schedule out and hang it prominently in the kitchen.
- Check that your child has all his notebooks and ensure he has a system of keeping them together.

- Use five-subject notebooks to reduce the number of moving parts. A binder that contains all your child's school subjects may also be used.

- Your child will earn a point for every notebook he writes in every day. If he had math, science, history, and social studies today, he has the potential to earn four points.

- Your child can look at his daily schedule in the morning, before heading out to school, to begin planning how he will earn maximum points.

- When he comes home from school, he must present you with the four notebooks and show you that he has copied from the board or written notes or done the assignment in each class. If he fills more than one notebook page, he will earn an extra credit point. If he still has all his notebooks every day, he can earn one additional point.

I have used this program with two of my children with great success. What was most fun was when my child followed me around the house, teaching me what he had learned that day. He got a great review, and I got to be on top of what he was learning and get some free conversation time.

2. Homework buddy

- Give your child a point for every item he copies from the board for homework and an additional point if the workbook or notebook are in his backpack. An extra credit point is granted if she has not brought home any books she doesn't need, and one more for a full pencil case.

- How will we know our child has written down the homework? He will check with a friend when he gets home from school to confirm the accuracy of his homework list. If he writes down everything, he gets an additional point. If he missed an assignment or left a book in school, he will either not get the extra point, or he will lose one.

3. Learning ahead

- Ask the teacher to keep you posted on what material your child's class will be covering this week in subjects that are particularly challenging for your child.

- Hire a tutor. I like to hire local high school students, to introduce the subjects that will be studied in class. When your child has a heads-up on what will be happening, he may be more motivated to pay attention.

4. Be involved with homework and preparation for tests

- We live in a technological age where even if your child did not take notes in class and is missing material, another student can send the material with ease. Obviously, we want to encourage our child to be responsible, and we are working on putting that in place. But until she gets organized, she should not be forced to fail tests.

- Keep up with her test schedule, help her get notes from friends, and set aside time to study with her. She can also study with a tutor (a high school student) or an older sibling.

- Homework should be done at a set time daily. Allow your child to take a break and have a nourishing snack when she comes home, and then sit down to homework.

- The ideal place to do homework is right in the kitchen or dining room, near a parent, and not in a silent, closed room. Phones of all sorts, tablets, or computers should not be accessible during homework time.

- Assess with your child how long she can stay on task right now. Right now, if she can sit and work well for ten minutes, set a timer for ten minutes of hard work. As soon as it rings, she will get a well-earned five-minute break. She will then work on homework for ten more minutes and call it a day. As the school year progresses, we will extend the on-task time slowly.

Be sure to explain to the teacher that you have a homework program in place to help your child develop homework responsibility skills. Add that by the middle of the year, the goal is for your child to complete her homework every night. Until then, you will ask the teacher to grant your child full credit for the homework she accomplished during the designated homework time.

Action Plan

1. Set up a meeting with your child's teacher.

2. During the meeting, agree to respectfully work together for the benefit of your child.

3. Do not get into arguments about medication, and never say you will never medicate.

4. Together, choose a formula for setting up a habit-formation chart. You will decide either to work on one skill for an entire lesson or choose three skills to work on in one lesson. Agree on what lesson each day would be the most effective for practicing the new skill.

5. Set up a daily discipline program with your child's teacher.

   - Discuss what behaviors should be complimented and how.

   - Build a punishment treasure chest together, choosing "community service" punishments as well as taking away a classroom privilege. Be sure the punishments are immediate, small, and uncomfortable but not painful. Punishments are reminders that we care and know that our child is capable of doing better. A small consistent punishment sends that message.

▫ Remember, the focus of our program is positive reinforcement and skill-building. Punishment should be reserved for classroom rule-breaking and can only be used if compliance with those rules is being reinforced with positive feedback.

6. Share some "set up for success" suggestions with the teacher.

▫ Choose a good location in the classroom for your child to sit.

▫ Discuss what may be standing in the way of your child succeeding. It may be disorganization. If so, set up an organization program together (backpack check to be sure she has the books she needs for homework and has returned the unnecessary books to her cubby; if he socializes on his way to his cubby, keep his books in a box under his desk; school supply check once a week).

▫ Perhaps your child has extra energy. Put a small podium in the classroom, or a figure eight, or both.

▫ Maybe he has social stress. He may need a few conversations with the school guidance counselor or a private therapist. There are so many ways to help a child remove obstacles to success. If the teacher and parent put their heads together many creative solutions will emerge.

7. Go home and photocopy your new chart many times. Place four charts in a notebook so you are ready for the next month.

8. Invite your child for a conversation about his new program.

▫ Always begin with a description of the prizes.

▫ Together choose prizes he will enjoy and write them down, along with how many points he will need to earn each prize.

9. Explain the "transportation points" to your child. Tell her she will get two extra points per day for handing the chart to the teacher and bringing it back home.

10. You may include a "school supply check" point or an organized backpack point to the chart.

11. As soon as the program begins, set yourself a daily reminder to check the chart.

    ◻ Make sure to compliment every success enthusiastically and purely. There is no value in adding a negative comment such as "too bad, you only got four points today." He knows he got four points! Celebrate his partial achievement and it will nourish even more success.

12. After running the program for a month, meet with the teacher to discuss either extending this program or choosing new skills to begin developing. The teacher will continue the positive verbal feedback for last month's skill and begin rewarding the new skill with points.

13. If the teacher can't participate in the program for some reason, choose one of the home-fueled programs, introduce it to your child, and get started.

THE CHEAT SHEET

Chapter Nine: The Bridge Between School and Home Program; Getting the Teacher Involved

- Your child's teacher is the most influential adult in her life besides you. You must become a team.
- The teacher is also generally the first to recommend a diagnosis for ADHD.
- What causes tension between parent and teacher?
    - The parent is not in school so can't see what's happening or help implement a program.
    - The parent feels very defensive when others evaluate her child.
    - The teacher believes the child should be medicated.
    - Our child is making the teacher miserable.
    - The teacher does not have the tools or time to attend to just one kid in the class.
- How can we overcome obstacles and work together as a team?
    1. Respect and listen to the teacher. Be less defensive.
    2. Discuss medication with the teacher. Never say you will never medicate. If you can't agree, agree to disagree.
    3. Take the lead in setting up the program so you don't overwhelm the teacher.
        a. Take only a few minutes of the teacher's time per day.
        b. Take responsibility for creating the program and rewarding your child.

    c. Make sure the program boosts communication between parent and teacher.

    d. Make sure the program helps the child develop missing skills.

☛ **Building the bridge**: This is a three-point plan.

  ▫ **Make a simple chart**

    a. Copy the chart in the book, focusing on one lesson per day.

    b. Either choose three different skills for the class or one skill that is reinforced three times throughout the lesson. This program will run at least a month.

    c. Prepare a notebook with at least three charts in it. The teacher's responsibility is to rate the behaviors at the end of the lesson and sign the chart.

  ▫ **Setting up a daily discipline program**

    a. Make the classroom rules clear and place them on the child's desk. Reword the rules if they are ambiguous.

    b. Before punishing for not following rules, compliment for rule following and good behavior.

    c. Catch a student doing well and leap at it with a compliment or prize ticket.

  ▫ **Setting the student up for success**

    a. Make sure she has all her books and supplies.

    b. Help her organize them.

    c. Get an additional set of textbooks to keep at home.

    d. Reward a child for having all books and supplies.

    e. Have extra school supplies at home.

  f.   Have books stored near his desk.

  g.   Look out for emotional or social stress and get help.

❑ **The punishment**

  a.   Plan A – community service, doing something for the
       classroom.

  b.   Plan B – taking away a classroom privilege for a short
       amount of time. Be consistent, and have parent and
       teacher agree on the punishments in advance.

❑ **Tips for teachers**

  a.   Privilege with responsibility: Allow a student to
       drink/stand/go out/walk on the figure eight as long
       as he has the responsibility for being quiet/coming
       back on time.

  b.   Allow a student to make comic strips or draw the
       lesson instead of taking notes.

  c.   Create an enrichment corner to boost motivation in
       the classroom.

  d.   Do deskercise between classes.

  e.   Stand to ask questions and get moving during the
       day.

☞ What if a teacher can't participate in the program? All is not
  lost. Implement one of these programs: homework buddy,
  learning ahead, or study help.

PART THREE

Check Your Environment

CHAPTER TEN

Your Second Brain: The Thirty-Day Challenge

MANY KIDS ARE struggling. ADHD diagnoses have reached epidemic levels. Our children are objectively doing worse than children just one or two generations ago. They are more allergic, spacey, hyperactive, autoimmune, tired, depressed, anxious, and physically ill than ever before. Why?

Part Three of this book, *Check Your Environment*, will tackle many of the environmental triggers and toxins that are directly causing ADHD symptoms and the plummeting of our children's well-being. We will examine diet, sleep, screens, nature, and how they affect your child and his behavior, health, and ability to learn. These chapters deal with specific challenges that children with ADHD symptoms *may* be facing. This section can be overwhelming! Too many triggers; too much to reconfigure.

We parents can start to feel that the world is a scary, toxic place and believe we need to make life-altering changes just so our children can function. Do not despair; not every aspect of your child's environment must be altered because not every environmental trigger is affecting your child with ADHD symptoms. Part Three is your opportunity to individualize the HyperHealing program to fit the needs of *your* child.

Read Part Three quickly to give you an overall picture of possible environmental triggers. If you hear me describing your child as you read each topic, that chapter and its recommended program are for you, and you should go back and review it more carefully. It will become clear to you what chapters are relevant to your child and what chapters you can omit.

The gut-health connection

The "need to feed" is the most basic desire for any parent. It's probably also the most challenging. The kids are hungry all the time! And we are busy. Don't we want them to eat healthy, nourishing food? Sure, but we also want them fed and happy without having to sprout or ferment something, look up recipes, and use every pot and pan in the house. A friend just sent me a quote that said, "Who knew that the hardest part of being an adult was figuring out what to cook for dinner every night for the rest of your life?" Isn't that the truth!

When it comes to our kids with ADHD symptoms, the challenge is even greater. She's a picky eater; he tantrums when there is no pizza in the freezer. Getting these kids fed the food you always dreamed your kids would eat seems like a distant fantasy. The food negotiations are not worth the effort, you may think. He's going to get what he wants in the end anyway because you won't let him starve, and your "need to feed" suggests that if only he consumes *some* food (read: empty carbs), at least he will be quiet, calm, and allow you to focus on helping with his homework or succeeding at developing good habits.

In this chapter we will take a close look at diet and its connection to behavior. We will examine scientific breakthroughs that make a direct link between people's gut health and their ability to learn, remember, and focus. We will review the symptoms that your child is struggling with, and if you choose to take the thirty-day challenge, you will see that it can alleviate ADHD symptoms in a significant number of struggling children.

Common wisdom on ADHD is that a change in diet will not alter behavior. We have been conditioned to believe that only the crunchy granola, grass-eating, tree-hugging types think behavior has anything to do with the food we eat. Doctors continue to insist that ADHD is a genetic, neurodevelopmental disorder. In other words, we can eat whatever we choose, within reason, because our food does not impact our behavior.

Leading researchers disagree. Cutting-edge research suggests that our gut has everything to do with our brain functioning and therefore needs our attention and care.

Allow me to introduce two sweet children. Perhaps you will identify with parts of their stories. Their symptoms may sound familiar to you. Once we get to know these kids, we will discover all the symptoms related to gut-brain breakdown. We will take a tour through the gut, understand the risk factors, see why kids with ADHD symptoms are more vulnerable, and finally begin our **Thirty-Day Challenge.**

Meet Anton:

Little Anton was a mess. He was in kindergarten, aged five, and the teacher was already hauling his parents in for meetings on a biweekly basis. He was bothering kids, throwing dangerous and large items around the classroom, and totally disregarding classroom rules.

When I observed Anton, a beautiful brunette with large deep brown eyes, he seemed uncomfortable. He pulled at his clothes and scratched his skin. He needed instructions repeated eight times before he responded; he touched everything, and had a whopper of a runny nose. He was very engaged when the teacher told a story, but sitting him down to write was a nightmare. He finally wrote his name down on a school assignment after being chided repeatedly by his teacher. He never completed the assignment.

Anton did not know I was in his classroom to observe him, but he came right over to chat. He asked charming questions and wanted to know everything about me and the computer I was holding. He was clearly an intelligent and engaging child.

The teacher, a talented and patient woman, was urging the parents to begin Ritalin, explaining that Anton was suffering, and he would fall way behind the class and feel terrible about himself if he had to be held back because he was not learning the skills he needed for first grade. The parents were on the verge of hysterics. This was their oldest child, and they were wary about tinkering with his young brain with stimulant drugs but could not offer any alternative solutions.

Now, meet Mika:

A young couple entered my office, looking exhausted and helpless. Their daughter Mika had just begun third grade, and the teacher was demanding an evaluation for their child's out-of-control ADHD. When I had spoken to the mother on the phone, she said she did not detect any offensive behaviors at home, but once I began asking questions during our meeting, she did recall some difficult symptoms. It seems Mika had trouble listening to instructions, even simple ones. She threw wild tantrums over small unmet expectations. Her reading was also not fully fluent.

Here is Mika's bio: She was a miserable baby who cried nonstop for the first few months of her life. As hard as the mother tried to nurse her, she just turned away and refused to eat. Mika had harsh sensory problems as a small child, most of which have since been resolved. She still plays with her food and makes a colossal mess at every meal. She also needs a window open, no matter the temperature outdoors. She had chronic strep throat as a baby and now has strep at least once every winter. She has recurrent bouts of worms. No medication clears her system of the worms. She swings between constipation and diarrhea. She has a phobia of being in small enclosed places, a fear of being alone, and sleeping out for the night. She gets a headache nearly daily after lunch. Mika has a family history of autoimmune conditions such as celiac, eczema/ psoriasis, allergies, and asthma. She gets rashes on her elbows that don't seem to ever go away.

These children are suffering! What is going on with them? We are seeing a mix of behavioral/emotional/physical symptoms.

As we go through this chapter, please do not feel defensive or guilty about the food your children have been eating for so many years. Your doctor probably has had a few hours of nutrition training at best throughout his entire medical school education, leaving the food industry to indoctrinate us for years. The cards are stacked against us as we feed our families the S.A.D. (Standard American Diet) or M.A.D (Modern American Diet) diet. This diet is indeed making us both sad and mad, but we have not accessed the information we have needed up until now.

My journey to improving the health of my family only began with sheer desperation, as I watched one of my children become very ill with no clear understanding as to why he was suffering. After many years, many blood tests and trips to the emergency room, my little boy was finally diagnosed with celiac and is now thriving, thank God. I am grateful for my wake-up call and hope that my experience will save you from the trauma of having to face poor health and a struggling child.

Back to sweet little Anton.

Let's take a fresh look at him. Here are some symptoms that may be connected to his difficulty focusing and completing tasks.

- He has a runny nose.
- He's touching everything.
- His clothes are bothering him.
- Following instructions and completing assignments is hard for him.

Now it's Mika's turn. Mika has:

- Alternating diarrhea and constipation
- Persistent intestinal worms
- Been exposed to antibiotics for much of her childhood
- Sensory processing issues
- Difficulties sitting in class and listening to simple instructions
- Daily headaches
- Anxiety.

These physical symptoms should be included in the complete evaluation of Anton and Mika's health and learning abilities. Both sets of parents may be told by the doctor evaluating ADHD symptoms that their child has ADHD plus a sensory processing disorder. Anton's parents may be told they should visit an ear, nose, and throat doctor or allergist to figure out why his nose is so runny. Mika may also be treated for anxiety with psychiatric medication or an emotional intervention.

Here is what studies have found about children with ADHD symptoms:

1. **Children with ADHD symptoms are more likely to suffer with bowel issues**: According to a study conducted on seventy thousand children diagnosed with ADHD, researcher Dr. Cade Nylund found that these children were significantly more likely to suffer from chronic constipation and fecal incontinence than other children their age. These children also visited the doctor more frequently for complaints of constipation and incontinence. Taking stimulant medication did not alleviate these bowel problems (McKeown et al. 2013).

2. **Children with ADHD symptoms are more likely to suffer from upper respiratory infections, colds, asthma, and allergic rhinitis:** It has been determined that, in China, many children with ADHD also have allergic rhinitis or asthma. These children are more susceptible to the common cold or upper respiratory infections compared with normal healthy children (Zhou et al. 2017).

3. **Attention Deficit Hyperactivity Disorder may be a high inflammation and immune-associated condition.** Participants in a Chinese study of 8,201 people were identified as having ADHD symptoms. In comparison to the normative control group, the participants with ADHD had an increased prevalence of allergic diseases, including asthma, allergic rhinitis, atopic dermatitis, and urticaria. The authors of the study concluded, "Our results supported the association between ADHD and allergic/autoimmune diseases. The

further studies will be required to clarify the underlying mechanisms" (Chen et al. 2013).

4. **Young children with ADHD may be at increased risk of deficits in various sensory processing abilities, over and above the core symptoms of ADHD.** In a study conducted in Israel, the researchers found that young children with ADHD symptoms were rated by parents and kindergarten teachers to have more symptoms of a sensory processing disorder than their normative peers (Yochman et al. 2014).

Why are children with ADHD symptoms struggling with these health issues?

I want to explore an answer to this question with you, which depends on the intimate connection between the gut and the brain. We will see that when the gut is not getting what it needs to thrive, the effects are noticeable throughout the person's body and behavior. Below is a list of symptoms your child may be suffering, which would indicate that her gut is calling out for help. I have included a brief explanation of the gut-brain connection that is causing each symptom, but if you want to understand them fully, see the deeper explanations later in the chapter:

- The child may be **anxious or depressed** because the gut neurotransmitters are not communicating with the brain through the vagus nerve. In addition, harmful bacteria in the gut can alone increase anxiety, according to a study at McMaster University in Ontario by gastroenterologist Premysl Bercik. He also found that good bacteria reduce anxiety (Carpenter 2012).

- The child may develop **learning problems** through leakage of lipopolysaccharides (LPS) into his bloodstream and across the blood-brain barrier. When our gut leaks, the LPS penetrates the blood-brain barrier and creates a vulnerable brain.

- She might struggle with **concentration** because her unhealthy gut produces less dopamine, the neurotransmitter that gets us going by stimulating the reward center and boosting our mood.

- His serotonin production becomes limited, thereby affecting his **sleep quality, memory, and cognition**. This may be why kids with ADHD often struggle with sleep. Sleep problems are not just one of the symptoms of ADHD!

- She may have an imbalance in her gut hormones, the ones that control appetite, leading to **unhealthy weight gain** and binge eating.

- You know that **picky eater** you have? His gut is demanding all those cookies and candies. His bad gut bacteria dictate what kind of food he would like to be fed.

- She may develop **food allergies**. When the gut gets leaky, food particles slip out into the bloodstream. The immune system sees these unharmful foods as an enemy and destroys them. From that time on, the food is marked as a dangerous substance, leading the body to overreact when the food is ingested. Food allergies can be deadly.

- A child's **sensory system** could be destabilized, affecting how comfortable he is in his clothing, when in contact with others, and his tolerance for being in any environment. Children with sensory processing challenges are also picky eaters and may gag on food that is intolerable to them.

- He may suffer from **more infections and illness**. Runny nose and strep and ear infections become common. He can also experience joint pain and acne.

- Children with sensory processing challenges are at **higher risk of developing autoimmunity disorders**. When a substance leaks through the gut lining, the body will identify and destroy it, commit the particle to its memory, and mark it as dangerous. The body sometimes goes one step further. It does something called molecular mimicry, meaning the food substance may have a similar structure to one of the organs in our body. If this is the case, our own immune system will identify this organ as dangerous and begin to attack it. Examples of autoimmune conditions that are on the rise in children are celiac, asthma, and eczema.

- Our gut produces our vitamins. When the gut is not functioning correctly, the child **does not get the vital nutrients** her brain needs to function sharply.

- A child may get **stomach and head pain** and have low energy.

- Finally, children with sensory processing challenges may develop **ADHD symptoms** such as inattention, distractibility, hyperactivity, and social challenges.

We will now go a little deeper to understand the science behind these symptoms and behaviors.

Many years ago, Hippocrates, the father of modern medicine, stated, "All disease begins in the gut." This was way back in the third century BC. Centuries later, the nineteenth-century Russian biologist Elie Mechnikov made a direct link between human health and longevity and a healthy balance of bacteria in the body. He famously said, "Death begins in the gut."

Something was indeed brewing in the gut, but modern medicine did not discover it for many long years. Phillipe Pinel, a psychiatrist who treated mental patients for many years, concluded in 1807: "The primary seat of insanity generally is in the region of the stomach and intestines" (Williams 2010).

Only recently did the gut come back into fashion. We are fortunate to have been born into a generation of explosive discovery relating to the power of the gut. David Perlmutter, MD, a leader in the field of functional neurology, wrote an eye-opening book called *Brain Maker: The Power of Gut Microbes to Heal and Protect Your Brain* (Little, Brown and Company, 2015). Dr. Perlmutter, along with many of his colleagues, has contributed to our understanding of the gut and its vital role in keeping us healthy and sane. This is a book well worth owning.

Dr. Perlmutter shares a list of environmental risk factors that, if present, indicate a person's gut needs repair immediately. As you read through the list, mark off what insults to your gut you may have suffered throughout your life.

- Mother taking antibiotics or steroids or acetaminophen while pregnant.[2]

- Child born by C-section

- Child not breastfed for at least one month

- Child suffering from frequent ear infections or strep

- Child needing ear tubes

- Tonsils removed

- Child treated with steroid medication even for one week

- Child prescribed antibiotics once every two or three years

- Child prescribed acid-blocking drugs for reflux or digestion issues

- Gluten sensitivity

- Food allergies

- Sensitive to chemicals found in everyday products

- Child diagnosed with an autoimmune condition

- Type 2 diabetes

- Being more than twenty pounds overweight

- IBS (irritable bowel syndrome)

---

2   "We found that using acetaminophen for 29 days or more during pregnancy gave a 220 percent increase in risk for ADHD in the child," Eivind Ystrom, a researcher at the Norwegian Institute of Public Health and the lead author of the study, told CNN. "This was after taking medical conditions and risk for ADHD in the family into account" (Tousignant 2017).

- Diarrhea or loose stools at least once a month

- Depression

- Sensory integration disorder.

- Constipation (having a bowel movement less than twice a day)

> It's now undeniable that our intestinal organisms (the roughly one hundred trillion bacterial creatures in us and on our skin) participate in a wide variety of physiologic actions, including immune system functioning, detoxification, inflammation, neurotransmitter and vitamin production, nutrient absorption, signaling being hungry or full, and utilizing carbohydrates as fats. All of these processes factor mightily into whether or not we experience allergies, asthma, ADHD, cancer, diabetes, or dementia. (Perlmutter 2015, 9).

If we can understand how a healthy gut functions, we will immediately understand the devastating impact of a sick gut. Let's get to know the gut a little better.

The gut is a closed system connecting our mouth and anus in one long, sealed tube. The surface is uneven, has many ridges and villi (fingerlike projections), and is nine meters in length. It has a surface area equivalent to two tennis courts, allowing for maximum absorption of food.

We understand why the gut is important in digestion and vitamin production. We get that the gut can be out of sorts and cause a tummy ache, gas, or reflux. But what does all of this have to do with brain function?

Michael D. Gershon, MD, famously called the gut our "second brain." How does the organ that is responsible for the "dirty work" of the body get such an elevated status?

The special status of the gut comes from its inhabitants. Large numbers of gut bacteria cling to the gut wall or float free. To put the numbers of gut bacteria inside of us in perspective, we have ten trillion human cells, and ten times that number of bacterial cells, which are significantly smaller than human cells. In total, the bacteria weigh between two and three kilograms (roughly six pounds).

The bacteria keep us healthy, and we reward them by feeding them the food they love most.

Our gut bug friends:

- Provide us with our daily energy
- Support detoxification in our body
- Keep chronic inflammation at bay. The source of all disease is chronic inflammation.
- Help protect our blood-brain barrier, keeping our brain safe from invaders
- Are responsible for healthy sensory functioning
- Direct our thoughts and feelings by producing the neurotransmitters used in our brain
- Communicate directly with the brain. The gut and brain work together to promote our physical and mental health.

Looking at this impressive list, we can see what Hippocrates meant when he said that the gut is fully responsible for keeping us healthy.

How is a healthy gut created and maintained?

The first few years of life are critical to developing an optimal bacterial ecosystem in the gut, which is one that is inhabited by many diverse and healthy bacteria. The environment a child grows up in will determine the make-up of her gut bacteria. Here are the guidelines for nurturing a healthy gut:

- **Mom transmits bacteria to her child through the placenta during pregnancy and in the birth canal during labor and delivery.** Mom transmits some microbes to her unborn child through the placenta. But the motherload (pun intended) is gifted to her child at birth. When our little ones are born by vaginal birth, Mom's birth canal bacteria immediately begin populating the baby's gut. What a great gift we give our children even before we meet them! When a baby is born by

C-section (a procedure which is sometimes unavoidable and can save the lives of both mother and child), the baby's first bacterial exposure is to the skin of the doctor, hospital staff, and parent.

- **The environment the child is born into contributes to the colonization of the gut.** Premature birth affects the healthy colonization of gut bacteria. When a child is born early, he cannot fully benefit from the bacterial exposure during pregnancy. Home birth versus hospital birth will impact the population of the gut because each environment has different bacteria. If a child requires intensive care shortly after birth, once again, she will be exposed to hospital bacteria, medication, and stress. Adrenaline in the gut is produced in response to stress, which affects the balance and viability of the bacteria. Surgery is a stressful experience that can also alter the gut population.

- **Antibiotic use alters gut balance.** Avoiding antibiotic use (which is not always possible) keeps our gut well balanced and strong. Unfortunately, western countries medicate with antibiotics far too frequently. Children who have a lot of ear infections and take antibiotics to treat the infections have been shown to have a higher risk of developing ADHD symptoms (Brody 2011). To add insult to injury, the meat we eat is loaded with antibiotics, excreted antibiotics get into our groundwater, and antibiotics in the form of pesticides and herbicides (i.e., RoundUp) are used in agriculture.

Food coloring, food additives, and preservatives wreak havoc on our gut bacteria. Antibiotics significantly reduce the diversity and health of our gut bacteria. Chlorine in municipal water also reduces the diversity in our gut.

> ... a link between antibiotic exposure and altered brain function is well evidenced by the psychiatric side-effects of antibiotics, which range from anxiety and panic to major depression, psychosis

and delirium. A recent large population study reported that treatment with a single antibiotic course was associated with an increased risk for depression and anxiety, rising with multiple exposures (Rogers et al. 2016).

- **The way a child eats after birth continues to dictate how his gut will be colonized.** Breastfed babies develop a much healthier microbiome than bottle-fed babies. Breast milk is loaded with prebiotics, the food our microbial friends eat, and the baby continues to receive his mother's bacteria from her milk and skin. Dr. Laura J. Stevens of Perdue University found that children who were breastfed were less likely to develop ADHD (Burgess et al. 2000).

- **Exposure to animals and nature matters to your gut.** Do you have a pet? Do you go to the petting zoo, out on hikes, or spend significant time in nature? We often think pets are great for kids because pets calm our children and teach them responsibility. What we didn't realize until recently was that we get so much more than that from our four-legged friends. It turns out that animal and nature exposure are key ingredients in vibrant gut health. We breathe in the microbes in the air, drink down microbes in natural water sources, and gain exposure to various healthy bacteria through our skin when we are out in nature. More nature and animal exposure directly leads to a more diverse and healthier microbiome. City dwellers have a less varied microbiome than the folks who live in the suburbs and on farms (Tun and Konya 2017).

- **The sterility of our environment reduces "food" for our gut.** Doctors Erica and Justin Sonnenberg explain that there is an incompatibility between our human DNA and that of our microbiome because our DNA has remained the same throughout the generations, but due to our poor western diet, our gut microbiome has changed. We no longer eat the foods that fuel our bacteria and are not exposed to healthy bacteria in our environment (dirt). **We are "starving our microbiome self"** (Sonnenberg and Sonnenberg 2014).

- **Diversifying our diet promotes a healthy, varied gut.** The more different types and colors of fresh vegetables and fruit in their original form we eat, meaning a whole food diet, the healthier our gut will be (Heiman and Greenway 2016).

- **What we eat affects the population of our gut.** The food choices we make also affect our gut bacteria's diversity. A plant-based diet, rich in colorful organic fruits, vegetables, and fibers, high-quality protein and complex (non-glutinous) carbohydrates guarantees a varied robust microbiome. Eating naturally ripened foods in season promotes diversity of our diet.

  Highly processed foods, sugars, simple carbohydrates, preservatives, and food coloring reduce the good bacteria in our gut and promote colonization of bad bacteria, thereby causing inflammation and illness. This bad bacteria makes us fat. When rural Africans who eat a mainly plant-based diet and have a very diverse microbiome migrate to western countries, their gut bugs are the first to suffer. Very soon after the relocation, diversity is replaced by a gut microbe monoculture (Davis 2016).

- **Stress affects our microbiome.** People who are exposed to more stress, abuse, or trauma have a less diverse microbiome (Karl et al. 2018).

- Consistency and frequency of bowel movements affect our overall health. Our body eliminates toxins through bowel movements. If a person has less than two bowel movements a day, the toxins his body is attempting to eliminate reduce health.

How many of us in the western world reach the age of three with a well-nurtured gut?

Almost none of us. If we did have a well-populated sealed gut, we could expect to have flawless communication between our gut and brain. But instead ADHD is on the rise, as are autism, autoimmunity disorders, and other psychiatric conditions in children.

> American children are not genetically different to any significant degree from children of other nations where ADHD is rarely seen. No one is asking the obvious billion-dollar question: why are children in Western cultures having such an issue [sic] as attention deficit, learning disabilities and impulsivity control problems? Obviously, what's going on here is something environmental (Perlmutter 2015, 90).

There are three major ways in which our gut can be injured. All injuries are environmentally caused, and all can be reversed.

1. **Gut dysbiosis:** The gut can have a very narrow gut bacterial population, or bad bacteria can overpopulate.

2. **Leaky gut:** The gut lining can begin to leak.

3. **Gut microbes can be starved because we are not providing them with the food they need to thrive.**

How do these problems develop?

Dr. Zach Bush explains that leaky gut is due to the opening of tight junctions in the gut lining (Vermette 2018). Tight junctions are like Velcro and are responsible for keeping things in and out of the gut. Dr. Bush explains that the loosening of these junctions has happened over time, as a result of factory farming and changes in the American diet since World War II. Firstly, the use of excess jet fuel in synthetic fertilizer destroyed the bacteria in the soil, the same bacteria that enriches the human microbiome. When the bacteria in the soil died out, we lost some vital nutrients we once got from our food. As an example, tomatoes used to have lycopene, which is a powerful cancer-fighting nutrient. Now tomatoes have nearly none of this nutrient.

In addition, our processed diet consists mainly of soy and corn.

These two products are loaded into our meats, bread, baked goods, etc. Also, animals eat corn and become processing plants for this exceptionally low-nutrient-dense vegetable. This has dramatically reduced the diversity of our microbiome. The less variety we eat, the fewer bugs we need to process our food. As a result, our gut becomes populated with a narrow selection of bacteria, mainly the kind that digests processed food and simple carbohydrates (think white pasta and processed cheese).

The next hit to our health came in the 1970s. Our gut had already become less diverse, and now the tight junctions in the gut lining came under attack from glyphosate, which was introduced to the farming market as a herbicide. It was considered a first-rate herbicide because it could be sprayed on plants and only kill weeds, leaving the plant intact. For this reason, it was a best seller because we finally had a herbicide that would not hurt the plant and that seemed safe for human beings. But while glyphosate was indeed killing the weeds, it was also causing the destruction of our gut microbes.

Researchers have suggested that glyphosate can cause dysbiosis, which is an imbalance between beneficial and pathogenic microorganisms. While it wipes out beneficial bacteria, the overgrowth of harmful bacteria generates high levels of noxious metabolites in the brain, which can contribute to the development of neurological deviations. Dr. Perlmutter explains that good gut bacteria are responsible for producing important brain chemicals like GABA and BDNF (brain-derived neurotrophic factor). The level of these essential brain chemicals is directly linked to the health of our brain. If we want to maintain a healthy brain, our gut must be treated well (Rueda-Ruzafa et al. 2019, 51).

Gluten was the next hit to our gut. I feel the eyeballs rolling already. We are all quite cynical about gluten these days because it seems that everyone is "sensitive" to it. How can an entire generation be intolerant to gluten when our grandparents ate gluten happily with no apparent adverse effects? Although I would agree that the gluten-sensitivity scare is overstated, we must focus on the population that seems to have a clear gut injury.

Dr. Alessio Fasano, MD, conducted research at Harvard University and published a paper showing that gluten in wheat causes permeability of the intestines of every human being. "Increased intestinal permeability after gliadin [gluten] exposure occurs in all individuals" (Holon et al. 2015). Does this mean that most people should stop eating gluten? Absolutely not. Our gut lining can heal quickly, and in many cases, despite momentary permeability and inflammation, the person will not suffer long-term negative effects from gluten.

There is no need for gluten-free hysteria for most of the population. When people go gluten-free but replace their bread with the gluten-free processed alternatives available now in every supermarket, they have done their gut no favors. As a matter of fact, the highly processed non-food gluten-free alternatives may be causing more harm to our health than gluten itself.

The intestinal wall is our gatekeeper. We know from Dr. Fasano that gluten permeates this lining. Zonulin is a protein that regulates the tight junctions of the small intestine. When zonulin is released in the intestines, the tight junctions open slightly and allow larger particles to pass through the intestinal wall. Gluten activates zonulin, leading to a cascade of gut leakage and a brain deprived of essential nutrients and vital neurotransmitters and the many difficult symptoms we have been discussing.

Unfortunately, the gut bacteria that would have protected our body from zonulin leakage have already been destroyed thanks to factory farming, explains Dr. Bush. He adds that the breakdown of the intestinal wall will also cause sensory problems, followed by ADHD symptoms. If the gut does not recover from the gluten/zonulin insult, depression and anxiety will soon follow as inflammation rises (Fasano 2012).

Why do children exposed to the same inflammatory environments develop different symptoms?

Dr. Tom O'Bryan, in his informative book *The Autoimmune Fix*, explains why some people are hurt by gluten and others seem to be just fine:

> Epigenetics teaches us that while genes influence our health, they are not our destiny. Studies of twins

give us a great example for how this works. If you were to take identical twins and keep them in the same environment, they would continue to look identical as they got older. But if you change the environments, including feeding them different foods and experiencing different stressors and different lifestyles, the twins will actually look different and their health will be different. These differences are caused by whether or not a certain genetic expression was activated, dependent on those external factors (Rodale, 2016, 42).

Our genes are fully loaded when we are born. The decisions we make for ourselves and our children in terms of diet and lifestyle will determine if certain genes will be activated or not. The factors discussed above (how and where a person was born, antibiotics, exposure to nature or animals, levels of stress, etc.) will either keep genes dormant or allow them to be expressed. Once disease is already present, we can reduce the damaging symptoms with better diet and lifestyle choices. Dr. O'Bryan reminds us that it is excessive chronic inflammation that is causing our child to feel out of sorts.

Now we may better understand why there is a modern epidemic of childhood disorders. Just one or two generations ago, our environment was cleaner, life was a little slower and less stressful, children played outdoors and with animals, elective C-sections were not popular, and we had a more diverse home-cooked diet, consisting mainly of fresh produce and whole foods. Much has changed, and our sweet children are paying the price. Today Dr. Bush estimates that about eighteen million Americans are sensitive to gluten. Our genes have not changed, but our environment sure has.

The difficult symptoms caused by gut dysbiosis can be reversed. Are you ready for the Thirty-Day Challenge to reverse the harm done to the gut and potentially eliminate ADHD symptoms?

Why thirty days?

Because it's a sure way of getting a sense if your child's symptoms are coming from his gut or not. Obviously if it took a few years to develop a health problem, it will take some time to repair the damage. But thirty days will indicate if we are moving in the right direction or not. We must find out if eliminating the inflammatory foods and adding healing foods will begin a restorative process in your child.

You have to be strong here!

All too often, parents will agree to jump on board for one month, but despite the obvious positive results they see right before their eyes, they then choose to discontinue the diet. Why? Because this diet requires some hard work, and sometimes we simply don't have the bandwidth to carry on. One example comes to mind.

I was meeting with the parents of a beautiful blond boy, aged eleven. The kid was fantastic! He was constantly pulling wild ideas out of thin air. He also had dyslexia and a nonstop runny nose. He literally bounced off the walls. The parents agreed to take their son off gluten for a short trial. Within a week, his nose stopped running completely. The boy was loving his snot-free face. After two weeks, he seemed calmer. Three weeks later, his nose was running again. "What's going on?" I asked. His sad response was that the holidays happened. His parents could not maintain the diet, and he was back to his original discomfort.

Another parent called at the end of the Thirty-Day Challenge to report that the entire family had gone off gluten for the month with great results all around. She, the mother, could finally focus for long enough to sit and read a book for more than half an hour. She had already finished a few good books. Her husband was much less constipated, and the kindergarten teacher was reporting that their daughter was less aggressive. She wanted to know when she could start reintroducing gluten because it was hard to maintain the diet when visiting grandparents and going out to eat.

I know how hard lifestyle change can be. I've done it and am still at it. It can take over our lives until we get it straight. It's a huge project. Which is why, if you discover that this will make all the difference to your child, you must be **strong!** Our child depends on us. Our chances of success are higher if we do it together as a family or with a friend or relative, so we can support each other.

What happens at the end of the month?

Simply put, if there were improvements, you need to keep at it.

1. Step one: Evaluating symptoms before and after the Thirty-Day Challenge

Before we get into the plan, please take some time to write a list of gut-related symptoms you or your child are struggling with. Make a separate chart for each family member participating in the challenge. Describe all the symptoms in detail.

The following is an example of what the chart should look like:

Gut-related symptom	Before Thirty-Day Challenge Date: _____	At the end of the challenge Date: _____
Constipation	Twice weekly	
Headaches	Every afternoon	
Concentration problem	Can concentrate for 10 min.	
Acne	(Take a picture)	

Ready to roll?

Great!

We are going to focus on three treatment areas, and in each we will discuss what we are eliminating and adding. The three categories are:

1. Resealing the gut lining to stop the leaking (what we will be removing from the diet)

2. Creating a diverse and healthy ecosystem in our gut (what brain-nourishing foods we will add)

3. Feeding our helper bugs the food they thrive on (adding extra support)

We will remove anything that causes inflammation (processed food, gluten, dairy, toxic animal products) and flood our child's body with nutrients to get his gut and brain functioning optimally.

2. Step two: Restructuring your diet
What must we eliminate? A printable version of both charts is available on my website, www.hyperhealing.org. Hang it on your refrigerator.

Food group you are eliminating	Forbidden	Permitted
Gluten	• All foods containing wheat, rye, spelt, barley, kamut • Look for a gluten-free (GF) label on any packaged food • Check spices, dressings, mayonnaise, soup mixes, and other products that may contain traces of gluten • Note: If the allergy warning states, "may contain gluten," it is usually produced in a plant that also makes glutinous foods and is permitted for gluten-sensitive kids but not for children with celiac	• White and brown rice, gluten-free oats, quinoa, buckwheat, millet, rice or corn pasta, potatoes, sweet potatoes • Flour that can be used for baking: potato, corn (non-GMO), rice, tapioca, almond, garbanzo bean, chickpea, lentil, soy • Beans and lentils • Although gluten-free products are usually very unhealthy, limited amounts of GF bread, rice cakes, cereal, and snacks are permitted for the transition period

Food group you are eliminating	Forbidden	Permitted
Dairy (and in more severe cases of autoimmunity or poor health, eliminate all animal products including meat, fish, poultry, and eggs)	• We want to remove as much dairy as possible. No drinking glasses of milk or using it on cereal.	• Choose milk substitutes like coconut milk, almond, or other nut milk • Use limited amounts of soy milk and soy products
Sugar and artificial sweeteners	• Eliminate added sugar in cake, cookies, candy, and other sweets • Children can have limited "treats" once or twice a week. Dark chocolate or GF baked goods are good options	• Honey, maple syrup, and date honey are permitted.
Food coloring, GMO products, processed "food" made in a factory instead of in a field	• Avoid as much as possible • These products offer no nutritional value and cause inflammation	• Natural food colorings are permitted

These are the major food groups you will be eliminating. It feels like a lot, and it is, especially when your child is a picky eater. To make this realistic for families with children on less than ideal diets, I try not to be too strict. Taking this program step by step for a few weeks before beginning the challenge is recommended, especially for kids who live on processed food. In our family, we started by removing dairy and adding coconut or nut-based replacements. Once the kids were used to that, we went gluten-free, making sure there were good home-baked options for the brave kids who were giving up their bread.

We must go 100 percent gluten-free. This part of the diet is not flexible. The good news for parents of kids with a limited tolerance for anything but carbs is that at the beginning of this dramatic shift, GF pretzels, bread, pancakes, cake mix, etc. will be allowed if you can't find anything else your child will eat. Please limit these items as they are loaded with sugar, simple carbohydrates, and preservatives. Try to provide home-prepared alternatives using nourishing GF flours. Some examples of these flours include almond, buckwheat, brown rice, oat, chickpea, tigernut, and coconut. Tapioca flour has little nutritional value but is useful as a binder or thickener. Chickpea, almond, and tigernut are great flours for sweet baked goods. The others work for savory dishes.

Dairy should be very limited. Kids should not be drinking whole glasses of milk. There are many substitutes today. Go with nut or coconut milk. Since plain yogurt and aged cheese have healthy probiotics in them, they are permitted in moderation on the dairy-free diet.

There is a raging debate about the health benefits of animal products. Some doctors, including Dr. Brooke Goldner (look her up on YouTube), recommend a plant-based, mainly raw, vegan diet, loaded with vegetables, greens, fruit, legumes, and healthy grains. Her research indicates that animal products cause substantial inflammation and should be avoided. Parents whose children have already been diagnosed with any autoimmune condition (celiac, psoriasis, asthma, etc.) should consider following Dr. Goldner's raw, vegan diet to reduce or even eliminate symptoms. Other doctors, specifically in the functional medicine world, recommend eating animal products in moderation. All agree that a healthy diet should be primarily plant-based and that processed and factory-raised meat should be avoided at all costs. If you would like to include animal products in your diet, be sure the food is pasture-raised and hormone- and antibiotic-free.

Completely eliminating sugar is the way to go, but it may be too challenging for your child socially and emotionally. He goes to birthday parties; she hangs out with friends. You may have a total rebellion on your hands if you try to eliminate sugar completely. The first two weeks of complete sugar elimination are difficult because your gut bugs will be tantrumming and demanding their sugar. Once you wean those nasty bugs, you will start to feel great. Try it! Be a role model and remove sugar from your diet first. Allow kids some 70 percent chocolate; make home-baked almond muffins with maple syrup; give them dried fruit or other less offensive GF snacks. If you do take the brave step of completely eliminating sugar, begin the process two weeks **before** the Thirty-Day Challenge. The first two weeks of sugar elimination are very difficult; you may feel sick, tired or very agitated. After two weeks, you will feel better than ever and be ready to begin the Thirty-Day challenge with energy you didn't know you possessed.

Another idea is to restrict sugar consumption to the second half of the day. As we know, sugar is very addictive. The minute we taste some in the morning, we are searching for more all day long. If we only permit ourselves to eat something sugary later in the day, we will naturally and gradually reduce our intake. If we go too extreme, we will lose our audience.

The following are the foods and supplements we will be adding during the Thirty-Day Challenge in order to promote gut healing and a diverse microbiome. I will be recommending supplements that I have studied and which I, my family, and many clients use. I have no financial relationship with any of these companies.

3. Step three: Adding gut health-promoting nutrients and activities to your diet
Add these foods and activities to your diet and lifestyle:

Probiotics and exposure to healthy bacteria in nature	• Yogurt, aged cheese
	• Sauerkraut (very easily made at home)
	• Kimchi (see if you can buy it locally)
	• Naturally fermented pickles
	• Pickled ginger or garlic or any vegetable, as long as it is not pasteurized
	• Kombucha
	• Coconut or dairy kefir
	• Hanging out with animals and hiking or walking in nature. Take your shoes off for best results (instructions from Dr. Bush)
	• Probiotic supplement (**Garden of Life** has a high-quality probiotic supplement. It is recommended to diversify probiotic supplements to expand your variety of gut bacteria.) The probiotics on the market today cannot provide us with the twenty thousand or so species of microbes, but the monoculture they build is a healthier one than we have now. Do not rely on probiotic supplements; be sure to eat probiotic foods whenever possible.

Healthy fats	• Enjoy all nuts and seeds
	• Plentiful olive oil, avocado oil, coconut oil, cold-pressed nut oil
	• Dried coconut
	• Avocado
	• Fat does not make us fat, and healthy fat is vital for gut and brain health
	• Avoid highly processed oil and fats including corn, soy, and canola oil, as well as margarine and lard
Fruits, vegetables, legumes, and GF carbohydrates	• Different-colored fruits, vegetables and leafy greens
	• Cruciferous vegetables are packed with healing nutrients (broccoli, cauliflower, cabbage . . .); eat them raw with an avocado or hummus dip
	• Have a fruit smoothie for breakfast or a snack. Fresh is best; frozen is fine.
	• Organic or locally grown produce
	• Avoid non-organic soy and corn
	• Beans, lentils, rice, quinoa, millet, buckwheat, and GF oats

Animal protein, eggs, and fish	<ul><li>Organic eggs (The pesticides in the chicken feed and possible hormones or antibiotics injected into the chicken are then highly concentrated in the egg)</li><li>Protein from chicken, lamb, duck, turkey, and other meats can be part of a healthy diet</li><li>No processed meat!</li><li>Avoid grain-fed meat, preferring pasture-fed</li><li>Organically fed chicken and meat</li><li>Wild-caught fish</li><li>Fish that is low in mercury</li></ul>
Gut-calming and nourishing foods and supplements	<ul><li>Omega-3 fatty acids</li><li>Vitamin D3</li><li>Magnesium</li><li>Take a high-quality multi-vitamin to replenish vitamins that are deficient in our food or not being produced by our gut microbes. **Hardy Nutritionals** makes a multivitamin that has been tested and proven to boost brain clarity and reduce anxiety and depression. I highly recommend it for the entire family. (See below for more information on the benefits of these supplements.)</li></ul>
Drink eight or more water daily!	<ul><li>Avoid soda, fruit juice, and other sweet drinks</li><li>Coffee and tea, especially green tea, are permitted</li><li>Don't drink any caffeine after noon to avoid interference with high-quality sleep. This rule applies to everyone, not just to those sensitive to the effects of caffeine.</li></ul>

These are all the gut-healing foods we should be enjoying. What about our helper bugs? Shouldn't we be feeding them as well?

4. Step four: Adding foods to our diet specifically to nourish our healthy gut bacteria
Prebiotics are the rich compost in the soil of our gut. They are the seeds that grow new vibrant microbes.

> Prebiotics are made up of nondigestible carbohydrates [fiber] that are used by bacteria in the colon to produce measurable health benefits. Naturally found in food, a prebiotic is not broken down or absorbed by the gastrointestinal tract. Beneficial bacteria use this fiber as a food source in a process called fermentation (Jockers).

The following is a list of prebiotic foods that taste great and are a gift to our healthy bacteria.
This list was provided by Dr. Jockers:

- Onions
- Leeks
- Radishes
- Carrots
- Coconut meat and flour
- Flax and chia seeds
- Tomatoes
- Bananas
- Garlic
- Chicory root
- Dandelion greens
- Jerusalem artichoke
- Jicama
- Asparagus
- Yams

I have added several supplements to this program, and I would like to discuss each one.

1. **Magnesium**: In a perfectly delightful book called *The Magnesium Miracle* (Ballantine Books, 2003), Dr. Carolyn Dean tells us that we shed a lot of magnesium, a trace mineral, daily. Magnesium should be found naturally in many foods, but it is depleted through sugar consumption, sweat, and stress. She also explains that magnesium is a vital element in the release and uptake of serotonin. Low levels of serotonin equal lower-quality sleep, memory, and emotional stability. In addition, children and adults who suffer from constipation (less than two bowel movements a day) get instant relief when they supplement with magnesium.

   If you detect sleep problems in your child, anxiety or depression, constipation or brain fog, magnesium is your best friend. Dr. Leo Galland, author of *Superimmunity for Kids* (Random House, 1989), recommends six milligrams per pound of weight per day, meaning two hundred and forty milligrams for a child who weighs forty pounds. He suggests a child take one tablespoon of magnesium citrate daily or one and a half teaspoons of milk of magnesia a day. It is preferable for a child to swallow a tablet, but the liquid works too.

   Magnesium can cause diarrhea in some children. If that's the case, split the dose in two. I highly recommend a magnesium supplement for moms and dads as well. We are major magnesium poppers in my house. If a child (or her parent) is not eliminating bowel movements twice daily, increase magnesium intake until elimination becomes consistent. This step alone can dramatically improve mood, behavior, and focus.

2. **Probiotics**: We do not consume enough probiotic foods per day. We are also not exposed to all the good bacteria from nature nearly enough. We have lost the art of preserving

food through fermentation. It is preferable to diversify and strengthen our gut bug helpers through food and natural exposure, but we must deal with what we have. In the words of Dr. Mark Hyman, best-selling author and leading functional medicine pioneer, "Think of your gut as an inner garden; just as with any garden—when you let the weeds take over, you get into trouble."

When we eat a processed diet, we consume pesticides and medications that ravage the good gut bacteria. Once the helpful bacteria are gone, the weeds—aggressive unhealthy bacteria—take over. Along with other gut-healing nutrients, a low-glycemic, whole-foods diet filled with healthy proteins, fats, fiber, and probiotics can improve the health of your gut significantly. Why?

> Because probiotics help to populate your gut with good bacteria, I recommend taking very high-potency probiotics (look for at least 25 to 50 billion live CFUs from a variety of strains). Start slowly and observe how the probiotics affect your gut. When you first start taking probiotics, you might notice some uncomfortable symptoms like gas and bloating, but if the symptoms persist for more than a few days, you may need to delay probiotics until your gut is more intact (Hyman).

Look online for Dr. Hyman's favorite brands. I recommend Garden of Life, developed by Dr. Perlmutter. My family and clients have used it with positive results.

3. **Vitamin D3:** In a study published online in 2018, vitamin D was shown to reduce the permeability of the intestinal lining in animal models. Interestingly, some probiotics increase serum vitamin D levels. In a multicenter study, oral supplementation with *lactobacillus reuteri*, a probiotic, increased serum 25(OH)D concentration (Tabatabaeizadeh, SA et al. 2018).

In an additional study headed by Bruce Vallance, PhD, investigator at the BC Children's Hospital Research Institute, University of British Columbia, researchers found:

> Vitamin D deficiency has been shown to promote an inflammatory environment which leads to dysbiosis of the gut microbiota, even in clinically healthy individuals. Oral vitamin D supplementation is known to be beneficial for individuals who suffer from chronic inflammatory diseases ... UVB exposure boosted the richness and evenness of their microbiome ... (Bosman et al. 2018).

In other words, exposure to direct sunlight for a limited time each day, or supplementation with vitamin D3 will strengthen your gut lining and enhance your gut microbiome. We are all deficient in vitamin D.

Between 50–80 ng/mL is considered an optimal level of vitamin D. Levels of vitamin D should be monitored. The following is the recommendation of the American College for Advancement in Medicine:

a. Healthy children under the age of 1 year – 1,000 IU.

b. Healthy children over the age of 1 year – 1,000 IU per every 25 pounds of body weight

c. Healthy adults and adolescents – at least 5,000 IU

d. Pregnant and lactating mothers – at least 6,000 IU.

Additionally, children and adults with chronic health conditions such as autism, multiple sclerosis, cancer, heart disease, or obesity may need as much as double these amounts. All of these amounts are per day that a person is not exposed to direct sunlight.

4. **High-quality micronutrient multivitamin**: While there are other quality micronutrient supplements on the market, I

discovered Hardy Nutritionals through a study I read a few years ago. The study tested the efficacy of micronutrients as a treatment for depression, anxiety, and ADHD symptoms. The study was a ten-week randomized double-blind placebo-controlled study led by research professor Julia Rucklidge of the University of Canterbury between 2014–2017. The original study concluded that preliminary findings indicated a trend in the improvements of ADHD symptoms of inattention, hyperactivity, ODD, and DMDD following treatment. A follow-up study was conducted recently, showing that children who chose to stay on the micronutrient regiment continued to improve. Those who want to supplement with micronutrients can rely on these vitamins to supply adequate magnesium, B vitamins, and vitamin D.

5. **Omega-3**: Omega-3 is a fatty acid that is essential to our diets and is not produced by our body. We must consume omega-3 in order to guarantee proper brain development and function.

In a recent study, the researchers found that children with ADHD have reduced omega-3 levels. They concluded that dietary supplementation appears to create modest improvements in symptoms. There is sufficient evidence to consider omega-3 fatty acids as a possible supplement to established therapies (Hawkey and Nigg 2014).

Amy Myers, MD, in her best-selling book *The Autoimmune Solution* (Harper One, 2015), tells us that omega-3 fish oil helps to decrease inflammation in addition to supporting brain function. This is precisely the support our gut needs on its way to healing. She recommends supplementing with one thousand to four thousand milligrams of omega-3 daily. This is an adult dose. Consult with your doctor for an appropriate children's dose.

Other excellent sources of omega-3 are chia seeds, flax seeds, and walnuts. Those who choose a vegan, plant-based diet would benefit greatly from these natural sources of omega-3. The seeds oxidize quickly, so Dr. Goldner recommends grinding a handful of seeds in a coffee grinder immediately before eating them. They can be added to a smoothie, made into a pudding or put in salad. Do not heat them. These seeds and walnuts are powerful anti-inflammatory supplements and can be added liberally to a healthy diet.

The Thirty-Day Challenge

The Preparation Stage

1. Discuss what you have learned in this chapter with your family and make sure everyone is on board.

2. Invite a friend or relative to join. It's easier and more fun to do the challenge with a supportive group of friends.

3. Get blood tests. Ask your doctor for a comprehensive blood test. Pay attention to vitamin D, the entire B group, and iron. Only 1 percent of magnesium is found in blood serum, so I recommend supplementing with magnesium no matter what the blood test reports if you detect symptoms of magnesium deficiency such as constipation or sleep problems.

4. Go to the grocery store and get to know the gluten-free and dairy-free products. Buy different flour alternatives and start to play with your existing recipes or look online for pancake, bread, and baked good recipes. Have your child bake with you. Do not buy sugar-free anything! The sugar substitutes used are very damaging to your gut. There are better sugar substitutes mentioned above. Once you see what is out there with a fresh new perspective, the Thirty-Day Challenge will seem less intimidating.

5. Take your child along to look for healthy snacks. Apple sauce, dried fruit, nuts and seeds are fantastic options. Trader Joe's is a great supermarket to visit. Check out <u>thrivemarket.com</u> to order affordable gluten-free and organic foods and products at competitive prices. They deliver directly to your home. Start trying new vegetables and creative salads. Eat as many raw vegetables as possible. Let the kids do the chopping. Make refreshing smoothies and add leafy greens to them. Our goal is to get the whole family to fill up on vitamins and minerals harvested directly from the ground and trees. These are the very foods our brains and bodies crave.

6. Get rid of the food you will not be eating for the next thirty days. Rid your pantry of all the junk!

7. Make a chart of all the neurological and gut symptoms your child is experiencing and describe them in detail (example above).

8. Join gluten-free groups on Facebook and look online for healthy meal options for a gluten-free plant-based diet. You are in luck! Gluten-free is all the rage, so you will be inundated with as much information as you need. There are online cookbooks and endless resources.

9. Start to stock food in your fridge that can easily stay fresh for a week, so you are not sweating over the stove constantly. Examples include a pot of quinoa, rice, or roasted vegetables. Chicken and salmon also can be refrigerated for a few days. Gluten-free soup is a great quick meal and can be made in large portions and frozen or reheated throughout the week. Make sure you have enough produce.

10. Don't skimp on healthy snacks. Feeling hungry on this challenge is not permitted! Remember, fruit is fast food, so place a bowl of fruit on the table. It *will* be eaten. I am always amazed that when I slice carrots and peppers and just place them near my children as they play a card game, the vegetables

get vacuumed up, even by the kids who theoretically don't like vegetables. A platter of melon is a great way to be greeted after school. Many supermarkets offer presliced vegetables and fruit and pre-mashed avocado. These are instant, effort-free snacks.

11. Focus on nutrient-dense whole foods, foods that can still be identified as their original form. As food is processed it loses its nutritional value. We want to flood ourselves and our children with abundant natural foods (fruit, vegetables, beans and lentils, organic eggs, pasture-raised meats and healthy grains). If a food is so processed that it can only be identified by the ingredient list on the package, it has no nutritional value and is harmful to our health.

Now, choose a date to begin. Do not launch your Thirty-Day Challenge until you have enough food in the house and a solid menu plan. Many families fail because they feel hungry and don't have an easily available snack.

You are now ready to begin your journey to complete physical health, mental clarity, and emotional well-being.

—————————————— **Action Plan** ——————————————

1. Review the chapter.

2. Take a week to prepare, with the instructions for the preparation stage, and then begin your epic Thirty-Day Challenge. If you feel your family needs more time to prepare, as mine did, make small changes every week for a few weeks (cutting out the processed stuff and adding new vegetables), and begin the Thirty-Day Challenge after those preparatory weeks.

3. When you complete the challenge at the end of thirty days, take out your symptoms chart and fill it out again. If you have seen improvements, keep at it.

4. If there have been no improvements, either continue the challenge for one more month to confirm that the symptoms your child is struggling with are not gut-related, or you can begin to reintroduce each food slowly. Take one week to reintroduce gluten and notice how you feel. The next week introduce small amounts of dairy, and once again observe how it affects your mood, energy, and ability to focus. You may decide to reintroduce all the whole foods you have eliminated if they do not cause you harm. Consider keeping processed foods, GMOs, and excess sugar out of your diet. Try to maintain a whole food diet, eating mainly foods that are rich in nutrients and have no chemicals added.

THE CHEAT SHEET

Chapter Ten: The Thirty-Day Challenge, Getting Your Brain and Gut Healthy

- ☛ The most basic need a parent has is to feed the family.

- ☛ When evaluating a child, we must look at behavioral, emotional, and physical symptoms.

- ☛ ADHD symptoms that indicate that the gut needs care include: runny nose, sensory issues, diarrhea or constipation, headaches, recurrent intestinal worms, bouts of strep or ear infections treated with antibiotics, anxiety, depression, food allergies, low energy, learning problems, sleep issues, and unhealthy weight gain.

- ☛ "All disease begins in the gut" – Hippocrates

- ☛ What triggers gut problems? Antibiotics, birth by C-section, not being breastfed, frequent infections, tonsils removed, steroid medication, acid blockers for reflux, gluten.

- ☛ How is health linked to the gut? Our gut bacteria are responsible for giving us energy, detoxifying our bodies, keeping inflammation at bay, keeping our brain barrier sealed, maintaining healthy sensory functioning, and producing neurotransmitters.

- ☛ How can we keep our gut healthy? Vaginal birth, breastfeeding, full-term birth, avoidance of antibiotics when possible, exposure to animals and nature, less sterile environment, eating a plant-based, very varied whole food diet, and calming down and relaxing.

- ☛ All insults to the gut that lead to health problems are environmentally triggered and can be reversed. When we change our diet, we can recreate our gut and brain health.

☛ Let's begin to heal our gut:

1. Foods we will eliminate: Gluten (wheat, rye, spelt, barley, kamut), dairy, sugar, artificial colors and flavors and preservatives, "food" born in a factory, GMOs, processed oils.

2. Foods we will eat:

   ◻ Grains: Rice, GF oats, buckwheat, millet, GF pasta, potatoes, sweet potatoes

   ◻ Milk substitutes: Nut milk, coconut milk, soy milk

   ◻ Sweeteners: Natural honey, maple syrup, fruit, dry fruit

   ◻ Fruit, vegetables, legumes, greens, broccoli, cauliflower and cabbage

   ◻ Animal products: Some choose to eliminate them altogether. Others eat eggs, meat, fish, and poultry in moderation.

   ◻ Healthy fats: Olive oil, cold-pressed nut oils, coconut oil, avocado, nuts, and seeds.

3. What we will add to boost health: Probiotics and more time with animals and in nature, omega-3 fatty acids, vitamin D3, magnesium, multi-vitamins

4. Drink a lot of water!

5. Eat prebiotic foods that feed our gut bacteria: Onions, leeks, radishes, carrots, coconuts, flax, chia seeds, tomatoes, bananas, garlic.

☛ Prepare for the Thirty-Day Challenge by eliminating all the foods you will not be eating for the month.

   ◻ Look up recipes

   ◻ Join Facebook groups for healthy gluten-free eating

- ◻ Get familiar with the foods you will be buying in the supermarket

- ◻ Let your kids help you choose healthy snacks

- ◻ Introduce milk substitutes slowly

- ◻ Be sure to explain the program to your kids, and don't just dump a total dietary change on them all at once.

☛ When the Thirty-Day Challenge is over, take out your symptoms sheet and evaluate if your child has made progress on his health concerns. If he has made significant progress, keep at it. If he has made a little progress, consider extending another thirty days, always keeping an eye on the symptoms. If there was no progress, check if you have truly flooded your child with vegetables and fruit and other nutrients and eliminated all inflammatory foods. If you have followed the Thirty-Day Challenge exactly with no progress, slowly begin reintroducing the foods that were eliminated. All children would benefit from less sugar and processed food, so consider not reintroducing them.

CHAPTER ELEVEN

Screens: The Creation of a Modern-Day Epidemic

LET'S TALK ABOUT how smart we are.

For many years the IQ scores of developed western countries had been climbing steadily. As a matter of fact, James Flynn, an intelligence researcher, noticed that over the previous century, IQ scores had steadily risen by three percentage points per decade. He named this phenomenon the Flynn Effect. Western society was getting smarter! As the scores began to plateau in the 1980s and '90s, the general assumption was that industrialized countries had hit their maximum scores, attributed to environmental improvements over the years, and that we were now as smart as people could be.

And then bad news rolled in like the London fog.

In 2007, researchers at Kings College, University of London, discovered that the trend was beginning to reverse itself. Western society was getting dumber. We were scoring significantly lower on math and science than we had in 1975. This was confirmed by researchers from the Ranger Frisch Center of Economic Research in Norway. They analyzed seven hundred and thirty thousand IQ tests and saw that the trend had steadily declined from the 1970s. The decline was universal, meaning both high and low scorers did more poorly, but boys' scores dropped more severely than that of girls (Smith 2018).

Kids in 2007 were performing at an academic level that was three years below their 1970s' counterparts. "A defining trend in human intelligence tests that saw people steadily obtaining higher IQ scores through the 20th century has abruptly ended, a new study shows," reported *Science Alert* (Dockrill 2018).

Lest we blame this trend on less intelligent people having bigger families (especially since I have six kids) or the West being inundated by less-educated immigrants, *Science Alert* continues,

> Researchers observed IQ drops occurring within actual families, between brothers and sons—meaning the effect likely isn't due to shifting demographic factors as some have suggested, such as the dysgenic accumulation of disadvantageous genes across areas of society.

If we were just getting dumber while our health, creativity, and gainful employment remained the same, we could happily continue life as our less-intelligent selves, probably never noticing the difference. Unfortunately, childhood IQ scores are directly linked to physical health outcomes at age fifty, according to a 2015 study. Help! We're losing our minds and getting sicker (Wraw et al. 2015).

Are we producing kids with lower cognitive ability today compared to past generations? The consensus within the scientific community is that environmental factors are pushing IQ down, just as they had nudged IQ up for many years.

What are the environmental factors contributing to the falling IQ in developed countries?

The following suggestions are based on a 2015 article in the *Telegraph* (Sturgis 2015), which offers some insight into the sagging IQ phenomenon:

- **The modern western diet slows us down:** A study by University of Montreal researcher Stephanie Fulton found that eating large quantities of **saturated fat** can have a significant effect on brain function, damaging the neural circuits that govern motivation and even leading to addiction. Saturated fats hamper the brain's dopamine function, a vital neurotransmitter responsible for motivation.

- **The brain is not wired to multitask**: "When people think they're multitasking, they are actually just switching from one task to another very rapidly, and every time they do, there's a cognitive cost," says Earl Miller, a neuroscientist at Massachusetts Institute of Technology. "Multitasking prevents deep, creative thought as we switch back and forth, backtracking, constantly starting from scratch each time. As a result, thoughts are less new and more superficial."

  Juggling too many tasks at once (working on your laptop, answering an email, jumping to a video conference while listening to the dings of text and WhatsApp messages coming in and checking the trending tweets) chronically floods our brain with cortisol and adrenaline, two stress hormones, which put our brains into fight-or-flight mode all the time (meaning that we feel we are constantly running from a tiger).

- **Google has replaced our memory**: Research by Columbia University showed that we are now more likely to recall where we save information, rather than the information itself. If we never have to rely on our memory, our brain and ability to focus suffer.. Our attention span is plummeting.

- **We are eating too much sugar**: Dr. Sarah Brewer, a medical nutritionist, warns of the damage sweet foods can do to your gray matter: "Brain cells need glucose to function, but too much in a short time will cause a sugar rush and make you feel over-wired."

- **Reality TV binge-watching replaces intellectual thought**: An Austrian study by psychologist Markus Appel showed eighty-one participants a fake reality-like screenplay based around what a football hooligan got up to during a day, then asked them to take a general knowledge test. Those who had seen the reality show beforehand fared worse than those who had not. What we see and hear influences our behavior. These shows are dumbing us down.

- **Sleep disturbances are slowing down our brains:** Studies on hamsters found that regular disruption to our internal circadian rhythm halves the normal rate of new neuron birth in the hippocampus (the area of the brain dealing with memory processing), and the effects last for many weeks.

- **Lack of exercise diminishes brain power and growth:** Dr. David Perlmutter tells us that BDNF (brain-derived neurotrophic factor), a brain-growth hormone, is amplified when we exercise. Aerobic exercise does the trick in just twenty minutes per day. It creates more brain cells in the brain memory center (hippocampus) and signals molecules to connect to each other, creating brain plasticity. We repopulate our memory center when we exercise. Those who do not do aerobic exercise (or sit around all day and don't move) have shrinkage of the brain. We have the power to grow and strengthen our brain (Perlmutter 2015).

Our brains are not doing as well as they used to. We are expected to multitask while being distracted by screens and getting much less sleep. The food we eat and the content of the shows we watch are making us dumber and slower. Many kids are not flourishing. New environmental factors have been introduced into our children's lives that we have never seen before, and they are causing our kids to struggle.

In this chapter we will focus on the dangerous effect screens are having on our children. We will understand the risks and dangers of screen addiction and learn to manage screens in a safe and productive way, so that our children can retake control of their minds and emotions. We will begin with a discussion of the devastating effects of screen addiction on children and their parents. We will examine the science behind screen exposure and our child's brain. We will understand the effects on our child of our own screen addictions and distractibility. We will see that screen addiction causes both ADHD symptoms and sleep disorders. Finally, we will make a plan to cure you and your child of your addictions.

As with all the chapters in Part Three of this book, not every child is affected by every environmental trigger. Not every child exposed to screens will become addicted. Read this chapter to determine if your child is being harmed by screens and whether they could be contributing to her ADHD symptoms.

If screens, movement, and sleep patterns are powerful enough to affect IQ across a whole generation, think of the impact they are having on our brains. The good news, though, is that since all these factors are environmentally induced, they are also reversible. In this book we have tackled diet thus far. Our children are already heading towards better brain and body health, but we still have work to do.

Is your child suffering from electronic screen syndrome (ESS), or as I like to call it, pre/post-screen personality disorder (PSPD)?

As a mom, I look back in shock when I think about how unprepared we were to parent this generation of children. We got caught by surprise, with no idea what was about to hit us when our kids were born. Could we ever have imagined how our children would be bombarded and tested by screens? Our life experience gave us no skills to guide our kids. How could we figure out how much and what kind of screen time was healthy for our kids when science was huffing and puffing, just trying to keep up with the trends?

Studies take years to conduct, and technology was being developed in a blink of an eye. Because of this, scientists could not tell us if the emissions from towers or phones could hurt us. The pace of technological development left scientists, parents, teachers, and medical professionals in the dust. Industry is leading the way, never a comforting feeling. So now we find ourselves with a generation of kids raised on Google, gaming, and YouTube. The results are worrying and demand intervention.

The following scene repeats itself in every home across the western world daily:

"Mom, can I watch a movie? Mom, Mom, are you listening? I want to play a game on the computer!"

"No, honey, today we are not watching movies or playing on the computer. It's a school night. You have homework to do, and I want you in bed on time."

"But Mom! You prooooomised! Yesterday you said you would give

us more time if we behaved well. See, we're behaving so well. Mom, you promised; you just don't remember."

"Not today, sorry. Let's get started on homework."

"How about if I do my homework really fast and jump right in the shower. Can we watch just one movie then?"

"No, it's a school night, and we are not watching a movie!"

"Okay, so I'm not doing my homework, and you can forget about me taking a shower! I'll shower when you let me watch a movie. I hate this house; there's nothing fun to do here! It's the worst house in the world! Everyone gets to have fun, but we NEVER do!"

"Stop throwing your toys; they will break! Did you hear me? I said calm down. Don't touch your sister; she is not in charge of the screens in this house. You will hurt her. Fine, if you get everything done quickly, you can watch a short movie."

What was that? It sounded like a hostage negotiation. Mom just caved to terrorist demands. Can we blame her? The little terrorist was not backing down; he had hijacked the evening.

You just witnessed the dangerous first stage of PSPD. It's a real disorder; I just gave it a name. This child is addicted to screens, desperate to get his fix. The hysteria completely altered his generally sweet personality. He took his mother hostage while in a disordered state, and she gave in to his demand. If we replaced "movie" with "heroin" and added a bit more violence, we would be describing a full-blown drug addiction. The symptoms of both are very similar. Although we would never let our children near hard drugs, we tend to nurture PSPD and then suffer the consequences.

What are the symptoms of Pre-Screen Personality Disorder?

1. **Anxiety**: A child comes home from school knowing he may have time on a screen at some point in the afternoon. He shows clear signs of **anxiety**, not knowing exactly when he will get his fix. This may include whining, crying, bothering a sibling, or generally stressed behavior.

2. **Addiction**: Symptoms set in. She starts crying, begging, and being willing to do anything it takes to get to her screen. Perhaps she will beg for chores, but most often our little

addict is willing to steal, lie, or cheat to get the parent to turn on the computer. She may tell her parents she has no homework; she already studied, etc. Alternatively, the house may get suspiciously quiet because she snuck into the den and turned the computer on all by herself. The child is willing to suffer the consequences of being caught. There also may be a silent exit from the house to a neighbor who always has a screen running.

3. **Aggression** is the natural next step, directed either at siblings or a parent, or both. It often includes foul language or violence, triggering a round of warnings and threats of punishment (including threatening to reduce screen time).

All of this is followed by a tense but magnificent calm as the exhausted parent finally gives in and turns on the computer for the very undeserving child. The parent may be lulled into the illusion that all is well in the world again, and her child will be happy and grateful after the allotted screen time . . . only to be crushed by the realization that there's no such thing as enough screen time!

The nightmare continues.

What immediately follows after turning off the computer is PSPD (post screen personality disorder). Here are some of the symptoms:

1. **Selective hearing**: Dad says, "Okay, time's up! Time to turn off the computer." Dead silence. No matter how many times that sentence is repeated, the child will ignore it and continue to squeeze out as much screen time as possible.

2. **Hysteria:** The child begins begging and pleading for more, promising to be a perfect child after just this one more game, or begins to be rude and angry.

3. Bursts of **anger** and **aggression** can carry on for the rest of the evening without fear of consequence. The aggression can include "You don't care about me" or "You never give me what I want" or the dagger, "My friend's parents let them watch whatever they want for as long as they want."

4. **Withdrawal** symptoms, such as being willing to sneak back to the screen, grab a smartphone when no one is looking, hide a tablet under the bed, or overall sad, depressed, and obnoxious behavior.

5. **Trouble falling asleep** due to the blue light from the screen disrupting melatonin production.

6. **Boredom** sets in. Nothing interests your child. He is so overstimulated that anything that does not mimic the fast-paced excitement of the screen is intolerable. This can include time with friends, listening to music, reading, playing a board game, etc.

Our Instant Gratification kid is most susceptible to the quick fix offered by screen time. Her PSPD may begin to affect her ability to focus, cause temper tantrums, and even aggression, which are then often misdiagnosed as symptoms of ADHD, OCD (obsessive-compulsive disorder), or ODD (oppositional defiant disorder).

Does this sound like a full-blown addiction to you? Indeed, PSPD mimics cocaine addiction in the brain. This is serious business. Will the DSM committee accept my contribution of a new disorder to their bible? I doubt it, because there is no pill for this ill. If our child is struggling with PSPD, we have hard work ahead of us, although not nearly as hard as nurturing and managing our miserable child and her addiction.

How does screen addiction affect healthy, normative people and their ability to function?

Elaine was an elegant, well-dressed mother of two young children. She had been diagnosed with adult ADHD when I first met her. Despite her polished outward appearance, Elaine was a mess. She didn't sleep well, often forgot to eat and had become too thin, was not attending to basic hygiene, and her husband was forced to shoulder all the responsibility of both children while holding down a job.

Elaine was a full-time mom and was therefore not contributing financially to the home. She had always been a poor student, preferring spending time with friends, sleeping, or reading a book to studying. There were few consequences to her poor behavior, so she had never learned responsibility at home or school. Now that she was a mother, life had become intolerable. She did not enjoy spending time with her kids or tending to her home. As a matter of fact, she could find very few activities that brought her joy. She felt bored all the time.

We worked hard together, Elaine and I. We made charts, created shopping lists and designated shopping days, evenings out with her husband or friends, an exercise routine, all to no avail. Elaine's functioning slipped so low that her psychiatrist added a second diagnosis, bipolar disorder. She was prescribed new medication, which she forgot to take, of course. She was temperamental and dismissive of her husband and kids, and downright unhappy.

Finally, we figured it out! At one meeting, her husband reported that Elaine often played video games through the night. She needed her screen time and would throw a fit if she didn't get it. She was willing to stay up all night and sleep through the day, as long as she got her fix. No price was too high.

We changed the diagnosis and devised a new plan. Elaine would begin a screen fast; she would remove every screen in her house for three weeks and promise not to seek out screens in other places.

The weaning period was a painful process. Elaine seemed to be suffering from physical drug withdrawal. She was only able to stick with the screen fast because the screens were not accessible. About three weeks into the program, a new woman emerged, calm and ready to engage her family. She still had very few caretaking skills, which she had not developed because of her addiction. But she was now ready to learn.

Addiction in children

A harried mother came to consult with me. She had her hands full with four children, all of whom seemed to whine all day long. Their fighting with one another had become intolerable. She spent her days breaking up fights between the children, shouting at them to stop any variety of bad things they were doing, and sticking them in front of a computer screen just to get some peace and quiet. The kids watched movies while they ate so that they wouldn't fight; the more volatile kids got to earn computer game time for acting in a vaguely civilized way. Mom wanted to know why her life was so crazy and if other families were as miserable as hers.

I reassured her that there were many miserable families and then asked her if she was up for a challenge. She told me that she hardly had the strength to shower at night, but she was willing to hear me out. We reviewed how difficult life was right now. I asked her if she believed she could turn it around. She wasn't sure. I asked her if she would be willing to make life much harder for just a few weeks so she could finally get some peace of mind by resetting her children in the right direction.

"Why would you do that to me?" she said with tears in her eyes.

I promised that I would be right there by her side and that she could blame the new program on me, but I also reiterated that the only way to reverse the difficult behavior would be by completely eliminating all screens for a month.

"Impossible!" she declared.

After much haggling we came to an understanding that she could yell at me as often as required for making her life a living hell, and I would forgive her. She marched into her house with resolve and gathered the laptops, tablets, and phones. The kids had a collective heart attack. There was not a quiet moment in that home. Day after day, the children punished their mother with aggressive behavior.

Mom begged me to let her stop. "Just a few more days. You can do this," I said. And she did! When they finally caught on that this was the new law in their home, the kids discovered friends and the outdoors and the books they used to love. And then there was calm.

How did I know to identify PSPD and treat it? All the credit goes to Victoria L. Dunckley, MD, who has probed this difficult new addiction in childhood. Her book, *Reset Your Child's Brain* (New World Library, 2015), presents definitive research about screens and the brain and guides us through a detox program. I highly recommend this book. You will refer to it often. I will present highlights of her research and program here.

Dr. Dunckley calls this disorder **electronic screen syndrome (ESS)**. She explains that there are different types of screen exposure.

1. **Interactive screen time**, which includes any screen activity where the person actively engages the screen. This includes playing a game, using a touchscreen, keyboard, sensor, or watching a movie on a handheld device such as a laptop, tablet, or smartphone.

2. **Passive screen time,** which includes watching a movie or episode on a television or computer without interacting with the technology in any way.

We often think that interactive screen time is less harmful, or even in some cases, beneficial or educational. We assume that if the child is active and his brain is working, he must be gaining some positive brain stimulation during the activity. We have been led to believe that passive TV watching is very harmful, but an active game gets the brain going.

Dr. Dunckley disagrees. According to the scientific evaluation, interactive screen time is much more damaging to the brain, behavior, emotions, and health of your child. Let's break this down:

What happens to the brain during interactive screen time?

*   Playing a video game mimics the body's **fight or flight response** to danger. When we interact with a screen, we move into **hyperarousal** or survival mode. This shuts down our higher-level cognition and ignites our primitive responses. The flight or fight response is healthy and helpful when we are in danger, but a feeling of constant hyperarousal, danger, or chronic stress leads to inflammation and directly reduces brain function. Back in the caveman days, when a person was being chased by a tiger, responding to hyperarousal by running away or fighting would eventually subdue the nervous system (if you didn't become the tiger's lunch) and bring a person back to calm and higher-level thinking. When playing a video game, we are in a similar state of arousal, but

with nowhere to run and therefore no ability to work off the stress.

- **Dopamine** (the feel-good hormone that we have already met) levels spike. Our child feels great about playing his game, earning points, and winning. But the exaggerated high level of dopamine cannot be mimicked in normal daily activity. This leads a child to seek higher and higher levels of stimulation from gaming of any kind and leaves her bored with normal daily activities.

- **The bright light of the screen** indicates that it is daytime, not bedtime. The circadian rhythm is disrupted (the natural rhythm of day and night). Since the body does not know if it is day or night, it does not produce adequate **melatonin,** and the child is set up for a poor and nonrestorative night of sleep.

- As a child's body moves into fight or flight mode, **blood flows away from his gut, kidneys, liver, and bladder,** and towards his heart and limbs. The thinking brain suffers from lack of blood flow, as does its partner, the gut. The primitive brain is now in charge, which is evident to any parent dealing with a child who just had her screen shut down.

- The child is now so pumped up, **he is fully ready for the fight, which will never arrive.** When the game is interrupted, only his primitive brain is working, so he becomes an irrational animal, ready for the attack.

- Even after the screen is shut off**, stress hormones remain high, making it hard for her to focus**. Eye contact becomes overstimulating and unbearable. Sleep gets interrupted with anxiety; he is full of cortisol even the next day. This leaves a child exhausted, sad, and craving carbohydrates and sweet snacks.

How similar are the symptoms we are seeing in screen-addicted children with the DSM symptoms for ADHD?

Here are the symptoms:

- Chronically stressed

- Sleep-deprived

- Irritable

- Mood swings (often mistaken for bipolar disorder)

- Tantrums

- Low frustration tolerance

- Poor self-regulation

- Disorganization

- Immaturity

- Poor eye contact

- Learning difficulties

- Poor short-term memory

- Parents and teachers describe the child as stressed out or revved up, wired or out of it

- Oversensitive. People feel they must walk on eggshells around the child.

- Sensory issues and poor coordination.

That's a lot of symptoms! Is your kid spending a significant amount of time on screens and exhibiting these crushing behaviors?

How much screen time is too much screen time?

- Just half an hour of interactive screen time was shown in a large study to disrupt natural sleep patterns. *The European Journal of Radiology* reports that interactive screen time actually causes brain damage (Weng et al. 2013).

- Any video games, not just violent or inappropriate ones, cause dysregulation, which is an inability to regulate and control emotional and physiological responses.

- Even reading from an e-reader (such as a Kindle) requires more cognitive effort than reading from a conventional book, thereby slowing down reading, reducing comprehension, and requiring harder work to process the information.

- Fast-paced cartoons are also cognitively fatiguing and damaging to the young viewer.

How can we know if interactive screen time is causing these symptoms?

The only way to know is by trial and error, removing the screens and seeing if the behaviors subside and only reappear when screens are reintroduced. We can also make an educated guess based on how our kids behave before and after they get their daily "dose" as described in the scenario above.

My kids were exhibiting some serious ESS until I was enlightened by Dr. Dunckley and ran her program in my home. We are all grateful, calmer, happier, and much more interesting people today. We have broken free of the interactive screen prison! And yes, when summer vacation arrives, and I get a little lazy and allow the kids to watch more movies together, we have to reset again before the school year begins.

Screens are part of our reality. Once we know that the screens are assaulting our kids and the kids are turning around and inadvertently assaulting us, we will understand that we must rescue our children. We would never leave them vulnerable to predators in the outside world. We should not tolerate those dangers inside the protective walls of our home.

There are three entry points through which interactive screen time causes toxicity to our child, says Dr. Dunckley.

Our **eyes** are particularly vulnerable: Screens emit unnaturally bright light, resetting our natural biological clock. Screens also alter normal eye muscle movement, which affects visual development, balance, cognition, and mood regulation. The unnatural visual stimulation, screen brightness, quick movement, and supersaturated colors, affect sensory and attention process. As screens get bigger and better, the arousal response will get more intense. Think about when your child interrupts you while you are sending a text. How much attention will that child get from you?

Finally, the LED light emitted from the screen has been implicated in retinal damage in animal studies. Excessive screen time may be narrowing retinal blood vessels, which is a marker for cardiovascular disease. Repeated exposure to screen time leads to an overactive visual system; the child will focus on everything in his surroundings, making it hard for him to concentrate on just one thing (like his schoolbook or the teacher).

The next hit is to our child's vulnerable **brain**. The brain has an orientation response, which is meant to react to visual input. This quick response to stimuli helped protect early humans who were hunting and gathering. This mechanism helps determine if we are in danger so we can decide how to best respond to stimuli. Computer screens artificially create stimuli, thereby overhauling our ability to assess danger and respond appropriately. Our brain is on heightened alert from the interactive game or movie on a tablet, but the sense of danger is not followed by a reset, which is the calm we feel after running or fighting.

When the brain is stressed, the blood flows away from higher-thinking areas and towards the more primitive areas so we can escape. When the prefrontal cortex, the higher-thinking frontal lobe, is deprived of blood flow, planning, thinking things through, attention, organizing, and impulse control are then suppressed. This can develop into a long-term problem. Once screen exposure is discontinued, the frontal lobe can begin to flourish again.

Dopamine is released, turning all of us into immediate-gratification seekers always looking for another surge of dopamine, which equals pleasure. Even the sound of an incoming WhatsApp or text gets dopamine activated and forces us to reach for the phone to get our reward. When the game is over and dopamine decreases, the brain experiences sensory deprivation, causing irritable behavior.

Finally, our child's **body** is assaulted. When we interact with the screen, blood flows away from the gut and reproductive organs and towards the limbs and heart (to release the energy to either fight or flee). Heart rate and blood pressure go up; cortisol is released. Some people suffer headaches or mild screen-associated tics. Sitting for too long, which most screen activities demand, is also harmful to our health. Screen time is associated with metabolic syndrome (high blood pressure and cholesterol, midsection weight gain, and precursors to diabetes, heart disease, and stroke). This syndrome was rarely seen in childhood until recently. Chronic stress and poor sleep are thought to be the precursors to metabolic syndrome. Both are caused by interactive screen time.

The fight or flight mechanism: How screens are creating anxious kids

We must understand this fight or flight mechanism better because it sits at the crux of the cascade of harm caused to our child.

Hyperarousal begins as soon as a person begins playing a video game. The physiologically engaging content or activity ups the arousal. Meaning, the more physically active the child is, the more his brain becomes flooded with cortisol, and he becomes more anxious. The competition, especially if the child is competing with others online, intensifies the stress-induced arousal. The possibility of earning points, progressing to the next level in the game, or improving one's score further intensifies hyperarousal.

Violent, sexual, interesting, vivid colors, and challenging and strange images all increase the fight or flight response. Have you met a game that does not include most of these stress-inducing, hyperarousal factors? Probably not, because those games are less addictive and therefore not profitable.

Media multitasking (when a child plays a video game while texting and using Twitter at the same time) adds to the cognitive demand and raises stress levels, sensory overload, mood swings, and lack of satisfaction from a job well done.

Poor sense of time and time management are affected by stress. When we are under high stress, we lose our concept of time. If you ask a child how long he has been watching something or playing a game, he will have no idea because his concept of time has evaporated. He is not just trying to make excuses for being on his screen two hours longer than you permitted; he honestly cannot sense the time passing. Being late, not calculating travel time or how long a task actually takes, missing appointments, etc., are all symptoms of high stress. Children who grow up in continually stressful circumstances tend to have a distorted concept of time, as do gamers and active screen users.

Fight or flight mode is a defensive stance that impedes social interactions. Anyone who approaches when a child is in high-stress mode will be considered a threat. Children in a state of hyperarousal often feel wronged and tend to cheat because they are willing to do anything to survive.

Socializing can be a stressful activity, especially for kids who are less socially graceful. Before the screen-saturation generation, children were forced to interact with others. The engine that propelled kids with social challenges to keep trying was their desire to fit in. Now socially anxious children can hide behind their games, which exacerbate their anxiety and make them retreat even deeper into screens. They also have their "fitting in" needs falsely met with online connections. They are never forced to confront their social anxiety and overcome it.

The violence of video games reduces empathy. If a child lacks empathy, he cannot relate to, or doesn't care about the situations that others are going through. He can't feel the other person's pain or joy. High stress and lack of face-to-face time exacerbate social and intimate bonding challenges.

Kids who are in heightened fight or flight mode often develop a fear of the dark, separation anxiety, and panic attacks. The panic attack is an alternative response to the cortisol rush. A person will either fight, flee, or freeze when he perceives danger. A panic attack is a freeze response.

Did our children already have ADHD, or are screens causing the symptoms?

As we have seen, children with ESS have all the symptoms of ADHD. Did these children already have ADHD symptoms that led them to poor screen choices? Studies would suggest that the screens are causing the symptoms rather than the other way around. Researchers have found that screen exposure in early life exacerbates the symptoms we have listed above. A large study in Singapore showed that gaming caused focus and concentration problems in children who had no history or genetic propensity to inattention (Jiayong et al. 2019).

In a study published in JAMA, researchers from California studied twenty-five hundred high school students and their digital media habits. The students did not have ADHD symptoms at the beginning of the study. The students were asked to report how often they engaged in fourteen different modes of digital activity per day. During the two years the study ran, researchers checked in with students frequently. They found that only 4.6 percent of teens who reported low-frequency use of digital media had ADHD at the conclusion of the study. The number climbed to 9.5 percent for teens who reported high use of seven digital activities. Of students who reported high use in all modes of digital activity, 10.5 percent had developed ADHD symptoms. The researchers found that high use of digital media increased the risk of developing ADHD by 10 percent (McCarthy 2018).

Parents addicted to their screens: How our screen addiction is pouring more fuel on the fire

The drawing I saw hanging in my child's kindergarten classroom haunts me. The teacher had asked her young students to draw a picture of their families. One piece of artwork stood out. Mother and children were holding hands and smiling while a very shrunken father was standing in the corner, holding his enormous phone. The father had diverted his attention away from his son, and the son responded by placing him in his rightful place within the family portrait.

Here's the problem. We parents have become terrible role models. Aren't most of us addicted to our phones? Once again, we had no idea that speaking on our phone, checking the mail, or texting would cause our children harm. How could we have known that our kids would get whinier, more demanding of attention, more depressed, or more accident-prone when we interact with technology? The rampant use of technology is one huge experiment being conducted on humanity, and we are the lab rats. Studies on technology use and parent-child bonding are displaying worrying trends. All statistics and studies below are cited in Brandon McDaniel's 2019 paper "Parent Distraction with Phones, Reasons for Use, and Impacts on Parenting and Child Outcomes: A Review of the Emerging Research" (Human Behaviour and Emerging Technologies):

- Research has shown that 73 percent of parents engage in phone use during time spent with their children in a restaurant (Radesky et al. 2014).

- Thirty-five percent of caregivers spend one out of every five minutes (or more) on their phone while at the park with their child (Hiniker et al. 2015).

- Sixty-five percent of mothers report technology intruding upon parent-child interactions during playtime with their young child (McDaniel and Coyne 2016b).

- There is concern that the increase in child injuries may be due to parent smartphone use (Palsson 2014).

- Thirty-six percent of American parents say they spend too much time on their phone (Jiang 2018).

- In parent-report data, an association has been found between greater parent difficulties with managing their phone use while with their children and worse overall parenting quality—i.e., greater parenting laxness and over-reactivity (McDaniel et al. 2018).

- Adolescents corroborate these findings, perceiving their parents to be less warm with them as a result of parental distraction with phones (Stockdale et al. 2018).

- Parents perceive technology interruptions happening in their interactions with their romantic partners, with their children, and in their parenting and coparenting interactions (McDaniel and Coyne 2016a; 2016b).

Parents who are busy on their devices have lower awareness and sensitivity to their children, fewer verbal and nonverbal interactions, and are less coordinated parents and coparents. Parents also have difficulty multitasking, meaning difficulty switching between paying attention to their device and being responsive to their child (Radesky et al. 2016). Multitasking causes us to make more errors and respond impatiently and without understanding to our children.

The kids absorb parental distraction and act out with negative and demanding behaviors. This often becomes a vicious cycle. As parents disengage, children fight for their right to be noticed in very childish ways. Parents, stressed and overwhelmed, react by escaping to their devices.

Granted, we parents have many pressures, both from work and socially, to be online and available all the time. We have limited mental and emotional energy, and we are now dividing it between old elementary school friends we reconnected with recently through Facebook, the adorable pictures coming in on the family WhatsApp, and carpool and work assignments that are no longer restricted to office hours. We are exhausted from all the screen time, so we retreat for some "relaxing" screen time, a good movie, or an educational TED talk. What remains, just that tiny little sliver of distracted energy, goes to our kid, who is less fun to hang out with because he is so demanding.

What happens to kids when their parents are distracted by devices?

Early childhood parent-child bonding is critical to children's development in many areas. They learn how to form relationships, how to treat others, and how they should expect to be treated based on these early childhood interactions with a primary caretaker. If this early bond is interrupted by a distracted parent, the child has reduced skills in forming relationships for the rest of her life (Sroufe 2005). Parents can't be attentive to child cues, be sensitive to child needs and communication, notice inappropriate interactions or social engagement, and respond appropriately when distracted themselves. Because of this distracted distance, the child forms a more insecure attachment with her primary caregiver.

Our teens are letting us know how they feel about our addiction and poor leadership. Fifty percent of US teens report that their parents are somewhat distracted by phones (Jiang 2018,) and 28 percent of our children feel we are addicted to our phones (Rideout and Robb 2018).

Overall, they are disappointed in our leadership, and wish we would be a good example of responsible phone use. We may notice that they are trying to get us to put the phone down. Parents notice a direct link between their heavy screen use and their child's behavior. On days that they are busier with their phone, kids act out more (McDaniel and Radesky 2017).

Infants can't tell us how they feel like our teens can, so we must guess based on their behavior. In a study examining child responses when a parent was in a noninteractive passive stance, if a parent engaged her phone, infants displayed increased negative affect, decreased positive affect, and increased bids for the parent's attention (Myruski et al. 2018). Children also don't learn well when we are distracted by our phones. One study demonstrated that when parents were tasked with teaching their kids new vocabulary words, if the learning time was disrupted with phone use, the child did not learn the words. Only parents who put their phones away were able to successfully transmit the information (Reed et al. 2017).

We mentioned above that kids with ESS tend to have sensory problems. It seems that we parents exacerbate these difficult issues by being distracted by our devices. Kids need many hours of unstructured physical play daily to activate and develop proper sensory integration, says Dr. Dunckley. They also need secure attachment with a parent or caregiver, positive physical touch, environmental stimulation, restorative sleep, conversation with adults, interaction with nature, physical movement, music, and dance. When a parent is on his screen, there is less touch, less eye contact, and more neglect. The more we bond with our children, the less they will turn to addictive activities and substances. When children are on screens, they are inside, not moving, not using most of their senses, and their eyes are being strained.

The entire family needs a major overhaul.

The brain of the child under the influence of screen time is struggling. Can we reverse the trend?

- We must reduce stress, because a brain cannot function under chronic stress.

- Our child's brain needs rest and healthy sleep to function properly.

- Our child needs us fully present and engaged. His brain needs nurturing through parent-child interaction and a warm, supportive relationship.

- A child needs to be touched, hugged, have eye contact, and be understood.

- Our child's brain needs natural stimulation through interaction with nature (green time).

- The body is not just the vehicle that carries our brain around; body and brain work together. The brain can only be healthy when the body is moving, getting exercise, and not sitting for lengthy periods of time.

Here's the plan: The Four Week Reset Program

Presenting Dr. Dunckley's four-week Reset Plan. (You can do it together with the Thirty-Day Challenge for best results ☺). Refer to her book *Reset Your Child's Brain* for more in-depth details of the Reset program.

Week One: Preparation

1. Make a list of the symptoms you are seeing in your child (and yourself) that you hope to address with the screen fast. List the symptoms and their severity as we did in the Thirty-Day Challenge. Track the severity of the symptoms throughout the Reset program and at its conclusion.

2. Get the whole family on board; this is a family project and cannot succeed in a vacuum. Both Dad and Mom must be involved for this program to work. Educating the family about the dangers of screen time and how the entire family is being affected will strengthen the program. Let the children

ask questions; let them get angry. Remain steadfast but open to conversation.

As a parent, you may need your phone for work. Before the screen fast begins, decide how much screen time is absolutely necessary, and be honest! Set guidelines for yourself and include a way to reinforce your rules. A friend or spouse can help strengthen your commitment. Set an alarm that reminds you to put the phone on airplane mode for the hours you are interacting with your child in the afternoon. Inform people who need to know that you will not be responding to messages of any sort until the evening. Get off Facebook, Twitter, Instagram, and other social media outlets. Silence WhatsApp groups so you are not constantly distracted by alerts.

This is a family project, and we are the leaders of our family. Our kids see right through us when we tell them we are involved in some serious work-related activity and then they catch a glimpse of the ball-game highlights we are watching. They don't respect our judgment then, and unfortunately, they copy us. We must disengage at least partially to be an example to our kids.

As we are more available, we will see miracles right before our eyes. Our child will stop competing with our screen. She will calm down, stop yelling and whining, and depend on us more. She deserves our undivided attention.

3. Make sure there are other modes of entertainment available in your home such as books, games, cooking or baking together, building toys, and ample opportunities to get out into nature with a parent. Make a schedule and plan activities throughout the three-week fast, such as Monday, making cookies with Mom; Thursday, football game with Dad. Plan game nights, reading books together, shopping outings. Schedule playdates with friends and active time outdoors.

Volunteering is very emotionally fulfilling and an activity your child will cherish. My kids get revved up when they know they can help someone in need. Just as with the Thirty-Day Challenge, where we are not permitted to be hungry, during the screen fast we don't want to have lots of open, boredom-inducing hours.

4. Other adults in your child's life must be informed because your child will be going through a detox transformation and may act out. We don't want teachers or friends' parents to be startled or respond harshly. Also, your child's environment must remain screen-free in all settings. Other adults can help by turning off the TV or computer when your child is around. Most adults are happy to help and may even be inspired to follow suit. Grandparents, counselors, coaches, and school staff can be particularly supportive.

5. Give yourself a break. Screens are very useful for us parents. When our kids are on screens, we know they are physically safe, not getting into trouble, and are very quiet. Screen time is calm time for us parents until . . . PSPD sets in when we try to disconnect them. We will be losing this quiet babysitting time during the fast. Of course, we will benefit very soon when the children stop demanding screens and find healthier ways to entertain themselves. During the transition, though, we must consider ourselves and our sanity. Go out with friends, hire a babysitter, find ways to decompress. You will be working hard, so cut yourself a break frequently.

6. Get friends to join you. If your child's friend is also doing the Reset program, it may be socially easier for both families.

7. Get rid of all screens, even the ones you forgot you own that are stashed under a bed somewhere. Physically remove them from the house. When your kid gets desperate, he will go searching for a screen. Screens must not be accessible at all.

What is permitted and what is forbidden during the Reset?

Permitted:

A minimal amount of television watching. Television watching is passive and does not have the same addictive impact as interactive or handheld devices. According to Dr. Dunckley, television watching should be limited to under five hours per week. The family can watch one or two movies together on the weekend. If you no longer have a television and rely on your computer for entertainment, be sure the child sits at least two-and-a-half screen lengths' distance from the computer screen. The child should not hold the remote control, and there should be no mindless flipping through channels during TV time. Plan what you will watch and stick with it. Ideally, a child should not watch TV alone; he should sit with a friend or family members, so the activity is more social. The TV may not be touched before chores or homework are done. If TV time is causing or exacerbating sleep problems, it should be discontinued during the Reset.

Forbidden:

No fast-paced modern cartoons, no violent content. Slow down the action. Focus on nature shows, older films, and older animated movies. No devices, gaming, or social media.

If your child has school-related computer assignments, be sure they are done early in the day, nowhere near bedtime. Check that your child is not getting extra computer time in school and is not being rewarded with games for good school behavior.

Begin the Reset

Your kids are not going to take this well. The younger kids will panic; the older ones will get angry; and they will all cry. Explain. Be clear, be loving, and don't back down! Your child will make you feel guilty like you are ruining his life and might try to punish you. Stay clear on your mission. You have young addicts on your hands, by no fault of their own. They were handed a test that was too hard for them to overcome. There are teams of brilliant women and men doing their very best to ensure maximum addiction to games, shows, and other screen interactions.

Look around at restaurants, ball games, waiting rooms, and parks. Every parent is fully engrossed in a phone. The child squirms in her seat, hoping to distract the parent for a moment. We are loving parents. Our kids are not natural addicts; they were tricked into this and have no idea that they are even suffering. We must be firm and not allow crying, threats, and bad behavior to deter us from our goal: extracting our sweet children from the claws of the technology monster and giving them back their happy, carefree childhood.

What withdrawal symptoms can we expect to experience?

Agitation, sleeplessness, depression, irritable mood, apathy, and lack of motivation.

How long will these symptoms last?

Young children: just a few days

Adolescents: a week or more, but their response may be more extreme, including more rage and crying. Of course, the longer a child has been engaging screens, the more intense the reaction will be. The dopamine pathway has been so desensitized in this child that she needs very intense stimulation to feel okay. Removing all the stimulation at once will cause serious stress to her system.

One important note: We began this book by discussing taking back control of our home, becoming the leaders in our family. We have discussed the importance of rules and follow-through. We simply cannot run a Reset program when a child is still running the home, when we still believe our child is disordered, and we don't really believe he can succeed. Your child will be angry, maybe even violent. If you are not in charge of your home and do not know how to reinforce behavior through compliments and punishment when necessary, the Reset will be very challenging, if not impossible.

If you see clear signs of ESS in your child and feel the Reset screen fast is the best way to help your child return to himself, review the earlier chapters of this book and only then begin the Reset.

Remind yourself that:

- Your child needs a leader and feels unsafe when he is permitted to make decisions or threats on his own.

- Your child is healthy and can do well when given the opportunity.

- This child is an Instant Gratification kid and therefore was easily sucked in by technology, but can also be extracted.

- You have the ability to help him turn things around, and you have gained the skills you need to help your child get through this. You are a tantrum-reducing pro; you notice every little positive choice your child makes and compliment it, so you're ready for this task.

- There are no quick fixes and you are engaged in a process of helping this wonderful child thrive. The first few days or weeks may be painful, but the long-term process will help your child grow up to be a strong and resilient contributor to society with the skills he needs to build a meaningful life for himself.

Be compassionate and be present. If your child is anxious, wants to hurt herself, or is acting depressed, be there to listen, comfort, and engage in an activity. Your child needs you by his side at the beginning. Don't abandon him or give up when he ups the obnoxious meter. He will get past this with you at his side.

As you and your family progress through the Reset, you will begin to see some welcome signs. Your child will begin to sleep better, become more creative, more energetic, more organized, and move quicker in the morning. She will be less argumentative and will find new activities to engage in or rediscover books or toys that used to be a lot of fun and which improve higher-order thinking. You will still get some intermittent tantrums, depressed behavior, and anger, but the improvements will far outweigh the stress. Communicate with your kids, share what has been hard for you, and listen to what they are struggling with. Point out how you are benefitting from this program and ask them to share what they have noticed is improving in their lives.

The three-week fast is over. What's next?

- Children who had a stronger addiction and are still showing signs of depression or anxiety need more time. Keep at it for a few more weeks.

- Some parents decide to stay the course and eliminate screens permanently.

- Some parents reintroduce screens but in a limited way. They may allow five hours of television watching per week, but never reintroduce games or handheld devices. Tablets and gaming devices are removed permanently. TV time is permitted after chores and responsibilities are taken care of, and not within two hours of bedtime.

- In my family, we have found that a weekend movie or two is a fun activity, but we do not allow screens during the week.

- Teens pose a challenge as they have their own smartphones and rely on them to travel, be in touch with friends, do homework, and overload on games and YouTube. When a teen is given a smartphone, ensure you establish some ground rules:

  a. Every phone must have a program installed to block out inappropriate content. There are many online programs that can be downloaded for free or upgraded to protect your family from invasion. Shop for the best option for your family. Make sure software is installed even if you have small children. The following are a few highly rated screen-filtering solutions:

    ◻ Qustodio

    ◻ FamilyShield

    ◻ KidLogger Wondershare Famisafe

b. No games may be downloaded onto the phone. If they are, the phone is returned to the parent.

c. YouTube is disabled.

d. The cell phone may not double as an alarm clock. The phone must be turned off at night, and a proper alarm clock should be used to wake your child up.

e. No screen time is allowed two hours before bed.

f. No phone use is permitted during school hours. A simple phone can be purchased for your teen to take to school. It's easy to switch the SIM card in the evening two hours before bed. This limits gaming access but gives your child a chance to catch up with friends in the afternoon.

Compliance with these rules will grant your child more weekend phone time (but never game time, or nighttime phone use). If your child doesn't follow the rules, confiscate his phone.

Dr. Dunckley recommends removing fluorescent lights from your home because the bright light causes additional stress. It is also recommended to switch off WiFi in the evening to avoid emissions.

Pornography exposure in childhood

There is one more screen-related topic that we must not ignore, and that is pornography exposure in childhood, or as I call it, "screen rape." Do I sound like a hysteric to you? First, let's align ourselves with the facts, and then you can judge for yourselves.

Wendy and Larry Maltz, in their book *The Porn Trap* (Harper, 2008), report that most people have their first exposure to porn when they are eleven years old. Many children are exposed even earlier. How many young children are watching an innocent show when an "advertisement" for available girls pops up on the screen? What will happen to that sweet, innocent child?

> Porn can have as powerful an effect on your body and brain as cocaine, methamphetamine, alcohol and other

drugs. It actually changes your brain chemistry. Porn stimulates the area of the brain known as the "hedonic highway" or median forebrain, which is filled with receptors for the neurotransmitter dopamine (Maltz and Maltz, 19).

Adults can still remember pornographic images they saw at age five in vivid detail. Adults of today still lived in more innocent times, when we kids had to be very motivated to find porn, and when we did, we most likely found a magazine rather than a video.

Imagine the impact of pornography in action on screen on a young mind. Kids think the images are mysterious and secretive, which makes it even more exciting. The children can't interpret what they are seeing, but the feeling they get sticks with them. Do you remember that first time you "discovered" sex, the giggling conversations with a friend or sibling? It was fun, exciting, interesting, "dirty," and only a conversation. Yet the memory lingers.

Our kids are in danger! They WILL encounter pornography, much younger than we expect.

What is our role in all of this? We can either mess this up completely or set our children on the right path. Our protective instinct and response to our child when he informs us that he has been exposed to porn will make a big difference. Blaming our children for being "bad" or "dirty" will shut them down and leave them with no parental support. Our children are not bad in any way; they are curious, which is completely healthy.

Why might our kids be exposed to pornography?

- **Our child will be curious**. All human beings are interested in bodies, differences between girls and boys, and how sex works, right? Your child should never be made to feel ashamed of her curiosity. She should hear that it is healthy to be curious and that she must learn to control her curiosity and respect others and their bodies. Kids must know that sexuality is beautiful, private, and most joyful when saved for the right person at the right time.

- **Our child will want to know about sex**, and that may be how she landed on a porn site to begin with. The less we share, the more our children will want to know. And they will fill in the gaps with their computer screen or phone if we are not forthcoming. The "sex" education kids get from porn is obviously skewed. There is no love, no relationship, no connection, no healthy touch. Children watching porn are exposed to bodies like animals, doing a physical act. Women are treated disrespectfully, to say the least, and this sends a message to our girls to be available bodies and also tells our boys to take advantage of those bodies.

- **Our child will want to be cool.** Kids and teens may be seen as part of the "in" crowd if they have seen porn or shared it with friends or brothers. Porn can become a secret code among friends. It feels like a rite of passage for boys, a warm welcome to the boys' club.

- **Our child may absorb the false message that sexual feelings are shameful.** He may not want to share his sexual confusion or his attraction to EVERYTHING that moves or doesn't move (during puberty) with an adult. But everything is permitted in the world of porn; there is no shame, no secret. It's all out in the open. This makes porn even more attractive, as a release from shame. Although our child must learn that sexual feelings are not shameful, and that these feelings are natural and good, this is the worst way he can go about reducing shame. He may feel less shameful by absorbing the porn messages, but he will be emboldened to become more aggressive, less sensitive, and more hurtful to others.

- **Our child will want to escape from the stresses of teenage life.** He can escape to gaming or TV watching, but once he discovers pornography, that may become his escape of choice. When a child lives with constant anxiety from an unsettled home, bullying, academic failure, criticism, lack of order or clear rules and expectations, porn becomes his best companion. It's his escape, the only pocket of life where he can privately feel good. People who became addicted to porn as an escape describe it as a drug, a substance needed to reduce the suffering of life.

- **Our child may have suffered sexual abuse and turn to porn to cope with the experience.** Children who have been sexually abused feel confused about their bodies and become highly sexualized. They turn to pornography in the hopes of calming their confusion.

- **Our child may be introduced to porn or abused by other children due to the confusing and alluring images they see on their screen.** Exposure to porn conveys the message that every sexual act, with anyone or anything, is encouraged and glorified. Kids cannot differentiate in their young minds between sexual touch that is permitted or forbidden. They have become so sexualized by what they have seen that they continue to imagine what they saw, even when the screen is turned off, and they may act it out on younger victims. Because of this, many children go on to hurt others. The cycle of violence is created and fueled by endless content flowing through the WiFi we pay for.

What is a parent to do to protect a child from being raped by screens?

Imagine a scenario where someone knocks on your front door. You look through the peephole, and the person trying to enter your home is completely nude. Would you let her in? Would he be offered a coffee? No, you would immediately call the police. There is one more "door" to our home that we fail to lock, and that is our technology. Kids can invite these nude people into a safe and protected home the moment they log on to the internet. Your house is no longer safe if your kids can swing the door wide open and party in the red-light district from the comfort of their own bed.

I beg you never to think that your child is a "good" kid and would never touch porn. Your child is a great kid, and he will still get to porn well before you formulate your birds and bees talk. She will be able to give you the talk from her own "research." Great kids get exposed to and addicted to porn. Is there a child who would not stare at a nude body, let alone a sexual act, right in front of her? Let us not be naive.

1. **Limit possible exposure to harmful content**. You, the parent, should have control over the content that is permitted in your home and on your phones. There are many solutions today that effectively block out the nude people trying to knock on the door. They can be installed on phones and all screens. This is not a suggestion; this is a must for any parent who truly wants to keep his child or teen safe. Every day that our screens are unprotected is a day our front door is wide open with a huge welcome sign perched outside.

2. **Deal with your own addiction**. Many parents have already been affected by porn addiction. We must be an example to our children that this garbage may never be permitted in our homes. When magazines are lying around, "girl" ads pop up on our screens, or we joke about intimacy flippantly, we are giving our children permission to copy us. Breaking a porn addiction is very difficult and requires professional help. If you cannot control the sites you wander to or the magazines you purchase, get professional help. Your child needs a clear message that you will never tolerate the degradation of women, people acting like animals, and sex without relationship or intimacy.

3. **Be an example of positive, loving touch**. Children should see their parents show affection to one another. A warm hug or kiss observed by a child goes a long way. Be careful with your limits. A child should not bathe with parents or watch them get undressed. This is not because our bodies are shameful; it is because they are private, and we are demonstrating healthy boundaries.

4. **Talk to your child!** Kids are exposed to sex and porn so young today. Start talking to them at a young age, as early as six or seven years old. Tell them, "No question is a bad question! You are welcome to ask me about anything you would like to know, and I will do my best to give you my most honest answer." Tell your children about sex, and explain how intimate, special, and private it is. Tell them how to respect their bodies and the bodies of others. Tell them that it is normal and healthy to have sexual desires. Tell them about the evils of pornography just as you would about cigarette smoking or using drugs. Keep the channel of communication open all the time.

5. **When your child does encounter porn, be there to support her**. Protect your child like you would from any dangerous invader. Kick the invader out and seal the entries. Be sure to limit further exposure. Talk to your child to discuss the arousal, the horror, or any other feeling she may have experienced. Help her put her experiences in words and help her understand how destructive continued exposure can be.

6. **If your child is addicted, get him help**. With all our good intentions, kids get addicted to porn. We may have safety-locked our computers and phones, but our children babysit, visit grandparents, and spend time with friends. We cannot hermetically seal any environment. If your child is showing symptoms of porn addiction such as sneaking around, spending hours in front of screens, disappearing to friends' houses for long periods of time, aggression, depression, or obsession with sexuality, get your child help. It is never shameful to admit that a child has an addiction and needs help. It *is* truly shameful to ignore the addiction and allow a child to continue to suffer alone.

Action Plan

1. Examine your home and see how each member of your family engages with screens. Are they exhibiting symptoms of ESS?

2. Are we as parents dividing our time between screens and kids? Is our distracted attention affecting our children? Be honest! We must set the example in our home by getting our screen addiction under control.

3. Follow the instructions for a screen fast carefully and begin healing your family from the strangling grip of screen addiction.

4. Put filters on all devices in your home. Your child will trip on inappropriate and damaging content at a very young age if she is not protected.

5. Pay close attention to your child and her behavior to see if she is showing signs of pornography addiction. Get professional help.

6. Always keep channels of communication open with your child. No question is illegitimate; no topic is off-limits.

THE CHEAT SHEET

Chapter Eleven: The Screen Addiction Repair Program

- ☞ What environmental factors are lowering our IQ and slowing us down? Our western diet, multitasking expectations, using our memory less and googling more, reality TV binging, sleeping poorly, and exercising less.

- ☞ What is electronic screen syndrome? There are two types of screen time: interactive and passive. Interactive screen time (video games, even the physically active ones) is more dangerous and causes many health and cognitive problems.

- ☞ Instant Gratification kids are more susceptible to becoming addicted to screens.

- ☞ What happens to a brain during interactive screen time?

  1. The child gets a rush of cortisol (stress hormone) and goes into fight or flight mode.

  2. The child becomes hyper-aroused and goes into survival mode. His thinking brain shuts down, and he can only access primitive responses. He is emotional and irrational.

  3. Dopamine levels spike; he is getting constant high-level pleasure feelings, and real life can't mimic these feelings. He is always searching for more. Regular activities become boring.

  4. Sleep is disturbed; melatonin (sleep hormone) is not produced because of the blue light.

  5. Stress hormones remain high, even after screens are shut off, making it hard to concentrate.

- ☞ Some symptoms of screen addiction include high stress, sleep deprivation, irrational mood swings, tantrums, low frustration tolerance, poor self-regulation, disorganization, immaturity, poor eye contact, learning difficulties, poor short-term memory, being spaced out, oversensitive, poor coordination, sensory issues. Nearly identical to ADHD.

☛ Half an hour of screen time in the evening disrupts sleep. Any video game causes dysregulation. An e-reader slows reading and processing abilities.

☛ How can we know if our child is exhibiting symptoms of electronic screen syndrome? Trial and error. Notice if the symptoms are reduced when screens are removed and return when kids get back on screens.

☛ Three areas are assaulted by screens: our eyes, our brain, and our body.

☛ Kids who suffer socially are particularly hurt by screen addiction. They hide behind their screens and even feel like they fit in with their online "friends," but never practice real socializing. Kids who are addicted to screens feel wronged and misunderstood.

☛ Parents must be role models to our children of healthy screen use. When we are addicted, our kids are neglected, create weaker attachments with us, have more accidents, and are more unhappy and demanding. They are touched less, spend less time speaking to an adult, less time active, and less time outdoors. Without our focus, their development in every area is stunted.

☛ The four-week Reset program: Take a week to prepare by informing and discussing the program with the family, preparing other modes of entertainment, informing other adults, inviting another family to join, and getting rid of ALL screens.

☛ What is permitted during the Reset program? Up to five hours of television watching per week or sitting far from a computer screen. No games and no small screens! Your children will exhibit many withdrawal symptoms. Stay strong; be a leader.

☛ Kids get exposed to porn ("screen rape") exceedingly early. We must protect our children by installing screen filters, keeping open communication, being an example, and being present. Porn for children is as dangerous as drugs, alcohol, or cigarettes. Don't tolerate it in your home.

CHAPTER TWELVE

The Walking Dead

SANDRA, THE MOTHER of a six-year-old boy, was visibly tense as she described her son's daily routine. Bobby was unfocused, tantrummed all day, teased his siblings incessantly, and didn't listen to anyone.

"How does he sleep at night?" I asked.

"Funny you should ask," she responded. "When he gets up in the morning, his bed looks like it has been through World War III. His sheets have fallen off or are twisted around his body; both blanket and pillow are on the floor. He wakes up with a bad hair day every morning. He looks like a wild child."

"Does he sleep through the night?"

"I don't think he has slept through the night since he was born," was his mother's exhausted response. "He wakes up to visit us or to go to the bathroom or from a nightmare almost every night."

"Does he snore?"

"Oh yes! He sounds like an eighteen-wheeler."

Did the boy have all the classic ADHD symptoms? Absolutely! Was the mother told that his difficult sleep was just a symptom of his disorder? You bet!

I told this brave mother that stimulant medication would just exacerbate her son's difficult behavior because it would reduce the already pitiful quality and quantity of sleep he was getting. This child was probably suffering from obstructive sleep apnea, which causes all the ADHD symptoms and more. She made an appointment with an ear, nose, and throat doctor at once, and due to the fantastic treatment her son got, I never met with her again.

We all know that sleep is important, don't we?

Not really. Most of us have terrible sleep hygiene, like sleeping a few hours per night during the week and "catching up" on the weekend. We also spend time on screens at night. We are an awful example to our children. We have somehow become confused by messages from the modern twenty-four-hour world and think that those who sleep less get more done and are therefore to be revered. We may think that sleep is for the weak. Is sleep that important? Nothing serious can happen if we are a little sleep-deprived, right?

Wrong!

Dr. Matthew Walker invites all his audiences to doze off during his lectures. He sees this as the ultimate compliment because he knows that sleep is so vital to every area of our health; he would rather we get a good solid nap than keep our tired selves awake to hear what he has to say. In his international best-selling book, *Why We Sleep, The New Science of Sleep and Dreams* (Penguin Books, 2017), Walker lets us know that there is no more valuable protective and restorative system in our body than sleep. He then scares us directly into bed on time by letting us know what will happen if we push our bodies and brains too hard without stopping to recharge.

In this chapter we will discuss sleep and its vital link to ADHD symptoms. Not all children with ADHD symptoms suffer from poor sleep, and not all children with sleep disturbances develop ADHD symptoms. As you read this chapter it will become clear if a possible cause of your child's symptoms is his lack of sleep. Continue reading to discover if your child is getting the sleep she needs, and if not, how to assist her in restoring restful and sufficient sleep.

First, we will examine the risk factors that lead to sleep deprivation and ADHD symptoms. We will then analyze what causes children and adults to get too little sleep, and finally, we will discuss what we can do to repair sleep and dramatically reduce or eliminate ADHD symptoms. Walker will be our guide. He is much more generous than I am. I would rather you remain awake throughout the entire chapter and climb into your cozy bed right after we have devised a plan together to guarantee you and your child more restful sleep.

What does sleep guru Matthew Walker have to tell us about the link between sleep and ADHD?

> A... reason for making sleep a top priority in the education and lives of our children concerns the link between sleep deficiency and ADHD. Children with this diagnosis are irritable, moodier, more distractible and unfocused in learning during the day, and have significantly increased prevalence of depression and suicidal ideation. If you make a composite of these symptoms and then strip away the label of ADHD, these symptoms are nearly identical to those caused by lack of sleep. Take an under slept child to a doctor and describe these symptoms without mentioning the lack of sleep, which is not uncommon, and what would you imagine the doctor is diagnosing the child with, and medicating them for? Not deficient sleep, but ADHD. (Walker 2017, 314).

> There is more irony here than meets the eye. Most people know the name of the common ADHD medications: Adderall and Ritalin. But few know what these drugs actually are... Amphetamine (Adderall) and methylphenidate (Ritalin) are two of the most powerful drugs we know to prevent sleep and keep the brain... wide awake. That is the very last thing that such a child needs. (Walker 2017, 315).

> I am in no way contesting the disorder ADHD, and not every child with ADHD has poor sleep. But we know that there are children, many children, perhaps, who are sleep-deprived or are suffering from an undiagnosed sleep disorder that masquerades as ADHD. They are being dosed for years of their critical development with

amphetamine-based drugs. (Walker 2017, 315; bold added).

Based on recent surveys and clinical evaluations, we estimate that more than 50 percent of all children with an ADHD diagnosis actually have a sleep disorder, yet a small fraction know of their sleep condition and its ramifications. (Walker 2017, 316; bold added).

Signs of Sleep Complications in Children, provided by WebMD:

- Snoring

- Breathing pauses during sleep

- Difficulty falling asleep

- Problems with sleeping through the night

- Difficulty staying awake during the day

- Unexplained decrease in daytime performance

- Unusual events during sleep such as sleepwalking or nightmares.

These are not simply irritating behaviors of childhood that children will grow out of as they get older. These signs are also not just "psychological" or "manipulative" issues coming from the child who is suffering from FOMO (fear of missing out) and wants to stay up a little later. Children naturally crave sleep, so if this process is being stolen, we should not blame the child for her struggles. She would sleep if she could.

These symptoms are an indication that your child has an undiagnosed medical problem that must be addressed immediately. What happens when poor sleep persists for a length of time, untreated? Let's answer this question by first looking at why we need sleep so much. Walker will make it abundantly clear why sleep is too important to skip.

Why do we need sleep?

All the areas of our brain are restored during sleep, and we need every stage of sleep to accomplish this task. We have three stages of sleep: light non-REM (rapid eye movement) sleep, followed by REM sleep, which is understood as the time we dream, and finally, a deeper non-REM sleep. These three stages repeat themselves throughout the night. As our brain cycles through these stages, old memories clear (the brain takes out the garbage), thoughts are organized, and new memories are solidified. We require each stage of sleep to achieve the restorative needs of different functions in our brain. Our brain needs many hours to accomplish all of these important tasks. In other words, **we need a full-length, complete night's sleep to keep our brain functioning optimally**.

Our memory is particularly affected by sleep. When we sleep, we solidify and store memories we want to keep and clear out memories we no longer need. There is a mad reorganization and filing of experiences process going on throughout the night. We don't want to disrupt this process by sleeping too few hours. A mess in the brain has dire consequences.

Let's understand the sleep brain-organizing process this way. Imagine if we hired a company that provided a memory storing and clearing service every night. The nightly work requires eight hours, so we are paying for the organizers to stick around and work hard for the full length of time. The organizers have a lot of work to do, filing new experiences, cleaning up and discarding old useless information, and connecting new experiences to the memory web that already exists in our brain. Instead of allowing the brain organizing team to do what they do best, unhindered, for the full eight hours, though, we decide we don't need all the help, and kick them out after five and a half or six hours.

Think of the pile-up mess accumulated day after day, the chaos that ensues after even two consecutive short nights of sleep. We get confused, don't remember valuable information, still have the clutter of old telephone numbers and details about people we have not interacted with in years, and hang on to painful memories which our cleanup crew should have taken out with the memory trash last night.

Sleep also strengthens our muscle memory, meaning the learning we do that involves motion. Examples of this are learning to ride a bike or play a piano piece. If a child learns a new physical skill during the day, after a good night's sleep, he will be able to perform that physical/brain activity with more ease than if he is sleep deprived. These memories are solidified in the last two hours of an eight-hour sleep. Waking too early and cutting out the final hours of sleep deprives us of honing our physical skills.

This memory- and brain-organizing mechanism is just the tip of the iceberg when it comes to keeping us healthy and well. Read on. When we understand what happens to the sleep-deprived, we will fully understand how vital quality sleep is to our health, success, and longevity.

What happens when we don't sleep?

1. **Our ability to focus is diminished**. Lack of sleep slows our reaction time (while driving, studying, or attempting to follow a complex lesson in class). Our focus begins to lag even after one shorter night's sleep. Scientists have found that even sleeping a mere six hours a night for a few consecutive nights brings people to a state of fatigue and lack of focus and concentration on critical tasks, including life-or-death ones like driving or operating heavy machinery. Many of us who are used to getting shorter nights of sleep and have already adjusted to the constant low level of fatigue will no longer feel tired and therefore blame our lack of focus on other factors like "our ADHD" or aging. We are, in a certain way, permanently drunk, but always feel fit to drive. In a frightening study, people who were drunk and people who were sleep-deprived performed similarly poorly on driving tests. The sleep-deprived group had been awake for at least nineteen hours but had consumed no alcohol (Tefft 2016).

2. **We become emotionally irritable**. When a person who is sleep-deprived experiences an emotionally loaded situation, the emotional area of the brain, called the amygdala, which is linked to strong emotion and fight or flight, becomes very

amplified. The emotional region becomes 60 percent more active in people who missed a night of sleep. Those who get a full, satisfying night's sleep have a more measured emotional response to provocation (Beattie et al. 2015).

3. **Lack of sleep is linked to aggression, bullying, and behavior problems in childhood** (Kubiszewski et al. 2014). Tired people tend to have less patience and judgment and therefore process social interactions more aggressively.

4. **Sleep-deprived people are hypersensitive to pleasure experiences**, which obviously looks like impulsivity to us. When a person does not sleep, he swings from a highly aggressive angry state to a happy, pleasure-seeking state. This experience can lead to risk-taking, sensation-seeking, and addiction (Walker 2017, 149).

5. **Lack of sleep can trigger psychiatric symptoms.**

   Psychiatry has long been aware of the coincidence between sleep disturbance and mental illness. However, the prevailing view in psychiatry has been that mental disorders cause sleep disruption—a one-way street of influence. Instead, we have demonstrated that otherwise healthy people can experience a neurological pattern of brain activity similar to that observed in many of these psychiatric conditions simply by having their sleep disrupted or blocked. Indeed, many of the brain regions commonly impacted by psychiatric mood disorders are in the same regions that are involved in sleep regulation and impacted by sleep loss (Walker 2017, 149).

6. **Sleep deprivation shuts down our ability to retain information.** Whatever we try to learn when we are tired cannot be retained. Kids often stay up into the night to study for tests, but this is always counterproductive as they can't store the information or recall it the next day. Even if a

student can hang on to some facts to spit out during the test that morning, the information will be forgotten soon after.

7. Dr. Robert Stickgold of Harvard Medical School found that if students do not sleep a full night's sleep after learning new information or studying for a test, even if they get a few full nights of sleep following the all-nighter, they still will not recall the information they studied. Memory storage does not heal following catch-up nights of sleep (Wamsley and Stickgold 2011).

8. **When we sleep shorter nights, we live shorter lives**. A large study indicated that those who slept less than six hours a night were 400–500 percent more likely to suffer a heart attack (Mazzotti et al. 2014).

9. **Lack of sleep affects the sympathetic nervous system, putting the sleep-deprived person into a state of fight or flight** (like the effect of screen time, especially video gaming). Cortisol is released, constricting already stressed blood vessels, leaving the tired person stressed and anxious.

10. **Less sleep, fatter body**. We eat more when we are sleep deprived, and our tired body cannot process the extra calories effectively. When we haven't gotten a full night's sleep, we get hungrier due to a shift in the hormones leptin and ghrelin, which control feelings of hunger and satiety. We also pack in an average of three hundred more calories per day when we have slept less than a full night.

11. **Men who don't sleep enough suffer from a drop in testosterone** and have the level of testosterone of men fifteen years their seniors.

12. **Women also pay a price, with more fertility challenges** when they sleep less than six hours per night.

13. **When we sleep less, we get sick more often.** Sleep boosts our immune system. Those who get five hours or less of sleep

per night are therefore more prone to getting ill. In addition, while we sleep, we have natural immunity-promoting cells that target and destroy precancerous cells developing in our body. When we don't sleep a full night, we block the power of our cancer-fighting cells, thereby preventing them from protecting us from this devastating disease.

14. **Sleep is the ultimate therapist**. While we sleep and dream, we absorb and reduce the impact of stressful events that accrued during the day. Those who do not sleep enough and therefore don't experience dream-inducing REM sleep are more anxious. Dreams also help us make sense of the experiences of the previous day and help us connect our new experiences to our memory grid.

One of the biggest disasters of childhood is lack of restorative sleep. Kids come to school and pass out, drooling on their desks by midday. Parents swear their children go to bed on time and sleep a full nine hours, but these children are NOT rested. What's going on?

Why are our kids not getting enough sleep?

- According to the National Sleep Foundation, many children suffer from **sleep apnea**. In childhood, the cause of this sleep disorder is generally enlarged tonsils. When tonsils swell, they can block air passages and cause the sleeping child to stop breathing. This child wakes up for a very short amount of time to regain steady breathing and then falls back asleep. This child has not experienced a good night's sleep and will suffer irritability and ADHD symptoms until he receives treatment.

  The most recently published data suggests that more than two hundred and eighty-nine thousand children in the US have tonsillectomies each year, and sleep apnea is a major reason (Hall et al. 2017). In one eye-opening study presented at the American College of Chest Physicians, children who snored loudly were twice as likely to have learning problems. Kids with sleep apnea snore loudly, gasp or snort during the night, sleep restlessly and in strange positions, and may sweat during sleep. During the day they may be very sleepy or even fall asleep, suffer from headaches, speak with a nasal voice, have trouble waking up, and have behavioral, learning, and social problems (Davila 2009).

- **Screens in the evening are destroying our children's sleep,** says Dr. Victoria Dunckley. The problem is that unnatural light can reset our circadian rhythm (sleep-awake cycle) and sleep hormone (melatonin) production. The blue light of the screen mimics daytime. If we are on screens in the evening, even the type that have adjustments for lower light, our body does not produce melatonin. That can be truly devastating because low melatonin levels are linked to depression and inflammatory states. (Let us not forget that inflammation is the cause of all disease.) When one hormone system is interrupted, the others follow. The sex hormones are the next to be suppressed. Growth hormones follow. We grow when we sleep, which means we need ample melatonin to produce ample growth hormones.

Let's imagine that a child does get his nine hours of sleep. How high is his sleep quality after he has been on his screen at night, even only for a short amount of time?

When a child is exposed to the light of the screen at night, even for fifteen minutes, his body will not go into deep sleep for an adequate length of time during the night.

Electromagnetic radiation from cell-phone towers suppresses melatonin production. Exposure to radiation and blue light has a combined toxic effect, adds Dunckley, noting that there is no safe amount of after-dark screen exposure. Any exposure at night will directly prevent restorative sleep, leading to anxiety, depression, and lack of focus.

Modern lighting is also disturbing our sleep, adds Walker. Even a hint of nighttime electric light can inhibit the natural production of melatonin. We need darkness to sleep. LED lights, invented in 1997, are even more invasive and disruptive to sleep than previous lighting. The blue LED lights suppress melatonin twice as effectively and are therefore twice as harmful (Bradford 2016).

Reading from an iPad at night suppresses 50 percent of melatonin release (Chang 2015). The light emitted from screens delays melatonin release by three hours. When people read from screens right before bed, they lose a significant amount of REM sleep; they are less rested the next day; and the effect of later melatonin release lasts a few days after exposure to screens at night. The melatonin release effectively resets itself, and we and our child pay the price.

Two key sleep-related terms you should know:

- **Somnambulism**: Activity during sleep, such as sleepwalking or talking. A person who has this condition is trapped between deep sleep and wakefulness during episodes of activity.

- **Insomnia:** Many people claim they have insomnia. Walker explains that insomnia describes either difficulty in falling asleep, staying asleep in the middle of the night, or remaining asleep for the duration of the night but waking up too early. This lack of sleep must cause significant impairment; a person must have this sleep distress at least three days a week for over three months. The doctor must also check for other medical causes for this lack of sleep before diagnosing insomnia.

About one in nine people suffer with insomnia. Often it is caused by emotional concerns or worries, anxiety, or stress. We have such busy, multitasking days, we have no time to process before we climb into bed at night, and then all the stress, anxiety, and worry collapse upon us like a ton of bricks. We are so overly accomplishment driven; our minds race as we think about what we did not check off our lists or how we have failed to achieve a specific goal today.

Remember the sympathetic nervous system that puts a person in fight or flight and is easily triggered by video games and lack of sleep? This same system is affected by high stress, which then prevents quality sleep. Fight or flight raises our core body temperature, and our body needs a drop in temperature to initiate sound sleep. In addition, excess cortisol production raises our heart rate, while our heart rate must drop to allow us to drift into dreamland.

Those who suffer from chronic lifestyle stress or posttraumatic stress have brains that follow an unnatural pattern when trying to get to sleep. A healthy brain will tone down the amygdala (emotional area) and the hippocampus (memory retention area) so that the body can initiate sleep. These two areas remain active in people who suffer from insomnia. The thalamus, the sensory area of the brain, which normally shuts down completely for healthy sleep, remains fully active in the insomnia patient, ready to defend and protect. People with insomnia are always on alert, worried, and stressed. Adding to this dismal picture of sleeplessness, an insomniac also does not achieve deep sleep even after finally successfully falling asleep. This leaves the person unrested, irritable, and even more stressed.

- **The bedroom is too bright:** We need complete darkness in our bedroom to get quality restorative sleep. Often children resist the darkness and want some light in their room when they sleep.

- **The bedroom is also too hot:** In order to fall asleep effectively, our body must cool two degrees Fahrenheit or one degree Celsius. Melatonin is stimulated by both the setting sun and the drop in our body temperature.

- **Consumption of alcohol**: Here's hoping that your small children are not drinking at all, and certainly not in the evening, but you and your teens probably are. Read this warning carefully, because our children pay attention to what we do and copy our poor habits: "Alcohol sedates you out of wakefulness, but it does not induce natural sleep" (Walker 2015, 271). Alcohol fragments sleep, inducing awake periods throughout the night. Because of the anesthetic nature of alcohol, the drinker is not aware of waking during the night, but restorative sleep will elude him. Also, alcohol suppresses restful REM dream sleep.

  It's fun to dream, but it's also essential. When dreams are prevented from taking place, there is a backup of pressure to dream. This can cause delirious daytime dreaming, experienced as hallucinations and other dangerous behaviors. Both daily alcohol consumption in the late afternoon or evening, and extreme sleep deprivation cause catastrophic results. This condition is called delirium tremens. Remember that REM sleep helps us solidify new and complex information into our memory. Even one night of drinking can wreak havoc on our memory storage from that day's learning.

It's clear that we need a good night's sleep and that many obstacles stand in the way of getting the quality sleep we need to remain healthy. What can parents do to help their child sleep well and therefore learn, grow, and develop well? Before presenting solutions to the sleep conundrum, let's understand how much sleep we really need.

The following are the National Sleep Foundation guidelines for sleep hours per age category:

- **Newborns (0–3 months)**: Sleep range 14–17 hours each day
- **Infants (4–11 months)**: Sleep range 12–15 hours
- **Toddlers (1–2 years):** Sleep range 11–14 hours
- **Preschoolers (3–5):** Sleep range 10–13 hours

- **School-age children (6–13):** Sleep range 9–11 hours
- **Teenagers (14–17):** Sleep range 8–10 hours
- **Younger adults (18–25):** Sleep range 7–9 hours
- **Adults (26–64):** Sleep range 7–9 hours
- **Older adults (65+):** Sleep range 7–8 hours

How can we help our children get more sleep?

First, we must address poor-quality sleep caused by external factors such as screens, LED lights, room temperature, and stimulant medication. We can then create a program for those with internal sleep problems such as insomnia and sleep apnea.

Solutions to external, environmentally caused sleep problems

The NIH has provided exhaustive recommendations for maintaining good sleep hygiene. Here is an edited to-do list for us to help our children with ADHD symptoms get the sleep they need:

- **Stick to a sleep schedule**: Go to bed and wake up at the same time each day—even on the weekends. This may be difficult for children who like to sleep in on the weekends. We don't have to be rigid, but we should ensure that our children get enough total hours of sleep on the weekend.

- **Exercise** every day, but not too close to bedtime. Allow your child about two hours to cool down from his sports activity before he climbs into bed.

- **Avoid caffeinated** drinks, especially after twelve in the afternoon.

- **Avoid feeding your child large meals and beverages late at night**: A large meal can cause indigestion that interferes with sleep. Drinking too many fluids at night can cause the child to wake frequently to urinate.

- **Avoid medicines that delay or disrupt sleep, if possible**: Some commonly prescribed heart, blood pressure, or asthma medications (and stimulant medication for ADHD), as well as some over-the-counter and herbal remedies for coughs, colds, or allergies, can disrupt sleep patterns.

- **Don't let your child doze off after 3 p.m.**: Naps can boost brain power, but late-afternoon naps will make it harder to fall asleep at night.

- **Relax as a family before bed**: Take time to unwind. A relaxing activity, such as reading or listening to music, should be part of your bedtime ritual.

- **Give your child a hot bath before bed**: The drop in body temperature after the bath may help him feel sleepy, and the bath can help him relax. Adding a few handfuls of Epsom salts to the warm bathwater makes for a truly relaxing experience.

- **Create a good sleeping environment**: Get rid of anything in your kid's bedroom that might distract her from sleep, such as noises, bright lights, an uncomfortable bed, or a TV or computer in the bedroom.

- **Keeping the temperature in the bedroom on the cool side can help your child sleep better**: A bedroom temperature of sixty-five degrees Fahrenheit or 18.3 degrees Celsius is an ideal temperature for initiation of sleep. Most people overheat bedrooms, especially for their children. Taking a hot bath or warming hands and feet before bed allows heat to move away from our core, thereby cooling the core for a good solid sleep.

- **Have the right sunlight exposure**: Daylight is key to regulating daily sleep patterns. Try to ensure your child is outside in natural sunlight for at least thirty minutes each day.

Dr. Walker adds one more "don't" to the list: don't take a sleeping pill, including "natural" melatonin!

Why?

Sleeping pills, much like alcohol, sedate us but do not put us into a deeply restorative sleep. Most classes of sleeping pills are addictive, thereby causing even worse sleep problems when the person stops taking them, even for one night. When a person skips a night, thinking she can wean herself from the strong sleeping pills, her addicted body needs the medication, and this poor tired person will have a terrible night's sleep, or even no sleep at all. She immediately assumes that she must use pills in order to sleep and runs right back to them for help. In reality, it was her addiction to the pills that disturbed her sleep. Once she begins taking her evening pill again, she will feel drowsy in the morning, drink more coffee to keep going, and the vicious cycle never ends.

What about melatonin? Doctors often prescribe melatonin to children who are struggling to initiate sleep due to taking Ritalin or other stimulant medications. Is this a good idea? Dr. Walker suggests that studies on melatonin use are not encouraging. At best the child falls asleep a few minutes faster, and most of the effect is placebo. In addition, because supplement manufacturing is not well regulated in the United States, it is unclear that there is a correlation between the dose stated on the label and how much you are really getting.

Is melatonin safe for children to take daily for a long period of time? WebMD weighs in:

> Melatonin is **POSSIBLY SAFE** when taken by mouth, short-term. Melatonin is usually well tolerated when taken in doses up to 3 mg per day in children and 5 mg per day in adolescents. There is some concern that melatonin might interfere with development during adolescence. While this still needs to be confirmed, melatonin should be reserved for children with a medical need. There isn't enough evidence to know if melatonin is safe in children when taken by mouth, long-term.

The following are two examples of external/environmentally caused sleep problems. We are all vulnerable to developing these sleep problems. But they are simple to repair if we are paying attention and identify the problem.

A few weeks after the birth of my third child, I was getting probably four hours of sleep a night, on a good night. One day, an acquaintance (who I thought liked me) sprang a most challenging question on me, probably knowing that there was no way for me to answer correctly. She asked what my husband's name was. How was I expected to know this information? I knew I had a husband; wasn't that sufficient? For a moment, I froze, but after a pregnant pause, I came up with a halting yet correct answer. Phew! I had not suddenly developed amnesia or dementia.

My lack of sleep for so many consecutive nights had literally stolen my memory capacity from me. I like to call this "mommy brain," and I assure all young mothers that their brain will eventually return. But this is not a sustainable situation. We must be sharp and alert so we can raise our kids. All you moms and dads, take care of yourselves! Turn the phones off in the evening, take a bath, read a book, and set an example by getting to bed on time.

One young client I met was so tired every day that her parents felt bad sending her to school. When this eighth grader did get on the school bus and enter the school building, she rarely made it to class. She dozed off on a bench outside her classroom. When schoolmates tried to wake her, she snapped at them or became irrationally furious. Her friends began to distance themselves from her because she was not fun to hang out with. Her schoolbag became a total wreck; she was no longer a functioning student. I suggested the parents take their child to the doctor to evaluate if the girl had a sleep disorder.

The doctor was much sharper than me. He sent the parents home to check if their child had a secret device she was interacting with well into the night. Sure enough, this clever kid had found an old laptop and gotten it up and running again. In the span of a few weeks, from watching movies late into the night and then being unable to fall asleep, this child had managed to alienate her friends and put her grades into freefall. Lack of sleep is just that powerful. Her parents did another sweep for screens and got her back on track with a bedtime routine and good sleep hygiene. The girl's friends were kind enough to forgive her as her well-slept personality came back. But it took some time.

In addition to environmentally caused sleep problems, there are children and their parents who are struggling with an internal sleep problem, either medical or psychological. We must address sleep apnea and insomnia.

Treating internal, non-environmentally induced sleep problems

How can an insomnia sufferer get some good sleep without the use of dangerous drugs?

Scientists understand insomnia to be a high-stress condition. This condition can either be imposed on a person who is affected by the high demands and expectations of this multitasking world or triggered by abuse or neglect from the past or present. It can affect a person at any age. Therefore, the best treatment option would be an intense and nurturing psychological intervention. Medication was thought to be the first line of treatment for insomnia until 2016, when cognitive behavior therapy for insomnia (CBT-I) was found by the American College of Physicians to be much more effective and longer-lasting than drugs. While the drugs clock a person over the head and force unrestful sleep on a sufferer with a real medical problem, CBT-I helps the person make real emotional and lifestyle changes and reclaim the restorative sleep she deserves.

How does CBT-I work?

There are two tracks to CBT-I. The first involves adjusting the physical environment and creating positive sleep habits. The second track is a therapeutic treatment for the emotional stress which is causing the lack of sleep to begin with.

The following are the steps taken to adjust the physical environment and create good sleep habits.

1. Choose a specific daily bedtime (even on the weekends).

2. Adjust the temperature in the bedroom.

3. Take a warm bath before bed.

4. Encourage moderate exercise daily, but not too close to bedtime.

5. Eliminate coffee and other caffeinated drinks, alcohol, and heavy pre-bed meals.

6. Make sure there is adequate daily sun exposure.

7. Eliminate naps.

8. Screen exposure is forbidden for at least two hours before bed.

9. All LED lights must be removed from the bedroom.

10. Remove clocks from the bedroom, so there is no clock-watching during the night.

11. If a person tosses and turns and simply cannot fall asleep, he is instructed to get out of bed and do something quiet and calming until he feels sleepy, and then return to bed.

12. Hours in bed are reduced at the beginning of the intervention program to only six, to allow for sleep pressure to build up and force the client into a natural sleep. As sleep is initiated more often, hours in bed are expanded to a full healthy eight hours of sound rest.

In parallel, client and therapist begin to unravel the emotional stress and anxiety that are preventing restful sleep. This may be a heart-wrenching process, but when the emotional pain is validated and resolved, the person will no longer feel constantly vulnerable and be in a state of high stress at bedtime. Once she feels safe and understood, she can sleep more soundly.

It's important to understand that the emotional stress is not simply in the insomniac's head. He has a genuine medical concern, and he can't just "get over it!" With proper care, the systems in our bodies that do not allow us to sleep due to stress and trauma will respond to treatment and allow for healing. We must have deep sympathy for a person who suffers from sleep issues and never blame the victim.

Do kids suffer from insomnia? If so, how can we help them overcome their stress and get the sleep they need to thrive?

Kendra was a feisty, friendly, and super-social sixteen-year-old. She seemed to have life totally figured out, but she was "just holding it together," in her words. What was going on? She climbed into bed every night at a reasonable hour, read a little, spoke to a few friends (actual talking, not texting or WhatsApping), and then she would try to get some shut-eye. Sleep didn't come until about three in the morning on most nights. Life started becoming unbearable. She could not function in school; she was fighting with everyone at home; and she even caused a totally avoidable car accident.

After checking in with the doctor to see if she had sleep apnea, which she did not, Kendra and I began talking. She was reluctant at first to discuss the verbal and emotional abuse she was suffering at home. She did not think it had anything to do with her sleep. We decided to stay the course, to unravel the daily trauma she was encountering and make some changes to her sleep routine. As she began to take more emotional control of her life and develop self-protective mechanisms, sleep came easier. She also learned to take a bath every night, get out of bed if she could not fall asleep right away, and listen to music for a little while. She was then able to get back into bed with better results.

Children most certainly can suffer from insomnia, as Kendra did. Kids may be carrying too much stress on their little shoulders. They may also have sleepless nights if they take stimulant medication, drink caffeine in coffee or soda, or if they drink alcohol, smoke, or spend late-evening hours on screens, especially if they are playing video games. We can help our child eliminate screens before bed and adjust physical barriers to falling asleep. The emotional stress requires sensitivity and attention.

Our children get into bed at night carrying all the stresses of that day. Has she been bullied? Yelled at by a teacher? Humiliated? Had trouble finding a friend to play with at recess? Did he understand all his lessons, or did he fall behind today? Was he self-conscious? Did she not have the right clothing to match the "cool" kids? That's a lot for our little ones to carry alone. What can we do to help?

Let's begin by creating a calm pre-bedtime environment. We must put our phones down and be available for any thoughts or feelings our child may want to express in the evening. Parenting is not a quality endeavor; it is all about the quantity. You see, our children are not robots; we cannot simply expect them to open their hearts and share in the half-hour timeslot we have allotted to them this evening. Before they agree to open their mouths, they need time and patience, and the feeling that if they do speak, they will be heard and respected.

Emotional "intervention" begins around dinnertime. Just chatting and sharing what happened in your respective days might allow for some sharing and reduction of stress. But sometimes that doesn't happen, and a child remains bottled up. Keep at it! After a warm bath with Epsom salts, your child may be ready to unload. Be ready to listen.

Reading a bedtime story to your child and talking a little about the characters in the book may be a fantastic segue into a sharing conversation. My children often have a long lecture to give right at lights out. We do want to listen for a few minutes, but it really is time for bed! For such situations, get a journal for your child. Take a few minutes to write down with him some of the topics he would like to discuss with you tomorrow. Jot down a few sentences, and then reassure him that all these topics are very important, and you will discuss all of them with him the next morning. Once his memories and experiences are recorded, your sweet child can drift off to sleep.

Are stimulant medications causing the sleep disturbances?

What do recent studies tell us about sleep and stimulant medication? Katherine M. Kidwell and her team analyzed all studies related to this important topic and reported her findings in the journal *Pediatrics*. They concluded that,

> Stimulant medication led to longer sleep latency, worse sleep efficiency, and shorter sleep duration. Overall, youth had worse sleep on stimulant medications. It is recommended that pediatricians carefully monitor sleep problems and adjust treatment to promote optimal sleep. (Kidwell et al. 2015).

Drugs such as Ritalin and Concerta list sleep problems as one of the potential side effects of taking the medication. Maybe we should start believing what they say about themselves instead of what "professionals" say about them? When we consider that we are administering these drugs to help children concentrate and behave better, shaving off hours of their precious sleep can be counterproductive. If our healthy children are struggling to fall asleep at night (after having a hearty meal well after dinnertime because their appetite was finally restored), we may want to reconsider our treatment of choice so that we don't inadvertently exacerbate the already challenging symptoms.

Does an instant gratification personality inhibit sound quality sleep?

Let's take a look at our Instant Gratification kid. He's not great at time management. He sets out to get a list of chores done, but one chore is more interesting or compelling than the rest. This chore draws him in, and before he knows it, four hours have passed; he has emptied the entire cabinet and still has to restock it. It's one o'clock in the morning! He just went with instant gratification and got a very short night of sleep. She may be watching a movie and promises herself she will shut the computer down by nine o'clock, and not one minute later. And then . . . uh-oh! She spots another great movie on Netflix and just wants to watch the first few minutes. We all know how this story ends, don't we?

Yes, our Instant Gratification, ADHD-symptom child will struggle to keep a schedule until we help her develop time-management habits. She will struggle even more with getting to sleep because the alternative activities are much more interesting.

In addition, often these little guys have been so active all day that they have not yet had time to process the events of the day. They experience everything in a very strong emotional way, so it all piles up. When they get into bed, all the experiences and emotions race to the surface at once, leaving them exhausted yet in a highly alert and stressed state.

We have four important tools to help our Instant Gratification child get quality sleep.

1. Make a sleep chart
2. Rein in evening screen time

3. Create a calming evening routine

4. Initiate bedside conversations.

We must first tackle the lack of good sleep habits with a behavior chart. This may be the most important habit you help your child develop, as it will keep him healthy and sharp for the rest of his life. Therefore, it should be the first habit you help your child develop. Remember, you may only run one habit-formation chart in your home at a time, so choose wisely. If a child continually gets out of bed to visit or get a drink, add a point to the chart for staying in bed from lights out until the morning, making sure he has gone to the bathroom before bed.

Here is an example of an evening sleep chart:

	All screens off 6:30 (including phones)	*Warm bath or shower and brushing teeth* 7:30–8:00	*Reading, relaxing, and talking in bed* 8:00–8:30	*Lights out* (after getting a drink and using the bathroom) 8:30	*Extra credit:* Staying in bed all night without coming to visit	*Practice:* Have child practice evening schedule and troubleshoot.
Sunday	✓	✓	✓	✓	✓	✓
Monday						
Tuesday						

One young client, who was an only child, was struggling nightly to fall asleep. She insisted every night that if her parents allowed her to sleep in their room, she would fall asleep immediately. And so she did. But she was already eleven years old, and her father couldn't stand it anymore. He felt his daughter was just spoiled while the mother thought she had a serious sleep disorder, ADHD, and anxiety.

Dad was right. Once we made a sleep chart, one of the rewards being a sleepover with friends or at her cousin's house, the girl began to calm down. Every night that she did not visit her parents, she got an extra point. After two weeks (and knowing that her parents no longer welcomed her in their room at night and would not change their minds despite her protests), the girl began sleeping alone in her room. When she woke up refreshed in the morning, she was greeted by two very proud parents.

We will gain control of screens in our home, making sure our child never plays video games and that all screens are switched off at least two hours before bed. Programing screens to shut down at the designated hour reduces arguments and negotiations. I highly recommend it.

Next, we will create a calming evening environment, allowing time for conversation, music, reading, and a hot bath.

Finally, we will accompany our child to his bed (but not jump in with him) and jot down his concerns from that day that he was not able to express earlier (remember to follow up with a conversation the next day).

The final sleep issue is **obstructive sleep apnea,** which both children and adults may suffer from. This medical concern is best treated either by an ear, nose, and throat doctor or through change in diet. If a child is eating foods that create inflammation (such as dairy, gluten, or sugar) and thus has a buildup of mucus, she will have trouble breathing at night. Before considering invasive surgery, first weigh the option of taking the Thirty-Day Challenge to see if the sleep apnea resolves itself. Many children I have had the pleasure to work with have been spared the knife by cleaning up their diet.

George was a mystery to his parents. He was a contented boy on the weekends, but during the school week, he had a terrible temper. He seemed so irrational and angry all week. When I started my hunt with the parents to try to discover the reason for his stress (and ADHD diagnosis), we discovered that George tended to sleep very late into the mornings on the weekend, when even a bomb dropping on the house would not wake him. His mother reported that he went to bed on time and fell asleep nicely, but he moved around a lot in his sleep and was exhausted in the morning. Dad, who got George up each weekday morning, said that it was the most stressful time of his entire day.

Was George generally healthy? Sure. And he also suffered from postnasal drip, which caused him to cough and sometimes have a runny nose. We decided to put George on the Thirty-Day Challenge. Two weeks in, we discovered why George was so much more pleasant on the weekends. It was the only time he was actually getting the amount of sleep his body needed. His postnasal drip had been disturbing his sleep, which he was unable to make up during the week as he had to get up for school. As his nose and throat dried up as a result of dietary changes, his sleep quality went up, and he was finally getting the sound sleep he deserved. This had a positive effect on his behavior and temper all week long.

Are there any natural supplements that can be taken to help people with sleep issues?

"Of course, I also believe that the underlying reason for most sleep disorders is magnesium deficiency, and **magnesium** is my first recommendation to anyone who can't sleep properly," says our magnesium guru, Carolyn Dean. She recommends taking a daily dose of magnesium. Her recommendations can be found in the Thirty-Day Challenge. If children have trouble swallowing the large magnesium pill, they can also bathe in an Epsom salts bath, which is essentially a magnesium bath. The magnesium is absorbed through the skin for a soothing, sleep-inducing experience. Epsom salts can be used every evening.

Action Plan

---

1. Evaluate whether your child is getting enough sleep per night.

2. If you find that she is not getting a full night's sleep, ask yourself why. Is there an environmental trigger (screens, diet, too-busy schedule, distraction . . .) or a medical problem such as sleep apnea or insomnia?

3. If environmental problems are creating the lack of sleep:

   ▫ First, follow the sleep hygiene guidelines.

   ▫ Next, make a sleep chart for your child and place a lock on your screens.

4. If you suspect sleep apnea, begin by doing the Thirty-Day Challenge as a family.

   ▫ If, after the month, the snoring persists, make an appointment with an ear, nose, and throat doctor.

5. If your child is struggling with insomnia, pay close attention to his sleep hygiene and either initiate a journal right before bed or find a CBT-I therapist to help you along.

6. Be a good example to your child by getting a grip on your sleep habits.

   ▫ Teach your child that sleep is too important to skip.

   ▫ Adjust the lights and the tone in the home in the evening.

   ▫ Do not catch up on work late into the night, and don't binge-watch shows you missed. Our kids are watching us, expecting us to show them how grown-ups make good decisions.

7. Take a magnesium supplement or an Epsom salts bath daily to boost sleep quality.

THE CHEAT SHEET

Chapter Twelve: The Sleep Program

- ☞ More than 50 percent of kids diagnosed with ADHD suffer from a sleep disorder.

- ☞ Kids who don't sleep enough suffer from moodiness, irritability, distraction, lack of focus, high emotions, and depression.

- ☞ The stimulants given to treat ADHD reduce the amount of time a child will sleep.

- ☞ Signs of a sleep disorder include snoring, paused breathing at night, difficulty falling asleep, not sleeping through the night, not performing well during the day, sleepwalking, and frequent nightmares.

- ☞ Why do we need adequate sleep? Our brain rests and is restored; old memories clear; new memories are solidified; our thoughts are organized.

- ☞ What happens when we don't sleep?

  1. Our ability to focus diminishes.

  2. We are more emotional and irritable.

  3. We are more aggressive and more likely to bully.

  4. We look for instant gratification experiences, thereby acting impulsively.

  5. We develop psychiatric symptoms.

  6. We forget things and have trouble retaining information.

  7. We live shorter lives and are more at risk for heart disease.

  8. We are more stressed and become fatter.

  9. We get sick more often.

☛ Why are kids not getting enough sleep?

1.   Sleep apnea blocks airways, causing a child to frequently wake up for a few seconds through the night.

2.   Screens in the evening destroy sleep. The blue light disrupts the wake-sleep cycle.

3.   Sleep apnea is an emotional sleep disorder suffered by kids with high stress or suffering from abuse or posttraumatic stress.

4.   The bedroom is too hot or bright.

☛ What can a parent do to help a child sleep better?

1.   Remove LED lights and screens from the room.

2.   Adjust the temperature in the room.

3.   Reduce or eliminate medications that inhibit sleep.

4.   Stick to a sleep schedule, going to bed at the same time every day.

5.   Exercise daily, but not near bedtime.

6.   Go outdoors in the strong sun for a short time daily.

7.   Avoid caffeine after noon, including chocolate, cola, and coffee.

8.   Avoid naps late in the afternoon, after three.

9.   Do not eat a heavy meal right before bed.

10. Unwind as a family before bed, giving ample time for your child to talk about his day. If it gets too late, write down the topics on your child's mind and bring them up again tomorrow.

11. A bath in the evening with Epsom salts induces high-quality sleep.

☞ If a child is suffering from insomnia, CBT-I is a very good intervention option. It includes therapy to understand the stress your child is carrying and works on proper sleep hygiene habits.

☞ Make an evening chart with your child to help her develop a strong evening routine habit.

☞ If a child is struggling with sleep apnea, the Thirty-Day Challenge may clear up the excess mucus causing part of the problem. If this doesn't help, consult an ear, nose, and throat doctor.

CHAPTER THIRTEEN

Get Moving and Get Outside!

Life is busy! I have a slim sliver of precious time to sit and write. Balancing a home, full-time motherhood of six remarkable children, lecturing, private practice, and saving just a bit of time for my neglected husband and a few friends leaves me with exactly fifteen minutes on a good day to focus. But there is a book that needs to be written, and I could find no excuse not to be the one to write it. With so little time, I need optimal focus.

Here's my secret to getting myself glued to the chair and committing words to paper: CrossFit. After a rigorous workout, my brain is calm and focused. I'm ready to write. I need no meditation, no soft music, just box jumps, weights, pull-ups, a few sprints, and yes, even burpees.

I learned this trick from my husband, a four-time New York marathon runner who continues to run daily, rain or shine. He was so energetic as a kid, he had to trace his shoes on the floor of the classroom so he could remind himself to place his feet exactly in their designated spot instead of everywhere else. He gives full credit for his success in every area of life to his consistent love of and commitment to sport; his rigorous hard work in building solid work habits, which, if you ask any of his teachers, did not come easily to him; and his remarkable, ever-supportive parents.

We both know how we feel after a workout; it is clear to us that we are more focused. But does exercise actually promote focus? Can it be used as a "drug" for ADHD symptoms?

In this chapter we will discuss the astounding scientific findings supporting exercise and its role in boosting focus. We will hear how the brains of kids who are in good physical shape compare to their less-active friends and uncover how stress and exercise are linked. Who knew that we needed exercise to remember things?

We will also learn that the great outdoors is the ultimate healer, and that this generation's unfortunate split from nature has caused some dire consequences. Linking the two factors, we can better understand why so many children are suffering from the unnatural demand of long hours in school.

Do you exercise? Did you buy yourself a great exercise outfit and the very best sneakers for the gym but have only tried them on once to show your sister how cute they are? Are you paying for a monthly gym membership but suffering from the daily nagging reminder that you are flushing that membership money down the toilet? Many of us know we should exercise, but do we understand just how important it is and why? Do we truly understand that our body is not just that thing that carries our brain around?

What does science have to say about exercise?

One psychiatrist has put more thought into this topic than most. John J. Ratey, associate clinical professor of psychiatry at Harvard Medical School, and author of the book *Spark: The Revolutionary New Science of Exercise and the Brain* (Little, Brown and Company, 2012), is bursting with scientific knowledge that he hopes we will all internalize and implement.

Ratey answers the questions:

- Why is exercise so important for us?

- How can exercise help our child, who is unfocused in school and temperamental at home, develop better skills?

We have previously discussed acute inflammation versus chronic inflammation in relation to our immune system. When our body is reacting to an invading harmful bacterium and we get a fever or feel sore, we don't like the achiness, but we understand that the fever is an indication that our immune system is doing its job. Once the danger passes, the immune response makes our body strong and resilient. This is how acute inflammation works. This process is good for us and strengthens our immune system. Alternatively, if our body is in a state of chronic inflammation due to poor diet, endless stress, loneliness, isolation, or bombardment from screens, we begin to suffer, and disease develops.

How does this relate to exercise? Firstly, exercise helps up control stress. When we exercise, we feel mentally and physically calmer and more able to concentrate. Additionally, exercise works on a deeper cellular level. When we stress our cells through exercise, we make them stronger. This concept brings us full circle. As we discussed at the beginning of the book, the challenging life situations we experience help up grow and learn and become more resilient. Our body does the same.

As we stress our body through exercise, our body becomes more prepared for any physical or mental challenge. The stresses to the body actually protect us long term, as long as they are in moderation and are not constant. Small bouts of stress on our immune system, on our physical body through exercise or from real-life challenges, build us. Constant physical, mental, or emotional stress breaks us down and leaves us weakened.

Now we can reflect back on the advice we often get to never allow our kids to struggle or be too challenged. How flawed this advice is! Our body is giving us a parenting lesson. If we protect our children from challenges, they will not have the opportunity to mature and become resilient. If we withhold physical exercise, our body becomes passive and unable to heal and protect itself. Body and mind are direct reflections of one another. Both need mild stress to become strong and self-protective.

Anita's story illustrates how toxic stress can hold us back from reaching our dreams. Exercise was her remedy.

Anita had a houseful of children; she was truly blessed. And her blessing was also doing her in! She loved her kids, she really did . . . But she could not manage to keep that house in order. She was probably one of the more intelligent and creative women I have met. She had a magic touch; anything she created was magnificent, be it a birthday cake or a dress. Unfortunately, due to the overwhelming mountain of work she had in her home, her creative side was gathering dust. What a shame!

Reorganizing the home, establishing routines, and giving the children more responsibility were all helpful techniques she implemented. Anita started feeling a bit lighter. But we weren't quite there yet. She still woke choked with stress every morning.

The next step in the plan was to get Anita out of the house every morning, the minute her youngest was picked up for kindergarten. My instructions were clear. "No matter how your house looks, when the kids pile out, you get on your sneakers and leave the house. Go for a brisk walk for half an hour, and if you have some extra energy, add some intermittent sprints. Only after you have exercised outdoors can you come home and begin your morning routine."

The walk/sprints were a game-changer. Anita was hooked. She could no longer begin her day without them. How did the walks affect her daily life? As she described it, the morning became a breeze; she got her chores done with ease and was able to carve out time to finally get back to her creative endeavors. She felt like a new woman.

Our brain needs fuel to function, and the fuel it uses is glucose. We must therefore feed it some natural sugar from complex carbohydrates and fruit (and not from added sugar in candies and cookies!). When a person is chronically stressed, all systems are on alert. The body understands that it must have available glucose on demand, and it will not release it for brain use, but rather stores it as fat around the belly. This ends up depriving the brain of functioning at a high level, which it can only do with fuel. When a person exercises, thereby managing stress, fuel can once again be directed to the brain.

How does exercise help children who are struggling to concentrate in class?

Exercise boosts dopamine, that same neurotransmitter that we hear a lot about in connection to ADHD. Dopamine improves mood and a feeling of well-being and gets our attention system going. Serotonin is also stimulated by exercise, and we need adequate serotonin for mood, impulse control, and self-esteem. As we remember, these neurotransmitters are also affected negatively when a person has a dysregulated gut. Adding exercise to the Thirty-Day Challenge heals the gut and brain together in a synergistic way.

A study out of the University of Granada, Spain, found that children who were in good physical shape had more gray matter in their brain in the frontal and temporal regions and the calcarine cortex. These areas are responsible for executive functioning (planning, inhibiting, organizing, completing tasks ...). When researchers compared kids who did sports regularly and their couch-potato peers, they found significant differences between the children. "The answer is short and forceful: yes, physical fitness in children is linked in a direct way to important brain structure differences, and such differences are reflected in the children's academic performance," said lead researcher Francisco B. Ortega (Esteban-Cornejo et al. 2017).

Our hippocampus is the brain area responsible for verbal memory and learning. Researchers at the University of British Colombia found that consistent aerobic exercise (the kind that gets our heart rate up and makes us sweat) makes this area of the brain larger. It is truly astounding that jumping rope, jogging, or speed walking grows the memory area of our brain (Godman 2018).

This research will explain what happened to a little boy named Garry.

Little Garry was struggling in class. He liked to learn but had trouble remembering what he learned. As a matter of fact, Garry sometimes forgot simple information that he was expected to know by third grade, like the name of his street or what era his class was studying in history class. He often felt confused and didn't like it at all! His mother saw his distress and hired a speech therapist to help boost his memory storage and retrieval skills. The work was slow but showing some progress.

One day his mother heard of a new karate class opening in the neighborhood. Garry's friends signed up, so the mom added her son to the list. Within weeks of beginning karate class, both Mom and therapist were shocked to discover that Garry started remembering better. He was able to answer information questions more quickly without the "um, um" pause first. Something fantastic was happening, but nobody understood what it was.

We may have guessed that team sports help children learn to socialize. Now, research has corroborated what parents have known for some time. Sports teach our children self-control, how to balance individual needs and group demands, how to handle defeat and celebrate victory, and how to reduce impulse control (Steinberg 2007). The data indicates that these skills are weak in all young children, and those who play sports and are physically active develop social and mental skills more quickly and effectively.

If we take a long hard look at the lives our children lead today, both in and out of school, it doesn't look like anyone is paying attention to the research. Our kids sit all day in school. When they come home, they sit some more. There is now a trend in United States and British schools to *decrease recess time,* despite the very clear finding that our children need to move more in order to learn! (Murray and Ramstetter 2013) This message cannot be more crystal clear, yet it is being ignored. Our bodies were programed to sweat and move vigorously many times per day, yet we rarely have the need to exert ourselves anymore.

We are told that we are the parents of deficient children who have not picked up executive function and maturity skills and therefore must be medicated to catch up. These children and the rest of us are suffering from an *exercise deficit disorder*! There is nothing wrong with the child or her brain. She is being deprived by her environment of physical exercise and therefore the power to concentrate! Without the steady flow of dopamine, serotonin, and norepinephrine, how can we expect her to learn? This is comparable to placing a kid in a straitjacket and expecting her to get her chores done anyway.

How does our modern world remedy this situation? We attempt to artificially tamper with the dopamine system through pharmaceuticals (a pill for every ill, even if we created the ill and can easily remedy it at no cost). A good rigorous run around the schoolyard at consistent intervals may be what's missing. Not only would exercise be cheaper and healthier, but the long-term benefits to our body and mind, including stress management, are innumerable. Compare that with years of stimulant treatment, which has been found to be damaging to this healthy child and her understimulated, stressed brain.

In addition, if our brain is not actively growing, it is shrinking. We know that we must keep our brain active by doing puzzles and learning new skills as we age, but studies have shown that regular exercise preserves our brain and keeps it sharp as we get older. This brain growth is happening to our kids as they get out on the basketball court or baseball field. Growth happens when children dance and practice martial arts. The brain slows when they play video games and tweet.

Bottom line: we all need to exercise. Kids who are not getting enough exercise are:

1. Depriving their brains of fuel

2. Not producing adequate dopamine, which helps with learning, focus, and concentration

3. Allowing stress to accumulate

4. Contributing to the passivity and therefore death of parts of the brain.

This is serious business. Our kids must get moving for the sake of their present school performance, positive mood, and future health.

What can we learn from the Finnish school system to help our children achieve more through exercise and nature?

The race is on in American schools. We want to cram in as much learning as possible and not waste any time. The student must get into an Ivy League, after all, right? The Finnish people disagree. As far as they are concerned, time is on their side. The child has all his school years to learn at his own pace. Students in Finland never sit in a lesson for more than forty-five minutes without a fifteen- to twenty-minute break between classes. Their American counterparts have heart palpitations (a high-stress response?) when they hear this. How can they waste so much time! How will they study everything on the curriculum?

The Finns plod along at this seemingly slow pace. The kids bundle up for recess and head outside every forty-five minutes! Many children walk far distances to school, and not for lack of bus service. In addition, students begin mandatory schooling only at age seven, and the students start school later in the day and end earlier, between 9:00 and 9:45 (meaning they are guaranteed a better night's sleep and a shorter school day). Science has shown that when students start the school day later, they learn more optimally (Urton 2018).

Finnish children bring home almost no homework... and they score significantly **higher** than their American counterparts on all international achievement tests. Oh, and one more intriguing aspect of Finnish education: only one out of one thousand students is medicated for ADHD (Grønli 2011).

Let's understand this. Finns are in school for fewer hours, do no homework, get double the amount of recess, have time to relax, stretch, and go outdoors throughout the day, and rank way ahead of their American counterparts? How is this possible? We had understood that if we pushed children to the max, they would excel. We understood wrong. The evidence is squarely on the side of the Finns (Colagrossi 2018).

An American investigator set out to unlock the secret of the Finnish school system and export it to the ailing schools in America. Anthony D. Pellegrini and his colleagues studied public elementary schools and how recess time impacted learning. Their findings were consistent with what Finland already knew; students were alert and ready to learn after breaks and were sluggish and tired before they were sent to recess. If a lesson dragged on past the forty-five-minute allotment, the teacher lost the students' attention.

Not only are there frequent breaks in Finnish schools, but the breaks take place outdoors, and the children can play freely, choosing their activity without the interference of a teacher. There is a teacher present to assure that the students are safe, but kids get to play like children. This free play allows children to socialize and learn life skills. Pellegrini and his colleagues found that when children were instructed to play organized sports during recess, as is a trend in American and British schools, recess lost its recharge-and-refresh value and kids returned to class still needing a break (Walker 2014).

Pellegrini has been fighting the good fight. He challenges principals and school administrators in America to defend their position on shrinking or eliminating recess in schools, despite the unequivocal evidence that children must be given breaks if they are to learn, absorb, and remember material, make friends, and socially mature. One man that Pellegrini locked heads with was Benjamin Canada, superintendent of Atlanta public schools.

Canada was a trailblazer in eliminating recess and replacing it with sports education. Why? He felt that in physical education class, the kids could learn new skills; the school could prevent bullying; and the kids didn't need to waste time jumping around and swinging from monkey bars, which had no apparent educational value. He proudly stated that he was raising the educational level of his school system. Canada could not produce any data to support his claim that children were learning better because the exact opposite was true. The unstructured frequent recesses were helping children learn, and he had sadly eliminated that.

Why are physical education classes not a good replacement for recess? Any class, including physical education, is designed to teach students new skills. Therefore, these classes do not allow the children to take a break, and the kids remain stressed and overworked. If a school is worried about bullying, the problem must be dealt with throughout the school campus because bullying can happen anywhere. If there is a teacher supervising free play, bullying on the playground accounts for less than 2 percent of the bullying in the school, according to Pellegrini (Pellegrini and Bohm-Gettler 2013).

Recess is the only time during the school day that children can interact freely with peers. This is the only time students have the opportunity to develop social skills. These skills are the most valuable life skills a child will learn in school. We must leave what remains of recess alone and add to it as the Finnish do. Maybe then our students will be less stressed, will enjoy learning, and will achieve better academic outcomes. With this understanding of the importance of recess, we can realize why we must never take recess away from a child as a punishment (Pellegrini and 2010).

Do extra sleep, more recess, and more time outdoors explain the low rates of medication for ADHD in Finland? Obviously, these factors all contribute. However, we must add that the field of education is highly regarded and well paid in Finland, and only the best and brightest are accepted as teachers. In addition, teachers spend many years with their pupils, so students and teachers become very familiar with one another and the teacher can tailor classroom demands to each student. The relaxed environment also helps, and the total lack of standardized testing means the teacher is teaching kids how to learn rather than how to take tests. The outcome is remarkable. Although there are not fewer students diagnosed with ADHD, the kids tend to grow out of their symptoms in a healthy and supported way.

A study comparing the use of ADHD drugs in Finland and America found that 60 percent of American students diagnosed with ADHD are medicated at some point in their schooling, as compared to almost no Finnish students medicated for the same symptoms. The researchers found that students in their late teens, both American and Finnish, had the same emotional, behavioral, academic, and social outcomes. Meaning, the medication use did not give the American students any edge over the medically untreated Finnish students.

We now have a better sense of what type of education would help our children flourish in school. Unfortunately, most western schools are so pressured to achieve on standardized tests that they work against those best interests. There is one school district that took matters into its own hands and made some seriously impressive changes.

Meet Debbie Rhea, Texas Christian University professor. Debbie is the founder of the LiiNK Project (liinkproject.tcu.edu), which she developed after returning from a six-month sabbatical in Finland. She was stunned by the incongruence of the short Finnish school day, with ample breaks, and their top international ranking in all academic subjects. Being a visionary, Debbie came home with fresh new ideas she was ready to implement. She saw clearly that the cutting of playtime in the long American school day was causing some serious harm. "The more the body sits, the more the brain stays stagnant—and the harder it is for that brain to take in learning," says Rhea on her website. She couldn't be more correct.

The great state of Texas was fortunate to have Debbie on the team. Two schools were chosen to participate in the first stage of the project, which began with kindergarten and first graders. The students would now have four fifteen-minute recesses in addition to a lunch break daily. A character-building curriculum was added three times a week to help children with socializing (without bullying) and improve self-esteem.

What are the results so far? Math and reading scores have gone up; students are more focused after recess and listening skills; and behavior has dramatically improved.

"You start putting fifteen minutes of what I call 'reboot' into these kids every so often and . . . it gives the platform for them to be able to function at their best level," says Rhea. The program is now being implemented in more than twenty schools in America. Here's hoping the trend goes viral.

What exercise would Dr. John Ratey recommend to 'reboot' the brains of our children diagnosed with ADHD?

1. Since we need both aerobic exercise and an activity that stimulates the brain, we should choose exercise that raises our heart rate and helps us develop a skill such as coordination, balance, or increased speed. All motor skills must be learned, and therefore present an excellent challenge to our brains. Tennis, martial arts, dance, aerobics, horseback riding, bike riding, running, jump rope, skating, trampolining, group sports, and swimming are all good examples of mind-activating aerobic exercises.

    How much exercise do our kids need to promote a healthy mind and body? We are meant to move a lot! Imagine how much cave kids moved. Think about how far people had to walk to get a meal back in the day. All of that exercise that kids in previous generations got just by living helped them remain focused and ready to learn. If we want to promote optimal focus, thirty minutes or more of vigorous exercise a day should be our target.

2. Our children should exercise with friends, not alone. Kids who are more isolated are less inclined to get moving. When they exercise with others, they become more social, thereby practicing good social skills and reducing loneliness. Those who sweat together stick together (literally). Exercise and friendship combined are a winning recipe for a great mood and positive attitude towards life.

3.   What is an ideal focus-boosting routine for our children (and
     their parents)? Ratey tells us to copy our ancestors: walk or
     jog every day, run a few times a week, and every few days
     push ourselves and do some challenging sprints.

This is all very nice advice, but how do we get the kids to participate?
And where do we find the time for yet another activity in our busy
schedules?

Trust me, I am highly motivated to get my kids focused. When
I became aware of the importance of getting my diagnosed kids
exercising, my oldest was probably twelve years old. I had three kids
who had to catch a 7:00 a.m. bus to the local elementary school, one
child in kindergarten, one in a playgroup, and the youngest was still
a newborn. When I learn something new that can help my children
thrive, especially something this astonishingly obvious and important,
I'm all in (perhaps a little too much!). My husband and I carried the
treadmill down to the dining room. We added a small trampoline, a
rip stick (similar to a skateboard), and a few weights, and we had a
morning exercise room.

Every morning I hauled the kids out of their cozy beds to get a good
start on the day. I would jog while they jumped. They would fly by
on the rip stick while I lifted the baby as a weight. I was determined
to get in those thirty minutes in the morning. But guess what? It was
impossible. You heard me: it could not be done. All I accomplished was
total mayhem and kids who thought their mother had finally fallen off
the deep end, which may not have been far from the truth.

I had to restructure my plan so that we would get the exercise we
need without loading on all the extra stress, which we most definitely
don't need. Here are a few of my guidelines that have worked.

-   **Choose a sport or physical activity that your kid enjoys**: All
    physical activity is good; we just need one that will keep the
    kids motivated to continue. Don't stress; they will probably
    have to shop around until they find a physical activity
    they enjoy. Eventually a child will know what feels right for
    him.

- **Sign your child up for a twice a week afternoon sports or exercise activity:** The activity should get heart rate up, and the child should have a great time, socialize, and further develop a physical skill. The goal is decidedly not competition, which will just add extra stress. Competition in sports is very valuable, as long as this does not turn into another chore for the child where he has to excel so he can add it to his résumé. This is meant to keep him a healthy, well-developing child. The exercise alone is what she needs, not awards and not stress.

- **Make the activity social:** Kids learn from their peers on the ball field to share, win, lose, reduce aggression, follow rules, and be socially appropriate. The more unstructured play kids have with one another, the more they will learn about socializing. They need less-sterile social skills classes and more time together playing, running, and sweating.

- **Have sports equipment available and visible in the home** so that during the time they are NOT on their screens, children can spot the jump rope or weights and begin playing with them. The best gift my kids ever got from their grandparents was a big trampoline. There are very few moments of the day when one of my children or a neighborhood child is not jumping on it. More often than not, I have to remind them to take turns so they don't overload the trampoline and injure themselves.

- **Choose hiking or the beach over shopping on the weekend:** If it's cold out, opt for an indoor trampoline park, ice skating or roller skating, or another indoor sports-oriented outing. Let your children know that you are making the shift and why, so they can help you choose activities. Pay attention to how they behave after leaving the ice-skating rink and compare it to their after-movie mood. It will become clear to you what a great choice you made.

- **Be a personal example**: Get out there and exercise. Kids are proud of their parent when the parent cares about himself and plays sports or exercises. When both parents are physically active, the kids see exercise as a part of life and not as a big bother that we are forced to do sometimes. They should hear the message that just like we eat and sleep, we move. The most fun I have ever had at my gym was when I took my older teenagers with me. I pretended that I had any chance of beating them with weights, push-ups, and sit-ups. We worked out so hard and had such a great time (and were sore for a full week afterward).

  I often race my kids to the house from down the block. They always win, and we always enjoy it. Choose to take the stairs in a building with an elevator. In our family, we call stairs an opportunity. Lifting heavy books, taking out the garbage, and walking to a nearby store instead of driving are also opportunities. Let your child know that you are fully dedicated to nurturing and strengthening your brain and body, and the only way to do it is by developing an allergy to "lazy."

- **Allow kids to play outdoors and discover things**: They are naturally curious about their environment, and when they can explore, they start to discover new shapes and textures, drag logs around, master the terrain, and develop all their senses. The highly controlled play our children are exposed to today does not allow for the level of activity, cognitive development, and socializing that free play provides. Taking children on a hike in the forest and letting them go ahead a little accomplishes this goal.

How did this plan turn out for my family? One child chose soccer. He now plays on a team twice a week and adds another four hours of soccer playing with friends at recess and after school. One daughter became a dancer. She attends a dance high school where she dances many hours a week while learning the rest of her subjects with ease (which was not the case before she started dancing more seriously). Another daughter took up eastern dance (belly dancing), a wild, fun, more freestyle dancing, which helps her express herself and build confidence, and she has a great time. One son became a workout guy. He is in the gym three times a week and runs or sprints the other days. The confidence and focus this has built in him is obvious. Yet another son is a horseback rider and rappeller. There is no greater joy than seeing a boy with the horse he loves so much, galloping through the fields. The youngest has taken up swimming, art, and dance.

As a family, we aim to go out on a hike together once a week. We are more consistent in warm months, but family time is outdoor time. The kids love to find wonderous things in the local forests, such as porcupine needles or beautiful leaves or berries. We call these "major finds" and get excited about each discovery. Rappelling boy is our guide and takes us all to conquer mountains on occasion. On our most recent trip, I lost my footing and descended the mountain on my husband's head. It was a great photo op. The kids, on the other hand, scampered up with ease like mountain goats.

Your child will happily play and be active if he does not have another more attractive activity waiting at home. **Sports will never compete with a video game.** If a child knows that he has no option of engaging with screens, he will very quickly discover how much he likes to move, learn, and create. If he has a group of friends with like-minded parents, there will be a pick-up game every afternoon. Be there to cheer, encourage, and support by getting a new ball when the old one pops. Play a game as a family and enjoy your child's growth. A great reward for a child who has a lot of points on his habit chart is going out to play ball with Dad or Mom. One more tip: put on some loud, pumping music and dance together!

Free play has all but disappeared from our children's lives. Why is free play so vital for their development, and how can we bring back the simplicity of free play?

A psychologist named Lev Vygotsky, born in 1896 in the western region of the Russian Empire, made some intriguing discoveries about how children develop cognitive functions (thinking skills). Vygotsky attributed full credit for children's mental and emotional development to their interaction with central adults in their lives, and their engagement in free, unstructured, make-believe play with their peers. He believed that if children do not interact in this way, they will not overcome the impulsiveness of childhood or learn the higher mental functioning skills required to attend and succeed at school.

Vygotsky's hypothesis was that the community contributes to helping the child make meaning of his thoughts and actions and therefore internalize them. When a child sees that an action or thought is meaningful to his family or friends, he connects to it, because we all need meaning, and thus he establishes his own social rule. Social learning with parents or friends leads the way, and once the child internalizes the importance of a new understanding, he translates it into the development of a new social/cognitive/emotional skill (Chaiklin 2003).

How is this accomplished?

Vygotsky tells us that this process begins with us, the parents. There are two ways we can help our child develop the skills she will need to be ready for school.

1. Get down on the floor with your kids. When we sit on the floor with our very young child and play "house" or any other imagination game, our language and cues to our child help him make sense of the world. He tests his understanding by setting up his own games. Pay attention to your children as they establish rules for games. They are often much stricter with their rules than an adult would be, because they are attempting to make order and follow it. The more they practice this understanding in interactions with us, the more they inhibit impulsivity and organize their minds.

    Vygotsky recommends that we use informal toys, like a stick or balloon for a doll or a broom for a horse. This way children learn to move from concrete thought to a deeper, higher theoretical level. When children make those substitutions, they learn to rely on thought and suppress impulses while they play. Games and toys today are very concrete. Look for toys that are simple, or just find items around the house and turn them into toys. A big box makes just as wonderful a dollhouse as the pink plastic Barbie one. My kids spend their lives playing with the broom (usually not to sweep the floor, more often to balance it on one finger or to turn it into an airplane).

2. The second way we can help our child develop higher cognitive, social, and emotional skills is to challenge her to engage in games that are slightly too challenging for her, but with our help. When we help a child strategize and figure out the game, she becomes competent. Once the child is competent at building a puzzle or playing a game together with a parent or teacher, she will progress more quickly on her own with our compliments and encouragement.

Piaget was a proponent of the idea of "self-discovery," that a child will learn new skills simply by interacting with the environment. Vygotsky disagreed, and modern observation is on Vygotsky's side. Studies conducted to test Vygotsky's theory have proven that when we play and talk with our kids, they become smarter and more capable of learning (McLeod 2018).

Kids learn how to learn through interactions with their peers. When children pretend-play with their friends, they learn to regulate their actions. Because of this, we must encourage free, unstructured play, where children can use their imagination and conjure up real-life experiences and try them out in their fantasy world.

Our children today are getting almost no free playtime at school, and screens have replaced that precious time at home. Also, when children do play, they are playing with action figures or Disney characters rather than their own imaginary friends. We see the consequences of the missing playtime in that kids are less mature, more impulsive, and sorely unprepared to interact and learn (Berk 2018).

Screen time must be replaced by "sit on the carpet and play make-believe" time, or board games/puzzle time, or a playdate with a friend that does not involve any screens. Kids need no instruction when they are left alone with a box, some wood, Play-Doh, and dress up clothing. We can sit back in awe as they create imaginary worlds that so closely mimic the world around them, thereby learning how to navigate the complexity of their lives. If only we allow for this simplicity, our children will show us how sophisticated they can be.

Nature Deficit Disorder: Where is Mother Nature hiding, and how is her absence affecting our child's development?

Do you remember wandering through the woods after the rain to catch salamanders when you were a child? How about garden snakes, the kind that are not poisonous? Did you stick them in your pocket? I sure did. And boy, was it fun! Kids today are so clean all the time; I don't know why we bother showering them. When I came home after a day of exploration as a child, I was covered in mud. Not modern kids.

Would we EVER allow our kids to wander through a forest near the house, get dirty, and come back with a pet snake? Most assuredly not. Why do kids today not get to have those glorious experiences that are seared into the minds of people just one generation older than them? Today we look at kids who wander over to the park barefoot with some bug in hand as dirty and unsupervised. We make a snooty comment to the well-manicured woman sitting next to us on the park bench surrounded by synthetic grass about that poor, poor child whose parents don't care about him.

The divide between our kids and nature is so large that kids these days seem incompatible with nature. We have rejected Mother Nature, and she is feeling snubbed. If my son brings over a group of friends, one is anaphylactic to peanuts, another to fish. My son can't touch gluten; dairy is out for all of them; one's eyes blow up if a cat walks by; and another begins to sneeze if the season is changing. We had a guest over recently who lost two nights of sleep after visiting our home, apparently due to the pet mouse in a cage in the opposite corner of the room (my daughter had rescued the mouse from a terrible fate and then got attached to it. We have also had a pet bat and many pet birds who had fallen from trees, and most recently a duck). The unfortunate gentleman sneezed and itched and was totally miserable. We are allergic to the world.

We already discovered the importance of nature when we discussed diet and health. Our body needs natural food to flourish. We need the microbes and germs from nature to nurture a healthy gut. Simply put, our physical health and emotional well-being depend on the loving embrace of Mother Nature. We can't live without her. Can anyone live without Mama?

How about our cognitive and emotional development; does Mama control that too? Anyone who has ever had a mama knows the answer to that.

Richard Louv, in his national best-selling book *Last Child in the Woods* (Workman eBooks, 2008), introduces us to nature deficit disorder, a condition (which he invented, a man after my own heart) of disconnect from nature that causes our children to be less alive, less vibrant. He describes the state of childhood today after its split from nature and discusses how that separation has impacted us so dramatically in just one generation. He analyzes the new era we have entered and describes what has happened to childhood and our ability to mature and develop in a nature-free world. He tells of children who cause trouble in class, but the minute they are out on a field trip, become leaders. Are we medicating nature-deprived kids?

Where has nature gone? Why are we no longer spending lazy afternoons with friends in nature, at the beach, or in open air?

According to Louv, we became fearful. We are a protective generation. Our understanding of nature, as parents, educators, and the media, is dark and frightening. Kids can't play alone outdoors because they may be hurt or kidnapped, God forbid. We must keep them safe at home (where they can encounter the internet with all its violence and sexual content, unsupervised) or in well-controlled, brightly painted Astroturf parks.

I'm all for safety. We should not allow our kids to wander too far, as not everyone has our child's well-being at heart. But the consequence of our fear is a locked-up child who cannot benefit from the necessary input of nature. We are extinguishing children's health and ability to learn while we inundate them with an electronic, fake world.

We may have thrown the baby out with the bathwater. We have "safer" kids, but "as youth spend less and less of their lives in natural surroundings, their senses narrow, physiologically and psychologically, and this reduces the richness of human experience," says Louv (2008, 3).

We recently took our kids out on a glorious springtime hike, where I saw the impact nature has on our children's cognitive development, creativity, and social skills. We found a remarkable trail, bursting with flowers and greenery. A stream ran through it. It took exactly one minute for all the kids to jump right into the rocky stream. How would everyone get across without falling? They worked together, hopping from stone to stone, carrying the youngest across (and their mother, who didn't want to get her new sneakers wet). They discovered a branch of a big, beautiful tree reaching across the stream right at an area where the water was deep enough to jump. Tarzan was the next game.

And then we hit the "major find"! A mulberry tree, overflowing with berries. Watching the kids strategize reaching the highest branches with the sweetest berries was fascinating. One found a stick lying on the ground that had a hook shape at the end. Another climbed the tree. A few kids took off their shirts, and the kid in the tree shook the upper leaves with his hook, allowing the berries to fall into their nets (shirts). Their focus and teamwork were such a pleasure to observe and participate in. As they worked hard to gather berries, one of my sons turned to me with a flushed-cheek smile and said, "This is really fun!"

Both staying indoors and venturing out have their risks. We sit too much indoors, which leads to disease. The air is more polluted indoors, adding additional risks to our health. In reality, the outdoors is no more dangerous than staying at home. Kids must be supervised in both environments, but they gain many more health and wellness benefits from venturing out into the big, beautiful world. They also learn to take small risks, like climbing a tree or starting a campfire or crossing a stream, which prepares them to be confident and capable of taking bigger, necessary risks in the future. Children who remain indoors become more fearful adults. Parents must make the choice to take the family outdoors and be present to supervise.

Kids are productivity-obsessed today. Nature is slow and unproductive in their minds and does not have the allure of the fast-paced world. We have discarded the art of slowing down and just "being" and replaced it with multitasking, checklists, and accomplishments.

This may explain the frantic push for medication, which is essentially a human-productivity steroid. Our message has been loud and clear: just being, taking your time, and enjoying the gurgle of a stream are unproductive and therefore not encouraged.

Almost too late, we discovered that it was nature itself that was promoting deep calm, and therefore more productivity. Schools are beginning to discover the same idea, that when they cut down on recess, they have wired, stressed students who simply can't absorb the material being shoved down their throats. Nature was exactly what we always needed to become our best. Without it, we are balls of anxious, insecure, stressed, medicated messes.

We need nature, and not just to have a quality diet and diverse gut. Research shows that we need the forest and the field for our mental, physical, emotional, and spiritual well-being. We come from nature; we are part of nature; and we pay a steep price when we are separated from it. Scientists tell us that exposure to nature can be positive therapy for ADHD.

A fascinating study was run by Dr. David Strayer, PhD, professor at the University of Utah. He took a group of students on a three-day backpacking hike into the wilderness. When he measured their brain waves after the excursion, he discovered that they performed 50 percent better on creative problem-solving tasks than the control group. He explained, "Our brains aren't tireless three-pound machines; they're easily fatigued. When we slow down, stop the busywork, and take in beautiful natural surroundings, not only do we feel restored, but our mental performance improves too." He calls this dramatic mental improvement "the three-day effect." It's a cleansing to our brain that happens with full immersion in nature (Atchley 2012).

In another study run by Strayer, two groups of adults were asked to walk through a nature reserve for a short amount of time. Their brain waves were measured by EEG throughout the walk and for an additional half an hour afterward. One group was told to hand over all devices and take the stroll screen-free. The other group was told to talk to a friend or colleague during the walk by telephone.

When the brain waves of the tech-free group were read half an hour after the nature exposure, their brains were calm and rested. The second group did not fare as well. Not only were their brains unrested, but they could not remember half of what they had seen during the walk. Multitasking while in nature was blocking the experience. What do we learn from it? We need to disconnect from technology to unwind. And we need to unwind to be healthy, growing, learning, and happy individuals (Gessner 2016, *YouTube*).

What does nature do for us that makes it so invaluable?

> Louv says it best:
>
> Nature inspires creativity in children by demanding visualization and the full use of the senses. Given a chance, a child will bring the confusion of the world to the woods, wash it in the creek, turn it over to see what lives on the unseen side of that confusion. Nature can frighten a child too, and this fright serves a purpose. In nature, a child finds freedom, fantasy, and privacy: a place distant from the adult world, a separate peace (2008, 7).

1. Nature is calming and relaxing. There is no rush, just sounds and smells and soothing colors.

2. Nature awakens all our senses. When we are in class or at a computer, we spend our energy shutting out distractions, shutting down our senses.

3. We become more creative and friendly. When we experience our own adventures, we create stories instead of living through the eyes of a movie character. When we compare kids playing outdoors in nature to kids playing in closed areas or concrete lots, the children playing in nature are far more likely to invent their own games and be creative. Kids are also more sociable with each other when they play in nature and are using their imaginations.

How do we get kids back into nature?

1. Sign kids up for outdoor programs, nature camps, Scouts, or other after-school nature activities.

2. Form family nature clubs by inviting friends or relatives to get out in nature together with you. You can garden, hike, clean a park, make campfires, or camp out as a group. Kids enjoy spending time with other kids in nature, so getting out with groups of families provides our kids and their parents with friends to roam and engage with.

3. Disconnect from the media messages of a doomed world, where nature is declining quickly. We must see our world as abundant and beautiful and accessible to us here and now. Cut the gloom and go for a hike or a rafting trip down the river. When our kids fall in love with nature, they will be sure to preserve it for generations to come.

4. Animals are not just good for our gut; they give us exposure to nature. We have a dog named Lucky. I did not adopt Lucky; my husband and kids conspired to sneak him into our house without me noticing. Good luck with that! You can't trick Mama Nature, and you can't sneak a dog by Mama.

   When the little puppy arrived, he arrived without a name. Choosing the right name led to a huge war in our home. No one could agree on what to name our mutt. Communication in the Gimpel home had completely broken down by the time we headed to bed that night. The next morning when I spotted the dog, I looked at him straight in the eye and said, "You are lucky that you are still in this house!" And that is how he was named.

   I have never regretted letting Lucky stay, but please don't tell my kids. Nor have I ever walked Lucky; he is the kids' responsibility. That gets my kids out the door every morning to walk him in nature. They roll around with him on the grass. We always take Lucky with us on family hikes and marvel at how happy he is to run around and soak it all up. His enthusiasm is contagious, and soon enough we are frolicking right beside him. Lucky has been our gateway to experiencing the absolute joy of nature.

5. Plant a garden or tend to plants at home. Planting vegetables reconnects us with our food source, and kids begin to understand that food is not grown in the supermarket. Raising chickens gives us the same message. Meat and poultry were once part of nature; they were not born plastic-wrapped in the freezer aisle.

6. Getting out in nature does not come naturally in our distracted world. Richard Louv commands us to just get out and do it. We must make a conscious decision, put it on our calendar, find a few friends, and explore God's beautiful world. Our children will thank us for it.

Action Plan

1. Make a choice today to be a leader in your family and begin exercising regularly. It can be as simple as speed walking a few times a week, preferably outdoors. Do it with a friend; I would never have changed my lifestyle without my friends at the gym.

2. Let your children know that they will not have to decide between being couch potatoes or getting up and moving, because there will be no screens to interact with, at least during exercise and nature time.

3. Sign your child up for active after-school activities. Group sports, martial arts, and dance are all good options.

4. Set up your home to be a place where movement happens. Stock the house with balls, jump ropes, and other sports equipment so that when the kids discover they have no access to the tablet and computer, they can make the natural choice to get active.

5. Invite friends and neighbors to get out in nature with your family. Allow the children to wander a bit ahead (without devices in their hands) and discover the surprises nature has to offer.

6. Discuss with your child's teacher options for more frequent breaks in the school day, or even just allowing your child to step out and run up and down the stairs to regain focus between classes. Our children are nature- and movement-deprived. The more we can reinsert these things into their lives, the calmer, happier, and more successful they will be.

THE CHEAT SHEET

Chapter Thirteen: The Exercise and Nature Intervention Program

☞ Why is exercise so important for us? Exercise controls stress; stressing our cells though exercise makes us physically stronger.

☞ Small bouts of stress to our immune system, life experience, and muscles make us strong. Constant stress to all three breaks us down. Kids' lives are too stressful; they must unwind!

☞ How does exercise help children focus?

  ◻ Exercise boosts dopamine, which helps a child feel good and more able to focus.

  ◻ Exercise boosts serotonin, which enhances mood, builds self-esteem, and reduces impulsivity.

  ◻ Children who exercise have more gray matter in the frontal region of their brain, which assists learning, planning, and executive functions.

  ◻ Consistent exercise makes the hippocampus area of the brain larger. This area is responsible for memory and learning.

  ◻ Sports teach social skills, motivation, goal setting, and self-control.

☞ In Finnish schools, kids have more recess, are outdoors more, start school later, and score highest on achievement exams in the western world. They medicate only one in one thousand children for ADHD.

☞ The best exercise for kids should raise their heart rate and develop skills such as balance, coordination, and speed. Tennis, jump rope, martial arts, dance, sports, swimming, and bike riding are examples. Thirty minutes per day is the minimum. Exercise is better with friends.

☛ Choose a sport your child likes; sign up for twice a week physical after-school activity; have sports equipment available at home; go to the beach or hike; shut off screens.

☛ Unstructured, imaginative play helps children make sense of the world, overcome childish impulsivity, and mimic adult life through play. When we play with our children, we give them cues to understanding what we value and what is positive behavior. Simple toys allow kids to develop their imagination and senses. Playing a challenging game or building a puzzle that is slightly too hard *together* with our child expands his mental capacity.

☛ We have become allergic to nature, seeing it as frightening and unknown. In an achievement-obsessed world, we see time in nature as pointless. Nature has become too slow for our fast-paced lives. But there is no stress in nature; it is where we used to go to calm down and meditate.

☛ Kids in nature become calm, focused, more social, more creative, develop their senses, and are more curious. They come alive.

☛ How can we spend more time in nature as a family?

1. Sign kids up for nature activities, camps, Scouts.

2. Make a family nature club where groups of families go out in nature together. It can be to garden, clean up a beach or forest, rappel, hike, or spend time at a park. Adding socializing to time in nature makes it more fun.

3. Stop fearing nature! Nature is nurturing. Home is more polluted; kids are exposed to real dangers on their screens.

4. Spend more time with animals or get a pet or two.

5. Plant a vegetable garden outdoors or plant vegetables in the house.

6. Turn off screens so children have a choice to get outdoors.

In conclusion . . .

Dear Parents,

What a jam-packed wild ride, huh? You must be wiped! There is a lot of information here, probably too much, but I had to include everything I felt could help you and your child. Before we part ways, allow me to indulge in a few more minutes to converse with you.

A book like this can be overwhelming. There are too many interventions; it seems as though our children need endless amounts of assistance. I made a promise at the beginning of the book that I would not add a moment to your day, and I intend to keep that promise. How is that?

Raising our children is a long and spectacular journey full of surprises, exhaustion, pain, joy, and everything in between. Our greatest goal is to get to know our children well and help direct them on the right path for *them*. No two children are the same; each is so precious and unique. This journey is not so much a fixing journey as much as it is a fact-finding and bonding mission. There *are* a lot of interventions in this book. So we don't get overwhelmed and burn out, the two things we must keep in mind are:

1. Not every child needs every intervention.

2. Every small improvement your child makes is a great leap. Even if you take one step, change one behavior of yours, love yourself more, establish one consistent rule in your home, remove one inflammatory food from your pantry, or give an extra compliment, you have done very well.

I included all the interventions not to intimidate you but to give you food for thought and goals to set for a later date. No one can implement all the interventions in this book at once. I didn't! Only the gradual changes stick. I know that from experience.

So take a deep breath, choose your first small goal, and then congratulate yourself.

One more very important message: Your child is a gift from God; he is exactly as he should be. He is a blessing to you and to the world. We are not fixing her; we are observing her personality, the strong and weak parts, and are guiding her towards the right path. That is our job. We must never think we should (or can) recreate this spectacular person. He arrived fully loaded. This book will help you meet and link hands with your child for the journey. He needs help to become *his* better self, not to be changed.

These interventions are hard to implement alone, as I have been saying all along. Going through the interventions with a friend or family member will give you much higher chances of succeeding. If you cannot create a local HyperHealing team, you are invited to join my HyperHealing workshops online. In my course, we go through all the interventions, strategize, ask and answer questions, laugh and cry, and most of all, practice! Find out about available workshops by visiting my website at www.hyperhealing.org or send an email to info@hyperhealing.org. You can also find me on YouTube at HyperHealing Mom.

I look forward to hearing your questions, reading your success stories, and being a vital resource in the HyperHealing journey you and your precious child are about to embark upon.

With much respect and gratitude,
Avigail

What people are saying about
HyperHealing

It is very rare to review a book that addresses so many important areas in such powerful and helpful ways! I love the section on helping parents recognize the negative cycle and how to change it. I love how deeply you understand what is happening inside the child and how to empower him. The section on nutrition also was a nice touch. You have an incredible book! Your approach has great wisdom, and I can see it working with tremendous effectiveness. I absolutely love it! May it help countless parents!

Your writing style is also very engaging and enjoyable to read.

Your writing also shows your deep understanding of both parents and children.

—David Hochberg, psychotherapist

Avigail's approach to ADHD is as simple and intuitive as it is groundbreaking. The impact of nutrition and gut health on behavioral conditions is extensive and scientifically proven but somehow often overlooked. This empowering approach addresses the root cause of symptoms and teaches people to heal, as opposed to masking symptoms and giving up. Important and powerful.

—Danya Saitowitz IIN-CHC, Empowered Health

As an educational psychologist and parent to children who are neurodiverse, I have grown to enjoy and appreciate people with neurodiversity and see it as a gift. It helps me understand my abilities as a mother to influence and assist my children in their struggles with Attention Deficit Hyperactivity Disorder (ADHD) and dyslexia.

This book is the compilation of several years of study and modification of findings on effective parenting as well as the interplay of nature and nurture on the final outcome of children with neurodiverse conditions, especially ADHD.

I hereby recommend this book as a must-read to all parents, caregivers, and stallholders in the educational sector. There is hope with *HyperHealing*.

—Ijeoma John-Adubasim, PhD

This book is breathtaking in its scope and passionate in its goals. Avigail Gimpel brings to the table knowledge, sensitivity, experience, and the desire to empower parents to trust their abilities and their intuition, while augmenting the latter with information and strategies to help them navigate not only their child's coping with ADHD, but their own coping, which is a major factor in achieving success. It is illustrated with fascinating stories and examples. A must-read for any parent or educator who has encountered this issue.

—Toby Klein Greenwald, veteran educator,
award-winning journalist and theater director,
and editor-in-chief of WholeFamily.com

This book is an invaluable tool for parents as well as therapists who work with children showing symptoms of ADHD. It is a comprehensive resource and includes practical advice and techniques that can be extremely helpful for our children. I highly recommend it!

—Ilana Sperer, OTR/L (occupational therapist and mom)

It was a pleasure to read such a well-presented book. As a mother, it taught me to develop some real tools, which Avigail has articulated beautifully. It is a must-read for family and friends that care, and not just for professionals . . .

—*Vivienne Glasser, owner Nusoil Technologies, mother of six*

HyperHealing is a comprehensive, practical guide for parents who believe in and are committed to bringing out the potential of their children with ADHD symptoms. It informs parents to make educated decisions, provides parent interventions with clearly laid-out strategies, and empowers parents to overcome the common stigmas created by our culture. A must-read for parents, educators, and professionals!

—*Tzvi Broker, director of Pilzno, <u>Work Inspired</u>, director of Career Opportunities & Professional Network @ <u>Shabbat.com</u>*

Endnotes

Chapter 10: Your Second Brain: The Thirty-Day Challenge

i. Our food begins to break down in our small intestines. The next station is the colon, which ferments the food, producing short-chain fatty acids. This gives us our daily energy. The bacteria in the colon are there to provide us with the ability to produce this energy.

ii. The gut microbes take on some of the role of the liver, thereby sharing the burden so the liver does not get overworked. In addition, researchers at three prominent universities recently discovered that gut microbiota regulate the glutathione and amino acid metabolism in our body. Why is glutathione so important to our health? It is the body's most powerful antioxidant, and our leading detoxifying agent. Glutathione is our internal hazardous materials truck; it clears out all the heavy metals and toxins. Glutathione is produced by every cell of the body, using the raw material provided by the gut bacteria's processing of our food. If we lack sufficient glutathione, our body cannot rid itself of heavy metals and other toxins we encounter in our daily lives (Jozefczak et al. 2012).

iii. Our gut bacteria help control inflammatory pathways, which reduces the risk of every disease. Our gut helps protect against inflammation by monitoring what enters the body and what is excreted. It also educates the immune system on the other side of the gut barrier, teaching it what is safe and what to destroy. It keeps the immune system from being under constant alert, causing a perpetual inflammatory response.

Dr. Zach Bush, a triple-board-certified medical doctor, explains that our immune system works by creating an inflammatory response, destroying any invaders. At that point, our immune system is meant to calm down and return to its pre-invasion state. This process is called acute inflammation and is very healthy for us. Let us imagine those soldiers located in our body. If there is an invasion, the soldiers respond with heavy artillery fire. Once the threat has passed, the soldiers rest, regain their energy, and prepare to be on alert for the next threat. This is healthy immune functioning. The immune system relies on the gut bugs to control the invasions so that they can remain vigilant but not at perpetual war.

Chronic inflammation occurs when the gut bugs stop excreting pathogens with bowel movements, thereby leaving the enemy inside the body and provoking constant warfare. To make matters worse, the gut lining can be penetrated, allowing for leakage of harmless yet unrecognizable substances into the bloodstream. When this happens, the immune system is vigilant all the time, never taking a break to reenergize. The immune system thereby exhausts itself, leading to devastating illness and autoimmune conditions.

iv. The brain, our command center, has its own impenetrable barrier of soldiers and surveillance around it. If penetrated, the brain can be attacked by any number of harmful substances, such as viruses and bacteria, or inflammatory toxins such as lipopolysaccharides (LPS), which are produced in the gut and are only harmful to a person if they leak out of the gut. Scientists have found that once LPS is injected into the bloodstream after leaking from the gut, it leads to overwhelming learning deficits. If the LPS passes the blood-brain barrier, it also causes a buildup of beta amyloids, which have been found to attack the memory center in the brains of rats (Sparkman et al. 2005).

An additional study demonstrated that LPS outside the gut decreases production of BDNF (brain-derived neurotrophic factor). Dr. Perlmutter explains that BDNF increases brain cells in the brain memory center (hippocampus) and signals molecules to connect to each other, thereby promoting brain plasticity. LPS is an important gut material that becomes dangerous only when released into the bloodstream. The gut bacteria ensure that it stays where it belongs. The gut also produces short-chain fatty acids, one of which is important in forming the blood-brain barrier. This fatty acid is called butyrate, and without it, the brain would be more permeable (Bourassa et al. 2016).

v. The gut/brain connection needs to be operational so that sensory information can be processed appropriately.

> In the brain are chemical messengers that transmit signals from one neuron to another, telling the brain and body what to do. These messengers are called neurotransmitters (NT), and they are also located in our gastrointestinal tract, which allows for communication with the brain. Amino acids, which come from proteins, feed the NTs, and the NTs in turn tell the brain cells how to motor plan, process sensory information, have appropriate behavior, formulate normal muscle tone, and so on (Kramer 2019).

vi. Our gut has neurons, which produce neurotransmitters. The gut produces half of the neurotransmitter dopamine (our reward and pleasure neurotransmitter). Serotonin, which is vital for sharp memory, cognition, sleep, a feeling of well-being and happiness, is almost completely produced in the gut. GABA, another neurotransmitter produced by our gut friends, boosts mood and has a calming effect on our nervous system. Low levels of GABA can lead to anxiety and chronic pain. Glutamate is another important neurotransmitter that is produced by gut bacteria and is dependent on a healthy gut. It regulates over 50 percent of our nervous system, including our sensory systems, and is considered the most important neurotransmitter for normal brain function.

It's also the precursor to GABA production. Our microbes also produce the vitamins that our brain needs in order to function well.

vii. How is this done? In three ways. First, those very neurotransmitters mentioned above stimulate the vagus ("wandering") nerve, a two-way street between the brain and abdomen. Most signals do not travel from the head to the gut, but from the gut to the head. About 90 percent of messages are conveyed from the vagal receptors to the central nervous system. The neurotransmitters coming from the gut control feelings and emotions. This communication happens within one hundred milliseconds—faster than a blink.

The second way the gut communicates with the brain is through hormones released into the bloodstream directly from the gut. This system is slower but no less impactful. These signals indicate to the brain whether a person is hungry or satiated. It is possible that serotonin or other nutrients that reach the brain through blood vessels may affect local neuron activity in the hypothalamus and modulate hunger.

The third hypothesized method of gut-brain communication proposes that gut microbes may stimulate the cells that work with the immune system, which could then signal the brain. When the gut releases cytokines, it is thought that the cytokines travel to the brain through the bloodstream and influence the microglia. The microglia in turn remove damaged cells at the site of injury. [See Jessleen K. Kanwal's (PhD candidate in neuroscience at Harvard University) presentation at http://sitn.hms.harvard.edu/flash/2016/second-brain-microbes-gut-may-affect-body-mind/].

Bibliography

Amabile, Teresa M., and Steven J. Kramer. "The Power of Small Wins." *Harvard Business Review* 89, no. 5 (May 2011): https://hbr.org/2011/05/the-power-of-small-wins.

Atchley, Ruth Ann, David L. Strayer, and Paul Atchley. "Creativity in the Wild: Improving Creative Reasoning through Immersion in Natural Settings." *PloS one* 7, no. 12 (December 2012): e51474, 10.1371/journal.pone.0051474.

Baumeister, Roy F., Ellen Bratslavsky, Catrin Finkenauer, and Kathleen D. Vohs. "Bad is Stronger than Good." *Review of General Psychiatry* 5, no. 4 (December 2001): https://doi.org/10.1037/1089-2680.5.4.323.

Beattie, L., Simon D. Kyle, Colin A. Espie, and Stephany M. Biello. "Social Interactions, Emotion and Sleep: A Systematic Review and Research Agenda." *Sleep Medicine Reviews* 24, (December 2015): 83–100, 10.1016/j.smrv.2014.12.005

Berk, Laura E. "The Role of Make-Believe Play in Development of Self-Regulation." *Encyclopedia on Early Child Development.* Illinois State University, February 2018, http://www.child-encyclopedia.com/sites/default/files/textes-experts/en/4978/the-role-of-make-believe-play-in-development-of-self-regulation.pdf.

Borlase, Nadia, Tracy R. Melzer, Matthew J.F. Eggleston, Kathryn A. Darling, and Julia J. Rucklidge. "Resting-State Networks and Neurometabolites in Children with ADHD after 10 Weeks of Treatment with Micronutrients: Results of a Randomised Placebo-Controlled Trial." *Nutritional Neuroscience* 23, no. 11 (March 2019): 876–886, 10.1080/1028415X.2019.1574329.

Bosman, Else S., Arianne Y. Albert, Harvey Lui, Jan P. Dutz, and Bruce A. Vallance. "Skin Exposure to Narrow Band Ultraviolet (UVB) Light Modulates the Human Intestinal Microbiome." *Frontiers of Microbiology* 10, no. 2410 (October 2019): 10.3389/fmicb.2019.02410.

Bourassa, Megan W., Ishraq Alim, Scott J. Bultman, Rajiv R. Ratan. "Butyrate, Neuroepigenetics and the Gut Microbiome: Can a High Fiber Diet Improve Brain Health?" *Neurosci Lett* 625. (Jun 2016): 56–63. 10.1016/j.neulet.2016.02.009.

Bradford, Alina. "How Blue LEDs Affect Sleep." *Live Science*, February 27, 2016, https://www.livescience.com/53874-blue-light-sleep.html.

Brody, Barbara. "Childhood ADHD—Explained. Find Out What's Behind a Diagnosis, and What Might Be to Blame." *Woman's Day*, September 8, 2011. https://www.womansday.com/health-fitness/womens-health/advice/a5871/childhood-adhdexplained-123305/.

Brown, Nicole M., Suzette N. Brown, Rahil D. Briggs, Miguelina Germán, Peter F. Belamarich, and Suzette O. Oyeku. "Associations Between Adverse Childhood Experiences and ADHD Diagnosis and Severity," *Academic Pediatrics* 17, no. 4 (May–June 2017): 349–355, https://doi.org/10.1016/j.acap.2016.08.013.

Burgess, John R., Laura Stevens, Wen Zhang, and Louise Peck. "Long-chain Polyunsaturated Fatty Acids in Children with Attention-Deficit Hyperactivity Disorder." *The American Journal of Clinical Nutrition* 71, no. 1 (January 2000): 327S–330S, 10.1093/ajcn/71.1.327S.

Carpenter, Siri. "That Gut Feeling." *American Psychological Association* 43, no. 8 (September 2012): 50, https://www.apa.org/monitor/2012/09/gut-feeling.

Centers for Disease Control and Prevention, "Preventing Bullying," October 21, 2020, https://www.cdc.gov/violenceprevention/youthviolence/bullyingresearch/fastfact.html.

Chang, Anne-Marie, Daniel Aeschbach, Jeanne F. Duffy, and Charles A. Czeisler. "Evening Use of Light-Emitting eReaders Negatively Affects Sleep, Circadian Timing, and Next-Morning Alertness."

Proceedings of the National Academy of Sciences 112, no. 4 (January 2015): 1232–1237, 10.1073/pnas.1418490112.

Chen, Mu Hong, Tung-Ping Su, Ying-Shue Chen, Ju-Wei Hsu, Kai-Lin Huang, Wen-Han Chang, Tzen-Ji Chen, and Ya-Mei Bai. "Comorbidity of Allergic and Autoimmune Diseases Among Patients With ADHD: A Nationwide Population-Based Study." *Journal of Attention Disorders* 21, no. 3 (February 2017): 10.1177/1087054712474686.

"Children and Sleep Apnea," Sleepfoundation.org, https://www.sleepfoundation.org/sleep-apnea/children-and-sleep-apnea.

Cloninger, Robert C. "A Systematic Method for Clinical Description and Classification of Personality Variants." *Arch. Gen. Psychiatry* 44, no. 6 (June 1987): 573–588, Doi: 10.1001/archpsyc.1987.018001800 93014.

Cloninger, Robert C., Dragan M. Svrakic, and Thomas R. Przybeck. "A Psychobiological Model of Temperament and Character." *Arch. Gen. Psychiatry* 50, no. 12 (December 1993): 975–990, 10.1001/archpsyc.1993.01820240059008.

"Cognitive Behavioral Therapy for Insomnia (CBT-I)," Sleepfoundation.org, https://www.sleepfoundation.org/insomnia/treatment/cognitive-behavioral-therapy-insomnia.

Colagrossi, Mike. "10 Reasons Why Finland's Education System is the Best." *Big Think*, September 9, 2018, https://bigthink.com/mike-colagrossi/no-standardized-tests-no-private-schools-no-stress-10-reasons-why-finlands-education-system-in-the-best-in-the-world.

Cornwall, Michael. "Does a Psychiatric Diagnosis Have the Impact of a Medical Curse?" *Mad in America*, September 24, 2017. https://www.madinamerica.com/2017/09/psychiatric-diagnosis-impact-medical-curse/.

Cowan, Nelson. *Essays in Cognitive Psychology: Working Memory Capacity.* New York: Psychology Press, 2005. https://doi.org/10.4324/9780203342398,

"Curse: Definition of Curse by Oxford Dictionary on Lexico.com Also Meaning of Curse." Lexico Dictionaries. English. n.d. Lexico Dictionaries. https://www.lexico.com/en/definition/curse.

Davila, David G. "Snoring in Children," Sleepfoundation.org, (December 2009). National Sleep Foundation.

Davis, Cindy D. "The Gut Microbiome and Its Role in Obesity," *Nutrition Today* 51, no. 4 (July 2017): 167–174, 10.1097/NT. 0000000000000167.

Dean, Carolyn. *The Magnesium Miracle.* New York: Ballantine Books, 2003.

Dockrill, Peter. "Science Alert IQ Scores Are Falling in 'Worrying' Reversal of 20th Century Intelligence Boom." *ScienceAlert,* June 13, 2018. https://www.sciencealert.com/iq-scores-falling-in-worrying-reversal-20th-century-intelligence-boom-flynn-effect-intelligence.

Duhigg, Charles. *The Power of Habit.* New York: Random House, 2014.

Dunckley, Victoria L. *Reset Your Child's Brain.* California: New World Library, 2015.

Dweck, Carol S. *Mindset.* New York: Ballantine Books, 2006.

Esteban-Cornejo, I. Cristina Cadenas-Sanchez, Oren Contreras-Rodriguez, Juan Verdejo-Roman, Jose Mora-Gonzalez, Jairo H. Migueles, Pontus Henriksson, Catherine L. Davis, Antonio Verdejo-Garcia, Andrés Catena, and Francisco B. Ortega. "A Whole Brain Volumetric Approach in Overweight/Obese Children: Examining the Association with Different Physical Fitness Components and Academic Performance. The ActiveBrains project." *NeuroImage* 159 (October 2017): 346–354,10.1016/j.neuroimage.2017.08.011.

Evans, Angela D., Kang Lee. "Emergence of Lying in Very Young Children." Dev Psychol. 49, no. 10 (October 2013): 1958–1963. 10.1037/a0031409.

Fasano, Alessio. "Zonulin, Regulation of Tight Junctions, and Autoimmune Diseases." Annals of the New York Academy of Sciences 1258, no. 1 (July 2012): 25–33, 10.1111/j.1749-6632.2012.06538.x.

Foxx, Richard M., and S.T. Shapiro. "The Timeout Ribbon: a Nonexclusionary Timeout Procedure." *J Appl Behav Anal 11*, no. 1 (February 1978): 125–136, 10.1901/jaba.1978.11–125.

Galland, Leo, and Buchman, Dian Dincin. *Superimmunity for Kids: What to Feed Your Children to Keep Them Healthy Now, and Prevent Disease in Their Future.* New York: Random House, 1989.

Gessner, David. "This Is Your Brain on Nature." National Geographic Video, YouTube, January 8, 2016, https://www.youtube.com/watch?v=CHkOk5gaxsM8.

Godman, Heidi. "Regular Exercise Changes the Brain to Improve Memory, Thinking Skills." *Harvard Health Letter,* April 9, 2014. https://www.health.harvard.edu/blog/regular-exercise-changes-brain-improve-memory-thinking-skills-201404097110

Greene, Ross W. *The Explosive Child.* New York: HarperCollins, 1998.

Grønli, Kristin S. "Large Differences in ADHD treatment." *Science Norway,* November 4, 2011. https://sciencenorway.no/disorder-forskningno-health-administration/large-differences-in-adhd-treatment/1373537.

Hall, Margaret J, Alexander Schwartzman, Jin Zhang, and Xiang Liu. "Ambulatory Surgery Data from Hospitals and Ambulatory Surgery Centers: United States, 2010." *Natl Health Stat Report* 102 (February 2017): 1–15, PMID: 28256998.

Hawkey, Elizabeth, and Joel T. Nigg. "Omega-3 Fatty Acid and ADHD: Blood Level Analysis and Meta-Analytic Extension of Supplementation Trials." *Clin Psychol Rev* 34, no. 6 (August 2014): 496–505, 10.1016/j.cpr.2014.05.005.

Hebb, Donald O. *The Organization of Behavior: a Neuropsychological Theory.* New York: John Wiley & Sons, 1949.

Heiman, Mark L., and Frank L. Greenway. "A Healthy Gastrointestinal Microbiome is Dependent on Dietary Diversity." *Molecular Metabolism* 5, no. 5 (May 2016): 317–320, 10.1016/j.molmet.2016.02.005.

Holon, Justin, Elaine Leonard Puppa, Bruce Greenwald, Eric Goldberg, Anthony Guerrerio, and Alessio Fasano.

"Effect of Gliadin on Permeability of Intestinal Biopsy Explants from Celiac Disorder Patients and Patients with Non-Celiac Gluten Sensitivity." *Nutrients* 7, no. 3 (February 2015): 1565–76, 10.3390/nu7031565.

Hyman, Mark, MD. "How to Feed Your Gut," https://drhyman.com/blog/2018/04/13/how-to-feed-your-gut/.

Jiayong, Lin, Iliana Magiati, Shi Hui Rachel Chiong, Swati Singhal, Natasha Riard, Isabel Hui-Xuan Ng, Falk Muller-Riemenschneider, and Chui Mae Wong. "The Relationship Among Screen Use, Sleep, and Emotional/Behavioral Difficulties in Preschool Children with Neurodevelopmental Disorders." *Journal of Developmental & Behavioral Pediatrics* 40, no. 7 (September 2019): 519–529, 10.1097/DBP.0000000000000683

Jockers, David, MD. "The Top 33 Prebiotic Foods for Your Digestive System," https://drjockers.com/top-33-prebiotic-foods/.

Jozefczak, Marijke, Tony Remans, Jaco Vangronsveld, and Ann Cuypers. "Glutathione Is a Key Player in Metal-Induced Oxidative Stress Defenses." Chalmers University of Technology. *Int J Mol Sci.* 13, no. 3 (2012): Kanwal, Jessleen K. "Why Poop Pills are in Trials as a Treatment for Obesity." Harvard University SITN Blog, August 22, 2016. http://sitn.hms.harvard.edu/flash/2016/second-brain-microbes-gut-may-affect-body-mind/.

Karl, J. Philip, Adrienne M. Hatch, Steven M. Arcidiacono, Sarah C. Pearce, Ida G. Pantoja-Feliciano, Laurel A. Doherty, and Jason W. Soares. "Effects of Psychological, Environmental and Physical Stressors on the Gut Microbiota." *Frontiers in Microbiology* 9 (September 2018): 10.3389/fmicb.2018.02013.

Kazdin, Alan E. *The Kazdin Method for Parenting the Defiant Child.* Massachusetts: Mariner Books, 2009.

Kidwell, Katherine M., Tori R. Van Dyk, Alyssa Lundahl, and Timothy D. Nelson. "Stimulant Medications and Sleep for Youth with

ADHD: a Meta-Analysis." *Pediatrics* 136, no. 6 (December 2015): 1144–1153, 10.1542/peds.2015-1708.

Kramer, Stephanie. "Gut Feeling: Curing the Mind Through the Stomach?" *Brain World Magazine,* August 12, 2019. https://brainworldmagazine.com/gut-feeling-curing-mind-stomach/.

Kubiszewski, Violaine, Roger Fontaine, Catherine Potard, and Guillaume Gimenes. "Bullying, Sleep/Wake Patterns and Subjective Sleep Disorders: Findings from a Cross-Sectional Survey." *The Journal of Biological and Medical Rhythm* Research 31, no. 4 (January 2014): 542–53, 10.3109/07420528.2013.877475.

Lavoie, Richard. *It's So Much Work to Be Your Friend: Helping the Child with Learning Disabilities Find Social Success.* New York: Simon and Schuster, 2005.

Louv, Richard. *Last Child in the Woods.* Workman eBooks, 2008.

Maltz, Wendy & Maltz, Larry. *The Porn Trap.* New York: HarperCollins, 2008.

Mazzotti, Diego Robles, Camila Guindalini, Walter André Dos Santos Moraes, Monica Levy Andersen, Maysa Seabra Cendoroglo, Luiz Roberto Ramos, and Sergio Tufik. "Human Longevity is Associated with Regular Sleep Patterns, Maintenance of Slow Wave Sleep, and Favorable Lipid Profile." *Frontiers in Aging Neuroscience* 6, no. 134 (June 2014): 10.3389/fnagi.2014.00134.

McCarthy, Claire. "Can Cell Phone Use Cause ADHD?" *Harvard Health Blog,* July 31, 2018. https://www.health.harvard.edu/blog/can-cell-phone-use-cause-adhd-2018073114375.

McDaniel, Brandon T. "Parent Distraction with Phones, Reasons for Use, and Impacts on Parenting and Child Outcomes: A Review of the Emerging Research." *Human Behavior and Emerging Technologies* 1, no. 2 (2019): 72–80, 10.1002/hbe2.139.

McKeown, Connor, Elizabeth Hisle-Gorman, Matilda Eide, Gregory H. Gorman and Cade M. Nylundet. "Association of Constipation and Fecal Incontinence With Attention-Deficit/Hyperactivity Disorder."

Pediatrics 132, no. 5 (November 2013): e1210–e1215,10.1542/ peds.2013–1580.

McLeod, Saul, "Developmental Psychology," updated 2017, https:// www.simplypsychology.org/developmental-psychology.html.

"Melatonin," WebMD, https://www.webmd.com/vitamins/ai/ingredient mono-940/melatonin.

Merzenich, Michael. *The Brain That Changes Itself: Stories of Personal Triumph from the Frontiers of Brain Science*. New York: Penguin, 2007.

Minde, Klause. "The Hyperactive Child." *Canadian Medical Association Journal* 112, no. 9 (February 1975): 1042, PMID: 20312652.

Murray, Robert, Catherine Ramstetter. "The Crucial Role of Recess in School." *Pediatrics* 131, no. 1 (January 2013): 183–188, 10.1542/ peds.2012-2993.

Myers, Amy. *The Autoimmune Solution*. New York: Harper One, 2015.

Nass, Clifford. *The Man Who Lied to His Laptop: What Machines Teach Us About Human Relationships*. New York: Penguin, 2010.

National Center for Victims of Crime, "Child Sexual Abuse Statistics," https://victimsofcrime.org/child-sexual-abuse-statistics/.

"National Sleep Foundation Recommends New Sleep Times," Sleepfoundation.org, (February 2015), https://www.sleepfounda tion.org/press-release/national-sleep-foundation-recommends- new-sleep-times.

Novotney, Amy. "Parenting that Works. Seven Research-Backed Ways to Improve Parenting." *American Psychological Association* 43, no. 9 (October 2012): 44, https://pa.performcare.org/self-management- wellness/parenting-tips/improve-child-behavior.aspx.

O'Bryan, Tom. *The Autoimmune Fix*. Pennsylvania: Rodale, 2016.

Palmiter, David J. Jr. *Working Parents, Thriving Families*. Minnesota: Sunrise River Press, 2011.

Pchelin, Paulina, and Howell, Ryan T. "The Hidden Cost of Value- Seeking: People Do Not Accurately Forecast the Economic Benefits of Experiential Purchases." *Journal of Positive Psychology* 9, no. 4 (March 2014): 322–334, 10.1080/17439760.2014.898316.

Pellegrini, Anthony D., and Bohn-Gettler, Catherine M. "The Benefits of Recess in Primary School." *Scholarpedia* 8, no. 2 (2013): 30448, 10.4249/scholarpedia.30448.

Pellegrini, Anthony D. "The Recess Debate: A Disjuncture between Educational Policy and Scientific Research." *American Journal of Play* 1, no. 2 (Fall 2008): 181–191, ISSN-1938-0399.

Perlmutter, David. *Brain Maker: The Power of Gut Microbes to Heal and Protect Your Brain*. Massachusetts: Little, Brown and Company, 2015.

Perlmutter, David, "Gut Bacteria & BDNF," Posted February 2015 at https://www.drperlmutter.com/gut-bacteria-bdnf/.

Peterson, Jordan. *12 Rules For Life, An Antidote to Chaos*. Canada: Random House, 2018.

Ratey, John J. *Spark: The Revolutionary New Science of Exercise and the Brain*. Massachusetts: Little, Brown and Company, 2012.

Reinberg, Steven. "Kids With ADHD Often Prone to Bowel Problems: Study." *HealthDay News*, October 21, 2013.

WebMD archive. https://www.webmd.com/add-adhd/childhood-adhd/news/20131021/kids-with-adhd-often-prone-to-bowel-problems-study#1.

Rogers, Geraint, Damien J. Keating, Richard L. Young, M-L Wong, Julio Licinio, and Steven Wesselingh. "From Gut Dysbiosis to Altered Brain Function and Mental Illness: Mechanisms and Pathways." *Mol Psychiatry* 21, no. 6 (June 2016): 738–48, 10.1038/mp.2016.50.

Rueda-Ruzafa, Lola, Francisco Cruz, Pablo Roman, and Diana Cardona. "Gut Microbiota and Neurological Effects of Glyphosate." *NeuroToxicology* 75 (December 2019): 1–8, Doi.org/10.1016/j.neuro.2019.08.006.

Ruiz, Rebecca. "How Childhood Trauma Could Be Mistaken for ADHD." *The Atlantic*, July 7, 2014, https://www.theatlantic.

com/health/archive/2014/07/how-childhood-trauma-could-be-mistaken-for-adhd/373328/

Sacks, Rabbi Lord Jonathan. 2010. "How to Praise." OU Torah, March 31, 2014. https://outorah.org/p/18440/.

Sacks, Rabbi Lord Jonathan. 2010. "It Takes Faith to Have a Child, Faith in Mankind's Purpose." Sunday Times (UK edition), May 21, 2010. https://www.thetimes.co.uk/article/it-takes-faith-to-have-a-child-faith-in-mankinds-purpose-5ng3njclp5s,

Sax, Leonard, and Kathleen J. Kautz. "Who First Suggests the Diagnosis of Attention-Deficit/Hyperactivity Disorder?" *Annals Family Medicine* 1, no. 3 (September 2003): 171–4, 10.1370/afm.3.

"Sleep Disorders in Children," WebMD, https://www.webmd.com/children/sleep-disorders-children-symptoms-solutions#1.

Snider, Vickie. E., Tracey Busch, and Linda Arrowood. "Teacher Knowledge of Stimulant Medication and ADHD." *Remedial and Special Education* 24, no. 1 (January 2003): 47–57, 10.1177/074193250302400105.

Sonnenburg Erica D., and Justin L. Sonnenburg. "Starving our Microbial Self: The Deleterious Consequences of a Diet Deficient in Microbiota-Accessible Carbohydrates." *Cell Metabolism* 20, no. 5 (November 2014): 779–786, 10.1016/j.cmet.2014.07.003.

Sparkman, Nathan L., Rachel A. Kohman, Vincent J. Scott, Gary W. Boehm. "Bacterial Endotoxin-Induced Behavioral Alterations in Two Variations of the Morris Water Maze." *Physiol Behav* 86, no. 1–2 (September 2005): 244–51. 10.1016/j.physbeh.2005.07.016.

Steinberg, L. "Risk Taking in Adolescence: New Perspectives from Brain and Behavioral Science." *Curr. Dir. Psychol. Sci.* 16, no. 2 (April 2007): 55–59, 10.1111/j.1467-8721.2007.00475.x.

Sturgis, India. "7 Everyday Ways You Are Ruining Your IQ." *The Telegraph*, July 30, 2015, https://www.telegraph.co.uk/health-fitness/mind/7-everyday-ways-you-are-ruining-your-iq/.

Tabatabaeizadeh, Seyed-Amir, Niayesh Tafazoli, Gordon A. Ferns, Amir Avan, and Majid Ghayour-Mobarhan. "Vitamin D, the Gut

Microbiome and Inflammatory Bowel Disease." *J Res Med Sci.* 23, no 75 (August 2018): 10.4103/jrms.JRMS_606_17.

Tefft, Brian. "Acute Sleep Deprivation and Risk of Motor Vehicle Crash Involvement." *AAA Foundation for Traffic Safety*, December 2016, https://aaafoundation.org/acute-sleep-deprivation-risk-motor-vehicle-crash-involvement/.

The Office of Rabbi Sacks. 2004. "In an Infantile Culture, Children Welcome a Chance to Grow Up." Last modified June 12, 2004. https://rabbisacks.org/in-an-infantile-culture-children-welcome-a-chance-to-grow-up/,

The Office of Rabbi Sacks. 2008. "The Best Present we Can Give our Children is the Chance to Do Something Great." Last modified December 12, 2008. https://rabbisacks.org/thought-for-the-day-12th-december-2008-the-best-present-we-can-give-our-children-is-the-chance-to-do-something-great/,

The Whole Child, "How to Identify Child Abuse Ages 6–12," November 24, 2018, https://www.thewholechild.org/parent-resources/age-6-12/how-to-identify-child-abuse-ages-6-12/

Tousignant, Lauren. "Chronic Acetaminophen Use During Pregnancy Nearly Doubles Risk of ADHD: Study." *New York Post*, October 30, 2017. https://nypost.com/2017/10/30/chronic-acetaminophen-use-during-pregnancy-nearly-doubles-risk-of-adhd-study/.

Tugend Alina. "Praise Is Fleeting, but Brickbats We Recall." *New York Times*, March 23, 2012. https://www.nytimes.com/2012/03/24/your-money/why-people-remember-negative-events-more-than-positive-ones.html

Tun, Hein M., Theodore Konya, Tim K. Takaro, Jeffrey R. Brook, Radha Chari, Catherine J. Field, David S. Guttman, Allan B. Becker, Piush J. Mandhane, Stuart E. Turvey, Padmaja Subbarao, Malcolm R. Sears, James A. Scott, and Anita L. Kozyrskyj. "Exposure to Household Furry Pets Influences the Gut Microbiota of Infants at 3–4 Months Following Various Birth Scenarios." *Microbiome* 5, no. 1 (April 2017): 40, 10.1186/s40168-017-0254-x.

Urton, James. "Teens Get More Sleep, Show Improved Grades and Attendance with Later School Start Time, Researchers Find." *UW News*, December 12, 2018. https://www.washington.edu/news/2018/12/12/high-school-start-times-study/.

Vermette, David, Pamela Hu, Michael F. Canarie, Melissa Funaro, Janis Glover, and Richard W. Pierce. "Tight Junction Structure, Function, and Assessment in the Critically Ill: a Systematic Review." *Intensive Care Med Exp.* 6, no. 1 (December 2018): 37, 10.1186/s40635-018-0203-4.

Walker, Matthew. *Why We Sleep, The New Science of Sleep and Dreams.* New York: Penguin Books, 2017.

Wamsley, Erin J., and Robert Stickgold. "Memory, Sleep and Dreaming: Experiencing Consolidation." *Sleep Med Clin.* 6, no. 1 (March 2011): 97–108, PMCID: PMC3079906.

Weng, Chuan-Bo, Ruo-Bing Qian, Xian-Ming Fu, Bin Lin, Xiao-Peng Han, Chao-Shi Niu, and Ye-Han Wang. "Gray Matter and White Matter Abnormalities in Online Game Addiction." *European Journal of Radiology* 82, no. 8 (August 2013): 1308–1312, 10.1016/j.ejrad.2013.01.031.

Whealin, Julia M, "Child Sexual Abuse," National Center for PTSD, US Department of Veterans Affairs. https://www.ptsd.va.gov/professional/treat/type/sexual_abuse_child.asp.

Wienen, Albert W., Maruschka N. Sluiter, Ernst Thoutenhoofd, Peter de Jonge, and Laura Batstra. "The Advantages of an ADHD Classification from the Perspective of Teachers." *European Journal of Special Needs Education* 34, no. 2 (February 2019): 1–14, 10.1080/08856257.2019.1580838.

Williams, Elizabeth A. "Stomach and Psyche: Eating, Digestion, and Mental Illness in the Medicine of Philippe Pinel." *Bull Hist Med.* 84, no. 3 (Fall 2010): 358–86, 10.1353/bhm.2010.0023.

Wraw, Christina, Ian J. Deary, Catharine R. Gale, and Geoff Der. "Intelligence in Youth and Health at Age 50. *Intelligence* 53 (Nov-Dec 2015): 23–32, 10.1016/j.intell.2015.08.001.

Yochman, Aviva, Shula Parush, and Asher Ornoy. "Responses of Preschool Children With and Without ADHD to Sensory Events in Daily Life." *American Journal of Occupational Therapy* 58, no. 3 (May–June 2004): 294–302, 10.5014/ajot.58.3.294.

Zhou, Rong Yi, Jiao-Jiao Wang, Ji-Chao Sun, Yue You. "Attention Deficit Hyperactivity Disorder May be a Highly Inflammation and Immune-Associated Disease (Review)." *Mol Med Rep.* 16, no. 4 (August 2017): 5071–5077, 10.3892/mmr.2017.7228.

CPSIA information can be obtained
at www.ICGtesting.com
Printed in the USA
LVHW101449251022
731527LV00005B/214